NETWORKED CHINA: GLOBAL DYNAMICS OF DIGITAL MEDIA AND CIVIC ENGAGEMENT

The Internet and digital media have become conduits and locales where millions of Chinese share information and engage in creative expression and social participation. This book takes a cutting-edge look at the impacts and implications of an increasingly networked China. Eleven chapters cover the terrain of a complex social and political environment, revealing how modern China deals with digital media and issues of censorship, online activism, civic life, and global networks. The authors in this collection come from diverse geographical backgrounds and employ methods including ethnography, interview, survey, and digital trace data to reveal the networks that provide the critical components for civic engagement in Chinese society.

The Chinese state is a changing, multifaceted entity, as is the Chinese public that interacts with the new landscape of digital media in adaptive and novel ways. *Networked China: Global Dynamics of Digital Media and Civic Engagement* situates the Chinese Internet in its complex, generational context to provide a full and dynamic understanding of contemporary digital media use in China. This volume gives readers new agendas for this study and creates vital new signposts on the way for future research.

Wenhong Chen is an assistant professor of media studies and sociology at the University of Texas at Austin. Her research focuses on the social implications of digital media.

Stephen D. Reese is Jesse H. Jones Professor of Journalism at the University of Texas at Austin. His research interests include media globalization, sociology of news, and framing of public issues.

New Agendas in Communication

A Series from Routledge and the College of
Communication at the University of Texas at Austin

Roderick Hart and Stephen D. Reese, Series Editors

This series brings together groups of emerging scholars to tackle important interdisciplinary themes that demand new scholarly attention and reach broadly across the communication field's existing courses. Each volume stakes out a key area, presents original findings, and considers the long-range implications of its "new agenda."

Ethical Issues in Communication Professions
Edited by Minette Drumwright

Global Communication
Edited by Karin Wilkins, Joe Straubhaar, and Shanti Kumar

Agenda Setting in a 2.0 World
Edited by Thomas J. Johnson

Identity and Communication
Edited by Dominic L. Lasorsa and America Rodriguez

Political Emotions
Edited by Janet Staiger, Ann Cvetkovich, and Ann Reynolds

Media Literacy
Edited by Kathleen Tyner

Communicating Science
Edited by LeeAnn Kahlor and Patricia Stout

Journalism and Citizenship
Edited by Zizi Papacharissi

The Interplay of Truth and Deception
Edited by Matthew S. McGlone and Mark L. Knapp

Sports and Identity
Edited by Barry Brummett and Andrew Ishak

New Technologies and Civic Engagement
Edited by Homero Gil de Zúñiga

NETWORKED CHINA: GLOBAL DYNAMICS OF DIGITAL MEDIA AND CIVIC ENGAGEMENT

New Agendas in Communication

Edited by Wenhong Chen and Stephen D. Reese

Routledge
Taylor & Francis Group

NEW YORK AND LONDON

First published 2015
by Routledge
711 Third Avenue, New York, NY 10017

and by Routledge
2 Park Square, Milton Park, Abingdon, Oxon, OX14 4RN

Routledge is an imprint of the Taylor & Francis Group, an informa business

Library of Congress Cataloging-in-Publication Data
Networked China : global dynamics of digital media and civic
   engagement / [edited by] Wenhong Chen, Stephen D. Reese.
      pages cm. — (New agendas in communication series)
   Includes bibliographical references and index.
 1. Information society—China.   2. Digital media—China.
3. Social media—China.   4. Mass media—Technological innovations—
China.   5. Information technology—Social aspects—China.
6. Communication—Social aspects—China.   7. Social change—
China—21st century.   8. China—Social life and customs—21st century.
 I. Chen, Wenhong, editor.   II. Reese, Stephen D., editor.
   HM851.N47675 2015
   303.48′330951—dc23
   2014043868

ISBN: 978-1-138-84002-7 (hbk)
ISBN: 978-1-138-84003-4 (pbk)
ISBN: 978-1-315-73307-4 (ebk)

Typeset in Bembo
by Apex CoVantage, LLC

To Hao and Daniel

To the twins

CONTENTS

FIGURES

TABLES

FOREWORD

This book is the result of a symposium organized by the two editors, Wenhong Chen and Stephen Reese. I had the privilege and honor of attending the symposium and reading the book manuscript. The symposium gathered some of the finest scholars working in the field of Chinese Internet studies and yielded a superb, agenda-setting volume.

If technological development may be studied in generational terms, then it is clear that the development of the Internet in China, as elsewhere, has undergone generational change. Online bulletin boards, personal home pages, and chatrooms were all the craze in the late 1990s. In 2002 and 2003, blogs began to catch on. Then came Sina Weibo, China's premier microblogging platform, until Tencent's WeChat arrived upon the scene as a serious business rival. Along with technological shifts, user habits change. People gravitate to different Internet or mobile platforms for different kinds of communication and interaction. Government attitudes and regulatory methods change, too. Bureaucrats in China find themselves constantly grappling with the exigencies that come with each new generation of digital media technologies, refining and modifying their strategies of regulating an ever-expanding cybersphere.

Like generational change in human societies, generational change in media technology is marked by both change and continuity. A new generation necessarily carries the imprints of earlier generations even as it blazes out its own path. A consequence of twenty years of Internet expansion in China is that the Internet is no longer a bare-bones technology, if it ever was. Instead, it has become fully embedded and encapsulated in the thicket of Chinese politics, culture, and society. It is as if the tree of the Internet were now wrapped in a deep forest. As a result, the Internet scene in China today is much more labyrinthine than before. The area of civic engagement and activism, the central concern of this volume, has become an arena of contestation.

The authors in this volume study the Internet by situating it within its complex social and political environment, revealing a dynamic and sometimes treacherous terrain of contention and political negotiation. They show that the actors in these interactions not only include state agencies and citizens, but also domestic and international business corporations and civil society groups. The state itself is not a static and monolithic entity but is multifaceted and changing. The networks in an increasingly networked China are multiple but unstable and often in tension. Global connections and cultural interactions exist side by side with the risks and threats of polarization, disenfranchisement, disruption, and disconnection. Only by situating the Chinese Internet in its complex, "generational" context is it possible to fully understand why it is where it is today and where it might be heading tomorrow. For anyone interested in joining this quest of critical understanding, this volume has set up vital, new signposts.

Guobin Yang

PREFACE

As part of the New Agendas series of the Moody College of Communication, this project draws on the expertise of our faculty, as we seek to showcase our own interests, attract the top young minds to Austin, and provide a catalyst for new paths of research in emerging areas. As it happens, we have begun to establish a growing community of scholars interested in communication and China, both faculty and graduate students. Like many universities, we have established collegial ties with Chinese academic institutions and begun to travel back and forth. All these developments have helped fuel an important research focus in our college, including among the editors of this present volume.

Wenhong Chen has both professional and personal interests in China and brings a network perspective to her broader research program. Stephen Reese came to his interest in China through a broader interest in journalism and media globalization, and he has shepherded previous volumes as coexecutive editor of the New Agendas series, along with dean Roderick Hart. Together, at Wenhong's instigation, we agreed that the time had come to combine our interests and began the process of identifying top young scholars who were carrying out research on the impact of digital media networks in China.

Our call for chapters brought more than 40 proposals. A global topic by nature, the project necessitated reaching out to scholars working both outside and within the United States, but we were able to bring 9 of the 11 chapter authors to Austin October 17–19, 2013, for a conference we hosted with the same title. In showcasing these young scholars, engaging with them personally—and they with each other—we hope to have collectively crystalized themes and perspectives for future research. We would like to thank our authors for their commitment and trust, and we look forward to more collaboration in the future.

We were especially pleased to enlist the help of the following distinguished senior colleagues as our keynote speakers: Zhongdang Pan (Wisconsin—Madison), Randy Kluver (Texas A&M), and Guobin Yang (Pennsylvania), who also graciously agreed to provide a foreword. We have benefited from the comments of our colleagues Iris Chyi, Tracy Dahlby, Joseph Straubhaar, Sharon Strover, and Karin Wilkins, in the Moody College, as well as Aynne Kokas (Virginia), Cindy Shen (California—Davis), and Cara Wallis (Texas A&M). We thank all of the authors who submitted a proposal.

Our undergraduate assistants Tianyuan He, Jason Kawalsky, and Emily Xiaoyige Wang as well as graduate students Kang Hui Baek, Hao Cao, Gejun Huang, Xiaoqian Li, and Fangjing Tu provided logistical or research assistance. Daniel Mauro performed proofreading and indexing. We appreciate the administrative assistance from Anne Reed and Genevieve Bittson in the Dean's Office, who helped with all the difficult logistics of holding a conference, which was made especially challenging because it included so many far-flung guests.

Wenhong Chen thanks her doctoral supervisor, Barry Wellman, who express-mailed a hard copy of a job ad from Toronto to Durham, which kick-started her journey in Texas. She appreciates many colleagues and students, whose support has made this journey meaningful. This book would not be possible without Stephen Reese's insight and wisdom. And most importantly, she thanks Hao and Daniel for their love.

Stephen Reese would like to thank Wenhong for proposing that he add to his role as series editor to actually venture a volume project of his own (why should other faculty have all the fun?). It proved to be a rewarding collaboration indeed, and he learned much through her expertise and their many conversations about China (among other topics). He also expresses his gratitude to his former doctoral students Jia Dai and Nan Zheng, who are both represented in this volume. They have helped guide him into the complexities of China as trusted colleagues, and helped challenge him to grow in trying to understand one of the world's most challenging social systems. In the academic ideal to which we aspire and sometimes reach, together we all have learned from each other. As always, he thanks Carol and Daniel as well as Aaron and Kate, and their twins, his new grandsons, James and Daniel.

Wenhong Chen
Stephen D. Reese
Austin, Texas
October 2014

CONTRIBUTORS

Wenhong Chen is Assistant Professor in the Department of Radio-TV-Film, College of Communication, at the University of Texas (UT) at Austin. Her research has been focused on social implications of digital media and communication technologies. Dr. Chen has published in top-tier journals in the field of communication and media studies, management, and sociology such as *Social Networks, Human Communication Research, Journal of the Association for Information Science and Technology (JASIST), New Media & Society, Journal of Computer-Mediated Communication, Management and Organization Review, Entrepreneurship Theory & Practice*, and *Journal of Social and Health Behavior*. Dr. Chen guest-edited the special issue *The Internet, Social Networks and Civic Engagement in Chinese Societies* for the journal *Information, Communication & Society* in 2014.

Yashu Chen is a doctoral student and teaching associate at the Hugh Downs School of Human Communication, Arizona State University (ASU). Her primary research areas of interest include intercultural communication; transnational communication; new media and social networking sites; new immigrants; and international students. At ASU, she teaches courses in business communication and human communication. She has presented papers at the annual conferences of the National and International Communication Associations.

Pauline Hope Cheong is Associate Professor at the Hugh Downs School of Human Communication, Arizona State University. Her multi-method and interdisciplinary research focuses on the social and cultural implications of communication technologies, including aspects concerning changing authority and community relations. She is lead editor of *New Media and Intercultural Communication: Identity, Community and Politics* and *Digital Religion, Social Media and Culture:*

Practices, Perspectives and Futures. Her award-winning research has been published in more than 60 books and international journals, including *New Media and Society, Journal of Computer-Mediated-Communication, The Information Society, Information, Communication and Society, American Behavioral Scientist, Chinese Journal of Communication, Journal of International and Intercultural Communication*, and *Journal of Communication*.

Jia Dai is Assistant Professor at the School of Journalism and Communication, Tsinghua University, China. Her research interests include media sociology, new media and social transformation, and environmental communication. Her published research includes articles in *Journalism & Mass Communication Quarterly, Journalism Practice, Asian Journal of Communication*, and *Chinese Journal of Communication*. Her recent research projects focus on the social and political implication of new media use in environmental contention in China.

Samuel Galler is a DPhil student at Oxford University, UK, where he is studying international development with a focus on the development of civil organizations, international funding, and technology in China. He also acts as director of Social Entrepreneurship for Sexual Health (SESH), an organization that is currently administering research funded by an R01 grant from the U.S. National Institutes of Health. He has previously done research on Chinese HIV organizations at Tsinghua University in Beijing.

Jun Liu is Assistant Professor in the Department of Media, Cognition, and Communication, University of Copenhagen, Denmark. His research areas cover digital media, political communication, and contentious politics. He has articles published in journals including *Television & New Media* and *Modern Asian Studies*. His work has won several awards, including the best dissertation award from The Information Technology and Politics Section of American Political Science Association (2014) and the best paper award from the 2014 International Communication Association Mobile Preconference.

Yuping Mao is Assistant Professor in the Department of Media and Communication at Erasmus University Rotterdam, the Netherlands. Prior to moving to Europe, Yuping worked as the academic developer in the Graduate Program of Communications and Technology at the University of Alberta in Canada. Her research focuses on intercultural, organizational, and health communication, and has been funded by various funding agencies such as Canadian Institute of Health Research and Kule Institute for Advanced Study. Her work has appeared in many peer-reviewed journals and edited books, including *Communication Research, Canadian Journal of Communication, China Media Research, Canadian Public Administration, International Journal of Health Planning and Management, Journal of Substance Use*, and *Italian Journal of Pediatrics*.

Ericka Menchen-Trevino is Assistant Professor at Erasmus University Rotterdam, the Netherlands. Ericka's research interests lie at the intersection of political communication and digital media studies, with a focus on methodology. She has published papers in journals such as *New Media & Society*, *International Journal of Communication*, *Journal of Information Technology & Politics*, *Information Communication & Society*, and *Policy & Internet*.

Stephen D. Reese is Jesse H. Jones Professor of Journalism and Associate Dean for Academic Affairs in the College of Communication at the University of Texas at Austin. He served as director of the School of Journalism for 7 years and has taught a wide range of courses. His research in political communication, press performance, and globalization has been published in numerous book chapters and articles. He coauthored, with Pamela Shoemaker, *Mediating the Message: Theories of Influence on Mass Media Content* (1991; 2nd ed., 1996), and a successor volume, *Mediating the Message in the 21st Century: A Media Sociology Perspective* (2014). He co-edited *Framing Public Life: Perspectives on Media and Our Understanding of the Social World* (1999) and, more recently, the "Media Production and Content" major section in the International Communication Association's *Encyclopedia of Communication* (2008/2015). Reese has been a regular faculty member at the Salzburg Global Seminar's Academy for Media and Global Change; has lectured internationally; and was the Kurt Baschwitz Visiting Professor at the Amsterdam School of Communication Research in the Netherlands.

Fei Shen is Assistant Professor at the Department of Media and Communication, City University of Hong Kong. His research interests primarily focus on new media and social transformation, civil society, public opinion, and the sociology of news. He has published articles in such journals as *Communication Theory*, *Journal of Communication*, *Communication Research*, *International Journal of Press/Politics*, *International Journal of Public Opinion Research*, *Asian Journal of Communication*, and *Chinese Journal of Communication*. He received the Google Faculty Research Award in 2014 for his project on freedom of expression and Asian values.

Rong Wang is a doctoral student at the Annenberg School for Communication and Journalism, University of Southern California (USC). Prior to USC, Rong worked at the International Development Research Centre (IDRC), based in Ottawa, Canada. At IDRC, she assisted in the development of new research programs to promote inclusive development in the network society. At USC Annenberg, Rong's research interests are focused on social media and collective action, crowdsourcing for innovation, network analysis, and organizational communication.

Guobin Yang is Associate Professor of Communication and Sociology in the Annenberg School for Communication and Department of Sociology at the

University of Pennsylvania. He studies social movements, mediated activism, environmentalism, and collective memory. He is the author of *The Power of the Internet in China: Citizen Activism Online* (2009) and co-editor (with Ching-Kwan Lee) of *Re-Envisioning the Chinese Revolution: The Politics and Poetics of Collective Memories in Reform China* (2007).

Xin Yu is a doctoral student at the School of Journalism and Communication, Tsinghua University, China. His research interests include communication technologies and social transformation, new media and social movements, and media sociology and public opinion. He graduated from Tsinghua University in 2011 with degrees in journalism and law, and was invited to be a Guest Academic Staff in 2013 at the Department of Political Science, Leiden University, the Netherlands.

Elaine J. Yuan is Associate Professor in the Communication Department at the University of Illinois at Chicago. Her research interests have included the interaction between audience agency and structural transformations of media fragmentation, polarization, and convergence. Her recent research focuses on the social implications of newer forms of communication in China. Dr. Yuan's work has been published in *Journal of Communication*, *New Media & Society*, and *Journal of Broadcasting & Electronic Media*, as well as other leading journals in the field of communication. She is also a research affiliate in the Web Mining Lab, City University of Hong Kong, and the Center for Intercultural New Media Research in the United States.

Fanxu Zeng is Associate Professor at the School of Journalism and Communication, Tsinghua University, China. His research areas are environmental communication, nongovernmental organization (NGO) communication, corporate social responsibility, new media, and public opinion. He is the author of *Negotiating Public Agenda in China: When NGOs Meet the Media* (2012, in Chinese), *Media as Mediators: Citizen Activism and Public Deliberation* (in Chinese, forthcoming). He has been published in academic journals such as *Chinese Journal of Communication*. He was a visiting scholar at Harvard-Yenching Institute, Hong Kong Baptist University, and Hong Kong City University.

Lize Zhang is a master student at the Department of Communication and New Media, National University of Singapore. She received her B.A. degree in journalism in China, and also had working experience in Chinese Internet industry. Her research interest lies in China and Internet, especially in China's Internet companies. Her current study is using a perspective of political economy to understand the role of Sina Weibo in interactions with society, market and state.

Weiyu Zhang is Assistant Professor at the Department of Communications and New Media, National University of Singapore. Her research focuses on civic engagement and information and communication technologies (ICTs), with an emphasis on Asia. Her published works have appeared in *Communication Research, Information, Communication, & Society, International Communication Gazette, Asian Journal of Communication, Chinese Journal of Communication, Computers in Human Behavior, First Monday, Journal of Media Psychology*, and *Javnost—The Public*, as well as many others.

Nan Zheng is Assistant Professor at the School of Media Arts and Design at James Madison University. Her research focuses on the impact of new media on global news communication and the economics of new media. Her work has been published in academic journals, including *International Journal on Media Management, Journal of Computer-Mediated Communication, Journalism & Mass Communication Quarterly*, and *Journalism Studies*.

Baohua Zhou is Professor at the School of Journalism, Fudan University, China. He is the director of the master's program of new media communication at Fudan. He is also a research fellow of the Center for Information and Communication Studies and associate director of Fudan's Media and Public Opinion Research Centre (FMORC). He studied at Nanyang Technological University of Singapore as an exchange student and was a visiting scholar at the University of Pennsylvania. His research focuses on new media, media effects, and public opinion. His research has been published in *Asian Journal of Communication, Chinese Journal of Communication*, and *Communication & Society*, as well as various communication journals in China.

INTRODUCTION

A New Agenda: Digital Media and Civic Engagement in Networked China

Wenhong Chen and Stephen D. Reese

Networks of communication have created new geometries of public deliberation and forms of civic engagement around the world, resulting in new dynamics for social change. Nowhere today is this process more vividly revealed than in China, an economically powerful, media-saturated, and connected society, with a leadership seeking to maintain stability while balancing rapid development with social control. As an important case and site for research, China challenges traditional approaches to understanding communication, media, and society—and requires new perspectives to adequately grasp these complex phenomena. This introductory overview aims to provide a guiding framework for the investigations in this volume.

Digital media in China reflect many contradictions of the Chinese society: rapid diffusion but glaring digital divides, significant economic freedom but strict political control, new opportunities for civic engagement but with pervasive surveillance. The mix of politics with market and the unique Chinese culture have created a multifaceted Internet, sometimes reinforcing while other times restructuring political and social inequalities, making research interesting and challenging at the same time.

Chinese Internet research, a crucial theme in its own right in understanding digital networks, has grown quickly since the 1990s (see reviews in Chen, 2014; Kluver & Yang, 2005; Yang, 2014). Almost every twist and turn in the tension between an authoritarian regime and the dramatic growth of Internet users has caught the sociological and communicative imagination. Scholars have been especially divided, debating whether the unprecedented levels of access to and use of a global technology may contribute to political change or social upheaval. Much of this discussion has revolved around issues of censorship and authoritarian controls, particularly in well-publicized cases involving foreign news organizations and information technology companies. Although the state still has enormous power to manage information flows, this focus on the more visible examples of top-down regulation and control understates how networked technologies have helped create new forms of civic engagement from the bottom up.

Journalism, as studied elsewhere around the world, has been the traditional media driver of citizen efficacy. And indeed journalists still have to deal with many political constraints in performing that role in China, but citizens the world over have been empowered to contribute to public discourse as never before (Reese, Rutigliano, Hyun, & Jeong, 2007). Indeed, Chinese citizens have become netizens (网民), media literate regarding the shortcomings of domestic and international news media as well as joining together to create their own forms of reporting. When online comments go viral via and beyond digital networks, they become "mass incidents," potentially stability-threatening out-pourings of social protests around corruption, threats to public safety, and other issues (Reese & Dai, 2009). As Reese (2009) observes, scholars need to recast their questions against the backdrop of these emerging deliberative spaces, "created by fluid networks of expression that don't always track national boundaries or traditional distinctions between the political and non-political" (p. 358), or even between journalism and other social practices.

This book examines the implications of digital media and the emergence of a global/transnational media space for civic engagement in a networked China. It asks whether and how mediated communication facilitates new patterns of civic practices and political association, which may contribute to an informed, con-nected, and engaged public in China. It explores how people and organizations use digital media technologies to navigate and negotiate their social landscapes. It aims to reveal the transformative power and the limitations of digital media technologies. We present 11 theoretically grounded, empirically based chapters, ranging from anti-corruption cases, campaigns of independent political candi-dates in local elections, grassroots environmental movements, and struggles of civil society organizations, to civic participation in memes, Twitter, protests, and fan communities. Chapter authors from Asia, Europe, and North America have used a variety of methods, including ethnography, interviews, surveys, and digital trace data. Undergirding these dynamic relationships are networks, based on digital media, which provide the critical component for civic engagement.

We start below, in laying out the context for these studies, with a mapping of the terrain, focusing on the historical development and current patterns of digital media access and use in China, as the results of and response to persistent censorship and aggressive marketization. Then we introduce two central themes of the book that organize the chapters: the implications, conditions, and contra-dictions of digital media technologies for civic engagement; and the emergence, composition, and function of a glocalized media space straddling boundaries of geography and issues.

Mapping the Terrain

Digital Media Adoption and Inequalities

By 1978, the Cold War had isolated China for almost three decades and the Great Cultural Revolution had the country teetering on the edge of economic bankruptcy. Far from achieving Chairman Mao's ambition "to surpass Britain and catch up with the U.S." (超英赶美), China found itself left behind by the West and many of its Asian neighbors. In 1978, China began the still ongoing state-initiated, gradual, and experimental transformation from a command economy to a market economy. Since then, the state has introduced a series of policies to "strengthen the nation through technologies" (科技兴国), encouraging investment and technology transfer from international corporations and the global Chinese diaspora. In particular, the state has been utilizing modern information and communication technologies (ICTs) as an engine and a symbol of modernization.

On September 20, 1987, with support from a research group at the University of Karlsruhe, professor Wang Yunfeng and his team successfully sent what is arguably the first e-mail from China to the world, fittingly titled "Across the Great Wall We Advance to the World" (越过长城, 走向世界). In 1995, Shuimu Tsinghua, the first bulletin board system (BBS) in China, was set up at Tsinghua University, quickly followed by a few other elite Chinese universities. In the same year, Jasmine Zhang, a private entrepreneur, started Beijing Information Highway Technology Company (瀛海威时空), the first commercial Chinese Internet service provider (ISP) and the first Chinese Internet café, located in Zhongguancun, a district in Beijing that eventually evolved into China's so-called Silicon Valley. Zhang advertised on a huge billboard at the main gateway of Zhongguancun in 1996, asking and answering a bold question: "How far is China from the Information Highway? 1500 meters north" (中国人离信息高速公路有多远? 向北1500米).

The rest is history. Although a relatively late starter, China has been catching up swiftly on the Information Highway. The number of Internet users in China increased from about 600,000 in 1997 to 632 million as of mid-2014, while the Internet penetration rate rose from 4% in 2002 to 47% in 2014, as documented by the semiannual reports issued by the China Internet Network Information Center (CNNIC, 1997–2014). As the world's largest mobile market, there are 572 million mobile Internet users, accounting for 83% of Chinese Internet users. The rapid diffusion of social media platforms, especially Weibo (微博), has significantly changed the media and communication landscape.

There have been, however, sharp digital divides and uneven Internet access and use, structured by education, age, gender, and regional differences (Chen & Wellman, 2004; Nam, Kim, Lee, & Duan, 2009). A typical Chinese Internet user is well-educated, urban, young, and male. Uneven telecommunication infrastructure, as well as income and education gaps, have resulted in significant differences in Internet access and use between the richer coastal region and the poorer hinterland, along with the divide between urban and rural areas (Pan, Yan, Jing, & Zheng, 2011). While more and more people gain home access, Internet cafés (or net bars, 网吧) have been unique and popular venues for Internet access and use, especially among young, working- or lower-income people (Qiu, 2013). Education, age, gender, and region affect not only access to digital media but also implications for civic engagement. For example, to use the Internet for their causes, rural activists have to rely on third parties (Wang, chapter 4). Since its introduction by Sina in 2009, Weibo has become an important venue of alternative news and information, political expression, and collective action (Chen, 2014). Yet, more than 80% of original posts in Sina Weibo are generated by 5% of users (Fu & Chau, 2013). Weibo campaigners during local elections were primarily young, male intellectuals or grassroots elites in the most developed regions such as Beijing, Shanghai, Guangdong, and Zhejiang (Shen, chapter 6).

The Complicated State-Society Relationship

Compared to the relative economic freedom in China, the Chinese Internet has been under strict political surveillance and censorship. In terms of infrastructure, the state owns and controls the few access points that link domestic and international Internet traffic. It has built a Great Firewall—a massive maze of laws, regulations, and administrative practices—to monitor ISPs and users. Facebook, YouTube, and Twitter have been blocked since the ethnic riots in Xinjiang in 2009. Instagram was banned during the recent pro-democracy mass demonstrations, the Umbrella Revolution, in Hong Kong in 2014. The state filters or blocks foreign news sites, social media sites, and sites carrying politically sensitive topics. All domestic and international companies doing business in China have to submit to censorship, which eventually contributed to Google's withdrawal of its Chinese search engine from mainland China in 2010.

The iron hand of the state has become increasingly covered in a velvet glove as it develops more sophisticated tactics to take advantage of digital media technologies. For instance, censors prefer misdirection over blocking, trying to make users perceive outright censorship as network error (Wright, 2014). A massive crew of online mercenaries is paid to monitor undesirable information and post pro-government/party messages in the government's effort to manipulate the online public sphere. In more recent developments, these control efforts have become more personal, with several opinion leaders in the Weibo-verse publicly shamed, and confessing on national TV business wrongdoings or paying for sex. Several editors and journalists were arrested in 2014 for alleged extortion or defamation. Both have sent chilling effects. The threat of permanent or temporary shutdown has encouraged widespread self-censorship among domestic ISPs.

The relationships between and among the state, corporations, and the emerging civil society have been complicated as they align and compete for new roles and opportunities in emergent networks enabled by digital media. This can be seen from at least three perspectives. First, the state can be the suppressor, the target, and sometimes the ally of social movements. Second, the state and its policies are neither monolithic nor omnipotent. For instance, a field experiment reveals that the policy and technological architecture of the Chinese national-level filtering system differs in targets and effects from region to region (Wright, 2014). Third, various institutional and individual actors have multiple, overlapping affiliations, commitments, and positions more nuanced than a binary stance of either with or against the state.

Indeed, there is a coevolution. A development cycle Qiu (2013) identified for Internet cafés in China is applicable to other digital media technologies: first, academics or entrepreneurs introduce an innovation, which may range from a copycat of original products or services in the United States or other markets, to a genuine indigenous service catering to Chinese culture and custom; second, the novelty triggers a phase of wide adoption that eventually attracts state intervention; and third, a revival occurs after a period of consolidation.

A few Internet firms have grown so fast and big that the state has had to adjust to them, which may erode its hegemony. For instance, while the state has rapidly expanded its censoring capacities and undesirable Weibo posts can be deleted within half an hour, the time lag allows hundreds of thousands of users to see and share those posts (Sullivan, 2014). The aggressive marketization and the intensive competition actually encourage Internet firms to test or push the boundaries of state censorship (Yang, 2009). For instance, Sina Weibo staff played the role of an organizing agent by setting up a page devoted to the high-speed train crash near Weizhou in July 2011, which trigged broader debates on national issues such as product safety, official corruption, and transparency (Bondes & Schucher, 2014).

An important premise for this volume is that, digital divides and political controls notwithstanding, digital media have opened previously unavailable space for citizens to seek information, share ideas, and shape public opinions. With the Internet giving millions of people a window to the outside world and more diverse perspectives, digital media have become the conduits and the locus where millions of Chinese engage in self-representation, creative expression, and civic participation.

Theme 1: Civic Engagement: Forms, Constraints, and Contradictions

The first theme embraces the new forms as well as constraints and contradictions of civic engagement enabled by digital media. We develop this theme starting with the big picture before turning to six specific cases, where we explore the issues, forms, and tactics.

Using a large-scale national random sample survey, Zhou (chapter 1) conducts a multilevel analysis of the relationship between Internet use and civic engagement and its variation by individual and contextual factors. Results suggest a positive relationship between Internet use and civic engagement (measured as voluntary association participation and opinion expression), which is moderated by political interest at the individual and the county levels, respectively. While a higher Internet penetration rate at the county level may indicate more local Internet users, greater exchange of information and opinion, and more opportunities for the formation of voluntary associations in the local context, it is not statistically significant to civic engagement. Zhou's chapter advances the debate on the Internet implications for civic engagement in China by highlighting the importance of contextual factors. As political interest plays a more important role than access to the Internet in affording civic engagement, the results support the normalization thesis that the impacts of the Internet have tended to be most salient for individuals who are already more active and who live in a more active local context (Chen, 2014).

Comparing social and environmental activism in Shanghai and Xiamen with ethnic riots in Tibet and Xinjiang, Weber (2011) found that the outcome of Internet- and mobile-mediated collective action depended on the nature of the issue rather than on how skillfully technologies were employed. Issues that fundamentally challenge the legitimacy of the current political power are harshly suppressed while livelihood issues, environmental concerns, and civil rights issues were more negotiable. Accordingly, Weibo posts criticizing the state, top officials, or policies are often left undeleted, but posts calling for collective action are swiftly deleted. In terms of issues, environmental and anti-corruption cases have been considered less threatening to the state and thus open up a new space for promoting political accountability, as demonstrated in the 10 anti-corruption cases in Dai, Zeng, and Yu (chapter 2); the three cases in Liu (chapter 5); and the environmental collective action in Wang (chapter 4).

Instead of organized or direct confrontation, connective action—self-organized personalized politics diffused via interpersonal networks enabled by digital, social, and mobile media—allows citizens to communicate, deliberate, and mobilize for new forms of grassroots civic and political activities (Bennett & Segerberg, 2011). Several chapters advance research on this kind of connective action by examining its mechanisms and contours in the Chinese context (Dai, Zeng, & Yu, chapter 2; Cheong & Chen, chapter 3; Wang, chapter 4; Liu, chapter 5; Yuan, chapter 11). In terms of mechanisms, digital and mobile media make the boundaries between the private and the public more porous and easier to switch (Liu, chapter 5). Digital media articulate lived, private experience and emotions in the public, allowing diverse voices to circumvent the strict scrutiny over traditional media and enhance the visibility of oppressed groups. Such infiltration and leveling up of the life world into the public sphere can trigger intensive public discussion and expression when individual grievances strongly resonate with larger sociopolitical issues, such as power abuse or inequalities (Dai, Zeng, & Yu, chapter 2). Satires, parody, mockery, homonyms, and puns are the most prevalent tactics used as expressions of dissent—bypassing, testing, and pushing the boundaries set by the state. For instance, most environmental activism has been spontaneous and pragmatic, using a moderate repertoire of communicative tactics to target specific polluters, corporate practices, or officials, collaborating with rather than challenging the legitimacy of the state (Yang, 2009).

Online anti-corruption is perhaps one of the most visible and successful forms of digital activism in China. Dai, Zeng, and Yu (chapter 2) use the concept of subactivism (Bakardjieva, 2009) to capture new forms of participation in public affairs or civic activities at the level of everyday life afforded by digital media networks. Analyzing online discussion centered on 10 high-profile online anti-corruption cases, Dai and colleagues shed light on the process and mechanisms through which citizens' expression of private concerns enters into public discursive spaces, as seemingly random exposure of private affairs sparks massive discussion and action on corruption. A "space of flows" (Castells, 1999), the dynamic arrangements of distributed yet simultaneous social practices supported by digital communication networks, enables and accelerates the circulation and interaction of distributed information and people organized around shared interests. It helps to link a variety of media spaces in order to form networked power that contributes to the downfall of corrupted officials.

Cheong and Chen (chapter 3) offer a unique perspective by examining how citizens—as producers, distributors, critics, and protestors—created and circulated two memes involving the notion of "mainland invasion" across multiple platforms in postcolonial Chinese societies, such as Singapore and Hong Kong, and their sociocultural implications across online-offline spaces. They theorize and demonstrate the creation, sharing, and remixing of satirical, emotionally charged, sometimes offensive memes as "middle-ground resistance" (Scott, 1995), an alternative form of civic engagement that can generate and sustain public discussion and political action on contentious issues filtered by mainstream media. The emotionally charged satirical discourse, as an alternative participatory form of personalized civic engagement that contests official policies and narratives, offers a middle path of resistance in societies with limited free press (Cheong & Chen, chapter 3). The derogatory portrayal of mainland Chinese may resonate with concerns about the rise of China or resentments of the inflow of mainland Chinese in Singapore or Hong Kong. While it may not change immigration policies in these places, the "locust" meme was a factor that contributed to the Hong Kong government's banning of mainland Chinese tourists buying and taking more than 1.8 kilograms of imported infant milk powder in 2013 (Cheong & Chen, chapter 3). The locust meme has appeared in recent protests in Hong Kong, including the Occupy Central protest in 2014. Such "weapons of the weak," however, can be a two-edged sword. Venting, vilification, and polarization involved in these comments may offer psychological catharsis but reinforce prejudices.

Drawing on in-depth interviews in four villages in Anhui and Jiangsu, Wang (chapter 4) advances a refined understanding of structural constraints that hinder Internet implications. ICT use was limited due to villagers' limited literacy and knowledge, the lack of leadership and political trust, as well as the perceived high cost of ICT use and its limited impact in public affairs. Multiple players, local and global NGOs, mainstream media, and local government officials were important in the success of the environmental movement in Village Q. NGOs, after learning the villagers' story from national TV, helped local activists to use digital media technologies, especially mobile phones, for communication, evidence documentation, and information searching. The pressure from mainstream media on the one hand and interactions between the state and villagers on the other eventually pushed local officials from a passive to a more active stance on environmental protection, which resulted in the relocation of chemical factories and villagers' greater trust in the government.

Mobile technology's effects on protest participation have been a perennial theme in the mobile communication literature since Rheingold's *Smart Mob* (2002). Qiu (2008) further demonstrates that mobile communication is used to engage, compete with, or bypass traditional and digital media, speeding and scaling up the formation of civil society. Few studies, however, have systematically examined mobile communication and contentious politics in China. Drawing on interviews, Liu (chapter 5) fills this critical gap. The embeddedness of mobile devices in interpersonal communication networks, as well as the mundane, pedestrian, yet diverse use of such devices, makes them a powerful tool for protest mobilization. First, the conversational, expressive, peer-to-peer communicative pattern afforded by mobile phones can articulate everyday experience and channel participants' "unrecognized, suppressed, and marginalized" emotions for contentious politics. Emotional mobilization has been one of the major repertoires of digital activism in China (Yang, 2009). Mobile phones enhance interpersonal communication especially among people who share strong ties, which has been identified in social movement literature as a key mechanism of recruiting and retaining protest participants. Liu reveals that mobile communication helps to maintain *guanxi* (关系), the Chinese notion of strong interpersonal relations that entail reciprocity and obligation, a crucial condition for citizens to overcome great risks and costs associated with protest participation in an authoritarian regime.

The Internet affords a growing awareness and a new venue of experimenting with possibilities of action previously inaccessible. Shen (chapter 6) investigates emergent politicians running for seats in district-level elections of the People's Congress in 2011 and 2012. Without the backing of the ruling party, they were so-called independent candidates. Analyzing Weibo accounts and posts of 130 independent candidates, Shen examines the candidates' social media practices and strategies for political expression and mobilization of the electorate, despite government censorship. Weibo posts of these independent candidates focused on election and social issues, offered opinions, questioned authority, and mobilized supporters but carefully avoided challenging the political status quo. Four types of candidates are identified: intellectuals, legal rights defenders, grassroots elites, and grassroots participants. The intellectuals tended to discuss more topics about the campaign, election law, and democracy, while legal rights defenders tended to be more cynical and angry. The dominant emotion expressed was anger, which might reflect authentic dissatisfaction but could be a strategy for gaining media and user attention. Shen also illustrates constraints of digital media for political participation. First, Weibo use had limited impact on the election result, as few independent candidates won, regardless of whether they had campaigned on Weibo or not. Second, lacking election success, a sign of the relative effectiveness of Weibo campaigns was whether the candidates drew mainstream or digital media attention: a quarter of them got mainstream media coverage while more than 60% were mentioned in online media such as blogs or discussion forums. Although the space offered by Weibo for independent political communication was precarious and subjected to state surveillance and crackdown—their Weibo accounts were often selectively and closely monitored—it did allow nascent politicians and their supporters to get around significant institutional and technical barriers, thanks to Weibo's relative affordability and accessibility compared to offline media or other digital tools such as BBS, IM, or Websites.

Drawing on a case study of the 2010 dispute between the Global Fund's Country Coordinating Mechanism (CCM) and representatives from the Chinese government and civil sectors, Galler (chapter 7) provides a rich account of the mixed effects of ICT-enabled networks of transnational civil society organizations (CSOs) in China. Facilitating the flow of knowledge and funding, the entry of transnational CSOs in China has benefited Chinese HIV NGOs, while indigenous NGOs have also benefited from ICTs for lowered costs of communication. Thus, to a certain extent, digital media allow local actors to form and participate in glocalized networks—combining intensive local connections and extensive global outreach (Chen & Wellman, 2009), which may contribute to long-term collective action and activism through organization and capacity building. However, the extent to which such glocalized networks affect access and mobilization of resources for development and social changes is ambivalent. The resource dependence of Chinese CSOs on transnational CSOs, combined with state restriction that has intentionally kept domestic CSOs weak, exacerbates interorganizational competition. Furthermore, ICTs could discredit consensus-based deliberation due to a lack of governance structures or discursive protocols for consensus building (Galler, chapter 7). Such unintended consequences show that the Internet may lead to polarization and disenfranchisement rather than improved communication or collaboration.

Theme 2: Glocalized Media Space: Emergence, Composition, and Function

Our second theme is situated in a larger global context, especially regarding how global forces interact with local phenomena to form global/transnational media spaces straddling boundaries of geography and issues of their composition and functions. In particular, we use the term *glocalized media space*—conceived of as the interactions between and among local, national, regional, and international media producers, distributors, and audiences—to explore how it has changed the ways citizens and activists and their organizations interact and deliberate. The term *glocalized media space* highlights the multivalent, multidirectional relationships between the local and the global, which may include acceptance, resistance, and appropriation.

The rise of China as a major global power in the last several decades has generated greater global demand of news about China. Yet, there are considerable logistic and linguistic challenges regarding covering China, which have created unique opportunities for "bridge blogs." Zheng (chapter 8) shows that as a form of global journalism practice, bridge blogs are operated by professional or citizen journalists or activists. As the name suggests, such blogs serve as bridges that connect otherwise disconnected components in the global media space and contribute to the transnational flow of news, information, and perspectives—especially in a time when many news organizations have to cut budgets and close foreign bureaus. They complement and compete with professional news coverage. Bridge blogs that occupy more central positions, however, are more likely to translate Chinese media content into English, exporting news and opinions on China—and made in China—to the world rather than engaging in original news-gathering or using referral practices (Zheng, chapter 8).

A glocalized media space becomes especially dense when major sociopolitical events attract tremendous attention from traditional and social media. One such event was the downfall of Bo Xilai, a prominent Chinese politician, charged and convicted for abuse of power. Building on theories of the global fifth estate (Dutton, 2009), Menchen-Trevino and Mao (chapter 9) compare topics and critiques on Twitter, both in English and Chinese, regarding the Bo case. Drawing on a dataset of over 10,000 tweets from January to March 2013, they demonstrate that English-language tweets were more limited compared to Chinese-language tweets. While tweets in both languages amplified mainstream journalism, Chinese tweets had more original commentary and were more likely to be critical of the ruling party and express skepticism of mainstream news media. In addition, political activists were only found in Chinese tweets. Contributing to these gaps are differences among users, mainstream media coverage, and the linguistic affordance of Twitter. English- and Chinese-language Twitter users differ in news tropes, background knowledge, and issue relevance. Mainland Chinese who have to get around the Great Firewall to use Twitter are likely to be more engaged in political expression that is prohibited in China. Given the significance of the Bo case in China, Chinese-language mainstream media offered more detailed coverage than their English-language counterparts, aided in part by the greater expression afforded by the character-based Chinese language compared to English within Twitter's 140-character limit.

Recognizing that civic engagement can come from unexpected places and actors, a growing number of studies have examined the civic and political potential of entertainment media. Many fans have bypassed political and economic barriers to access foreign reality shows not broadcast in China. In the penultimate chapter, observing and interviewing moderators and members of post bars (贴吧, a type of organized online forum) of foreign reality shows, Zhang and Zhang's ethnography (chapter 10) directs attention to these fascinating yet often neglected fandom communities and their civic potential. More specifically, situated at the intersection of media globalization and civic engagement, Zhang and Zhang examine transcultural media fandom and its influence on fans' reception and appreciation of local and transnational popular culture, showing that online fandom communities facilitate members' resource sharing, identity expression, and social interaction. Furthermore, online deliberation on the originality, authenticity, and monetization of entertainment media leads to a corresponding critique by members of the inauthenticity (假) and overcommercialization in programming of state-controlled mainstream media, such as CCTV or the more marketized Hunan TV.

Discussion: The Power of the Internet, Pendulum and Incremental Changes

The intellectual curiosity about the power of the Internet in facilitating social movements and regime change in China has been further fueled by the Arab Spring in 2011. On the one hand, the impacts of digital media technologies have been celebrated as transformational. The alternative public sphere can bypass the agenda setting and censorship of the mainstream media; make previously unseen or unknown dissent, resistances, and alternatives visible; and push the government for transparency and accountability (Tong & Zuo, 2014). Serving as prime portals for global dissemination of self-expression of personal emotions, concerns, and opinions on public affairs, digital media enable myriad self-organized, networked forms of contentious politics, aggregating and scaling up many micro actions from ordinary citizens without conventional organization, as chapters in this volume demonstrate. On the other hand, years after the Arab Spring, the Occupy Wall Street movement, and various other protests, enthusiasm for Facebook- or Twitter-type revolutions in China has faded—which highlights once again the importance of understanding the implications of digital media and technologies in specific social and historical contexts. For instance, due to a lack of institutional guidance (Galler, chapter 7), ICTs may lead to unintended consequences such as polarization, disenfranchisement, and funding shortages. The absence of vibrant civic organizations hinders the transformation of reactive, local protests into a normative political agenda.

While the pendulum may swing one way or the other, most analysts have taken the middle ground, with guarded optimism that the power of the Internet will contribute to democracy in China in the long run—and that the Internet plays a facilitating role rather than itself being the cause of sociopolitical changes (Yang, 2009). Moving beyond a binary, linear approach, a more interesting and challenging question is how to advance a better understanding of the paradoxical patterns of digital media appropriation as well as their nonlinear, contingent impacts (Chen, 2014).

In our final chapter, drawing on both structuralist and culturalist perspectives, Yuan (chapter 11) provides a broader perspective on our themes by offering a critical review of the literature on mediated activism in contemporary China, especially the construction of the public in China's rapid modernization process that has yielded new dynamics of social structure and cultural agency. While the structuralist perspective examines mediated activism in the large sociopolitical context and the changing relationships between the state and society, the culturalist approach centers on the production, distribution, and consumption of media text and events and their impact on individuals' identity, subjectivity, and ethics. Yuan further advances a multi-institutional approach (Armstrong & Bernstein, 2008; Yang, 2009), which helps to shed light on the historic and social significance of indeterminate, multivalent, tenuous outcomes in a mediated process in which power dynamics and cultural practices affect one another.

The literature has offered rich accounts of the aesthetics, genres, and strategies of online activism in China (Yang, 2009), and by now it is hard to imagine that any significant civic engagement, social movements, or sociopolitical changes could happen without digital media. Yet, as Liu points out (chapter 5), while many studies have examined the usage patterns of digital or mobile media in collective action, few have empirically evaluated the broader contributions and impact of such collective actions.

The concept of liberalization—defined as the growing respect for and reinforcement of citizenship and rights (O'Donnell & Schmitter, 1986; Wang, chapter 4)—may help to capture such ramifications that are "not inconsequential" (Cheong & Chen, chapter 3, p. 71). Used wisely, ICTs can contribute to liberalization, as cases in this volume have shown. For instance, the anti-corruption cases are relatively effective in terms of leading to the downfall—and sometimes conviction—of accused officials (Dai, Zeng, & Yu, chapter 2). Villagers' environmental activism, for example, helps to increase trust between the state and citizens (Wang, chapter 4). A global fifth estate enabled by digital citizen media increases public scrutiny and holds the powerful more accountable, as indicated by the Chinese court's unprecedented Weibo-cast of the Bo Xilai trial, almost blow by blow, which has been interpreted as a calculated move for projecting transparency (Menchen-Trevino & Mao, chapter 9). Fan activism finds a way to get around state control, and the post bar–enabled fan communities prepare them for civil discourse and collaboration, nurturing civic culture in the long term (Zhang & Zhang, chapter 10).

New forms of communication, expression, and association notwithstanding, significant structural changes come from changes in power dynamics in the communication networks that have been "programmed" to favor the political and business elites. Online anti-corruption action is relatively effective because it happens to be aligned with the interests of the regime: it can be readily used for cleaning up corrupted middle-level officials ("catching the flies" 打苍蝇) as well as for power struggles among the top leadership of the ruling party ("hunting the tigers" 打老虎). While the 10 cases studied by Dai and colleagues are more focused on middle-level officials, high profile anti-corruption cases involving top national leaders such as the Bo Xilai case and the unfolding case of Zhou Yongkang have recently emerged. It seems that the state may have learned from netizens to exploit the potentials of networked anti-corruption.

Conclusion: A New Agenda

The chapters presented here demonstrate the growing maturity and sophistication of the field and have pointed to promising venues for future research. First, it is crucial to understand the power of digital media in their complex diversity, as we examine the broader media landscape embedded in the Chinese social structure. While traditional and digital media in China are exploited by the state to enhance the rule of the Communist Party, a growing economy has created a vibrant marketplace for them to compete for audiences and advertisers. People use a repertoire of communication and media technologies for diverse purposes in a converging yet fragmentary media landscape. Growing repertoires of channels, platforms, media multiplexity, and multidirectional interactions between online and offline media call for studies that examine the implications of digital, social, and mobile media beyond a single, specific medium or technology. For instance, only in comparison do we learn that face-to-face meetings with local officials remained the preferred mode of communication of villagers (Wang, chapter 4). Shen's research on independent candidates points to questions about interactions between and among candidates, their supporters, and detractors beyond the Weibo-verse (chapter 6). Zheng's chapter on bridge blogs and the global media space suggests extending future analysis to offline networks of bridge bloggers and how they cooperate and compete with media organizations, activist groups, and NGOs across national borders (chapter 8).

Second, more research is needed to take into account mobile media use for civic and collective actions. The personal, pervasive, portable, and perpetual communication accommodated by mobile devices allows users to easily switch between the most private and the most public spaces, and gives members of disadvantaged groups a more accessible tool for civic engagement. The Occupy Central protest shows that smartphones have become indispensable tools for the mobilization and organization of protests and demonstrations, bypassing the state control of mobile telecommunication networks.

Third, comparative studies can reveal variations of digital media adoption, usage, and impacts. For instance, investigating differences between independent candidates on Weibo and those political candidates on Twitter in Western democracies can generate novel insights (Shen, chapter 6). The complexities and challenges of cross-linguistic comparisons may require cross-cultural collaboration among scholars who speak different languages as well as cross-disciplinary collaboration among scholars fluent with different methodologies (Menchen-Trevino & Mao, chapter 9).

Fourth, the case study approach has dominated existing studies (Yuan, chapter 11), a perspective that often seems to fit the contingent and dynamic phenomena we seek to explain in the Chinese context. While the scope, process, and implications of each case can be interesting and important, the literature will benefit from more large-scale random-sample survey data, as well as mixed methods that integrate qualitative, quantitative, and digital trace data for a layered, generalizable account of digital media technologies in China and beyond.

The Communist Party has built its legitimacy on economic growth and political stability. Most Chinese citizens, in particular the middle class, have benefited from the prosperity gained through more than three decades of economic reform, although the wealth distribution has been far from even. The vision of building a strong, affluent nation, which Xi Jinping, China's current president, has articulated as the Chinese Dream, still holds different social strata together. However, the cohesion depends on the state continuing to fulfill its economic promise and manage the many potential challenges and threats to that dream.

Digital media technologies per se will not trigger revolutions or deliver democracy, at least not as popularly imagined in the form of dramatic and sudden regime overthrow. New geometries of public deliberation and forms of civic engagement enabled by digital communication and media technologies will contribute to social changes at many levels and forms, visible or less so. But how they do so will depend on the negotiation and struggles, oftentimes digitally mediated, among the multiple institutions involved: the state, corporations, and an emerging civil society. We hope this volume provides new agendas to explore these dynamics as we seek to better understand Networked China.

References

Armstrong, E. A., & Bernstein, M. (2008). Culture, power, and institutions: A multi-institutional politics approach to social movements. *Sociological Theory, 26*(1), 74–99. doi:10.1111/j.1467-9558.2008.00319.x

Bakardjieva, M. (2009). Subactivism: Lifeworld and politics in the age of the Internet. *Information Society, 25*(2), 91–104.

Bennett, L. W., & Segerberg, A. (2011). Digital media and the personalization of collective action. *Information, Communication & Society, 14*(6), 770–799. doi:10.1080/13691 18x.2011.579141

Bondes, M., & Schucher, G. (2014). Derailed emotions: The transformation of claims and targets during the Wenzhou online incident. *Information, Communication & Society, 17*(1), 45–65. doi:10.1080/1369118x.2013.853819

Castells, M. (1999). Grassrooting the space of flows. *Urban Geography, 20*(4), 294–302. doi:10.2747/0272-3638.20.4.294

Chen, W. (2014). Taking stock, moving forward: The Internet, social networks and civic engagement in Chinese societies. *Information, Communication & Society, 17*(1), 1–6. doi:10.1080/1369118x.2013.857425

Chen, W., & Wellman, B. (2004). The global digital divide—within and between countries. *IT & Society, 1*(7), 39–45.

Chen, W., & Wellman, B. (2009). Net and jet: The Internet use, travel and social networks of Chinese Canadian entrepreneurs. *Information, Communication & Society, 12*(4), 525–547. doi:10.1080/13691180902858080

China Internet Network Information Center (CNNIC). (1997–2014). Semiannual survey report on the development of China's Internet. Retrieved from http://www.cnnic.org.cn/

Dutton, W. H. (2009). The fifth estate emerging through the network of networks. *Prometheus, 27*(1), 1–15. doi:10.1080/08109020802657453

Fu, K.-W., & Chau, M. (2013). Reality check for the Chinese microblog space: A random sampling approach. *Plos One, 8*(3), e58356. doi:10.1371/journal.pone.0058356

Kluver, R., & Yang, C. (2005). The Internet in China: A meta-review of research. *Information Society, 21*(4), 301–308. doi:10.1080/01972240591007616

Nam, C., Kim, S., Lee, H., & Duan, B. (2009). Examining the influencing factors and the most efficient point of broadband adoption in China. *Journal of Research and Practice in Information Technology, 41*(1), 25–38.

O'Donnell, G., & Schmitter, P. C. (1986). *Transitions from authoritarian rule: Tentative conclusions about uncertain democracies.* Baltimore: Johns Hopkins University Press.

Pan, Z., Yan, W., Jing, G., & Zheng, J. (2011). Exploring structured inequality in Internet use behavior. *Asian Journal of Communication, 21*(2), 116–132. doi:10.1080/01292986.2010.543555

Qiu, J. L. (2008). Mobile civil society in Asia: A comparative study of People Power II and the Nosamo Movement. *Javnost—The Public, 15*(3), 39–58.

Qiu, J. L. (2013). Cybercafés in China: Community access beyond gaming and tight government control. *Library Trends, 62*(1), 121–139.

Reese, S. D. (2009). The future of journalism in emerging deliberative space. *Journalism: Theory, Practice, Criticism, 10*(3), 362–364.

Reese, S. D., & Dai, J. (2009). Citizen journalism in the global news arena: China's new media critics. In S. Allan & E. Thorsen (Eds.), *Citizen journalism: Global perspectives* (pp. 221–231). New York: Peter Lang.

Reese, S. D., Rutigliano, L., Hyun, K., & Jeong, J. (2007). Mapping the blogosphere: Citizen-based media in the global news arena. *Journalism: Theory, Practice, Criticism, 8*(3), 235–262. doi:10.1177/1464884907076459

Rheingold, H. (2002). *Smart mobs: The next social revolution.* New York: Basic Books.

Scott, J. C. (1995). *Weapons of the weak: Everyday forms of peasant resistance.* New Haven, CT: Yale University Press.

Sullivan, J. (2014). China's Weibo: Is faster different? *New Media & Society, 16*(1), 24–37. doi:10.1177/1461444812472966

Tong, J., & Zuo, L. (2014). Weibo communication and government legitimacy in China: A computer-assisted analysis of Weibo messages on two "mass incidents." *Information, Communication & Society, 17*(1), 66–85. doi:10.1080/1369118x.2013.839730

Weber, I. (2011). Mobile, online and angry: The rise of China's middle-class civil society? *Critical Arts-South-North Cultural and Media Studies, 25*(1), 25–45. doi:10.1080/02560 046.2011.552204

Wright, J. (2014). Regional variation in Chinese Internet filtering. *Information, Communication & Society, 17*(1), 121–141. doi:10.1080/1369118x.2013.853818

Yang, G. (2009). *The power of the Internet in China: Citizen activism online.* New York: Columbia University Press.

Yang, G. (2014). Political contestation in Chinese digital spaces: Deepening the critical inquiry. *China Information, 28*(2), 135–144. doi:10.1177/0920203x14539910

PART I

Digital Media Technologies and Civic Engagement

Implications, Conditions, and Contradictions

1

INTERNET USE, SOCIO-GEOGRAPHIC CONTEXT, AND CITIZENSHIP ENGAGEMENT

A Multilevel Model on the Democratizing Effects of the Internet in China[1]

Baohua Zhou

Whether or not digital media, especially the Internet, have the potential to facilitate citizenship engagement has been argued as one of the most contested topics in Chinese communication research (Rosen, 2010) and has attracted many academic efforts (e.g., Chan & Zhou, 2011; Lei, 2011; Yang, 2009; Zheng, 2008). This chapter aims to further advance this line of research in two ways. First, it assesses the associations between Internet use and two dimensions of engagement (civic participation and opinion expression) in China with a nationwide random sample survey data set. Second, and more importantly, it will analyze how these associations vary by contextual factors besides individual characteristics. Unlike prior empirical studies in which China was treated as a singular entity, this study takes into account the heterogeneity across various socio-geographic units and examines the contextual effects of the influence of the Internet in China. In particular, I will focus on two factors—Internet penetration and the aggregate level of political interest—and explore whether or not either of them independently influences citizenship engagement and moderates the relationship between individual Internet use with individuals' engagement in public life.

Literature Review

Internet and Engagement: General Arguments and Chinese Context

The Internet's political and social role in facilitating citizen engagement has been extensively discussed by scholars in Western democracies (e.g., Boulianne, 2009; Xenos & Moy, 2007). One set of scholars contend that the Internet has the potential to encourage people to participate in the political process and civic activities. The major logical thoughts behind this positive effect include the following: (1) owing to its technological advantages, the Internet has lowered the cost for engagement and eased the socioeconomic restrictions on participation among citizens, especially money, time, and effort (Delli Carpini, Cook, & Jacobs, 2004); (2) as an information-rich medium, the Internet effectively promotes the flow of information and exchanges of opinion, which constitute the basic resource for democratic citizenship based on the informed citizenry thesis (Shah, Cho, Eveland, & Kwak, 2005; Weber, Loumakis, & Bergman, 2003); and (3) as a horizontal communicative space, the Internet also facilitates the development of social networks and the growth of social capital, which help people to coordinate their actions and engage in collective activities (e.g., Shah, Schmierbach, Hawkins, Espino, & Donavan, 2002). At the same time, another set of scholars argue that the Internet has negative impacts on civic and political participation. Major reasons include using the Internet primarily for entertainment (Putnam, 2000) and the fragmentation and polarization of online deliberation (Sunstein, 2001), as well as "slacktivism" or "clicktivism" in front of one's computer that results in defusing or escaping offline engagement and activism (Morozov, 2011).

Which story better reflects empirical facts? A meta-analysis examining 38 independent empirical studies conducted in the United States on the relationship between Internet use and engagement seems to support the camp of optimists (Boulianne, 2009). In all of the 166 Internet effects on engagement tested in Boulianne's study, 77% are positive.[2] The author concludes that Internet use appears to have a positive, albeit small, effect on citizen engagement.

Different from established Western democratic societies, China has traditionally been a society with a low level of engagement because of the long-term authoritarian political culture and strict state control (Wang, 2008). Things have changed since the marketization-oriented economic reform and open policy introduced in 1978. Although due to the authoritarian political system, the meaningful and sustainable participation based on stable and autonomous institutions remains lacking (Lieberthal, 2004; Shi, 1997), various forms of engagement have actually been developed in the era of social transformation, especially when the state has begun to relax its total control over society and people have begun to form a greater consciousness of their citizenship. Those activities could be categorized into two main types to be focused on in this study: the first one is civic participation, which is defined as individuals' involvement in the formal and informal social organizations or groups that are not dictated by the state, such as community homeowner associations, voluntary groups, fan clubs, and so on; the other one is opinion expression, referring to those expressive behaviors on a specific personal or social issue or problem via various channels such as governmental sectors, traditional media, new media, and so on (e.g., Chan & Zhou, 2011; Yang, 2009). Compared with other activities such as taking part in protests or engaging in collective actions, these two types of engagement require fewer costs and thus have more opportunities to take place. So they represent more regularly prescribed criteria for democratic citizens and could complement earlier studies focused on only political participation under some extraordinary circumstances (e.g., Cai, 2004).

Besides the general advantages of facilitating citizenship engagement in Western democracies, the Internet has special political and social significance in the Chinese context. It has been treated as one typical "alternative media" for Chinese society. As scholars have argued (Lei, 2011; Zheng, 2008), the emergence of the Internet in China does not merely mean an increase in the quantity of information but also suggests the possibility of having qualitatively different information and communication in terms of diversity and alternatives. There is no question that the Chinese Internet is subject to tight regulations that bar negative references to the top leadership, the legitimacy of the Chinese Communist Party (CCP), and other politically sensitive issues (Sohmen, 2001). Nevertheless, it is fair to say that cyberspace is much more abundant, liberal, and diverse than the state-controlled mass media and has raised information flow and opinion expression to an unprecedented level (Goldman, 2005; Yang, 2009; Zheng, 2008). Some qualitative analyses have found that the Internet could reshape social organizations and facilitate civic engagement in China; these analyses conclude that the civil society and the Internet are energizing each other in their coevolutionary development (Yang, 2003, 2009; Zheng, 2008).

Although still scant in numbers in general, there are already several quantitative studies to show that the Internet is positively related to engagement in the Chinese context (e.g., Chan & Zhou, 2011; Lei, 2011; Pan, Jing, Liu, Yan, & Zheng, 2012). Based on the current theoretical arguments and empirical findings, I will test the first hypothesis in this study.

H1: Even controlling for other individual and aggregate level factors, Internet use is positively related to both types of engagement (civic participation [H1–1] and opinion expression [H1–2]) in China.

Political Interest as an Individual-Level Moderator

Although optimists argue that Internet use can facilitate citizenship engagement and the existing majority of empirical studies seem to support this, a less studied question is whether or not the effects of Internet use are universal or conditional. A line of theoretical discussion related to this issue is the debate of the "instrumental approach" versus the "psychological approach" introduced by Xenos and Moy (2007). The models following the instrumental approach tend to see the Internet as an easygoing and low-cost "instrument" for all people to get information to facilitate engagement. That means the effects of the Internet are direct and universal. Alternatively, the psychological approach argues that the impact of the Internet is not evenly distributed but contingent upon several individual factors such as psychological characteristics (Bimber, 2003; Xenos & Moy, 2007). New media technologies themselves are not the sole source producing effects but always interact with individual characteristics shaping the power of effects. This kind of view is also echoed in the debates between "mobilization" and "activation" arguments (Boulianne, 2009). The mobilization view emphasizes that the Internet could mobilize politically inactive populations; the activation view posits that the Internet serves to activate those citizens who are already interested in politics.

Among various psychological factors, Xenos and Moy (2007) argue that political interest should be a significant contingent factor, given that whether or not people have an interest in public affairs is not only one of the most important influential factors for participation (Verba, Schlozman & Brady, 1995) or political discussion (McLeod et al., 1999), but also it drives people toward more active use of the Internet and engagement in online activities. By analyzing the 2004 American National Election Studies data, they find that although Internet use has direct effects on information acquisition and use, its effects on civic or political engagement do depend on levels of political interest, which supports the psychological approach.

In the Chinese context, political interest has also been proven to be an important psychological factor to encourage citizenship engagement (Lei, 2011; Pan et al., 2012). In the past, even Chinese people have had interest in engaging in public affairs, but they feel it is difficult to find a convenient way to do this. The Internet has for the first time provided a platform for ordinary people to express themselves and participate in politics (Hao & Li, 2001; Zhou, 2008). Even though the Internet has given every user an opportunity to engage, those who have greater interest in political and public affairs will be more motivated and able to make use of Internet resources, especially for political information and opinions (rather than other types of content such as entertainment), further improving the likelihood to engage in citizenship activities. So I posit that the higher level of political interest will interact with Internet use to produce more robust effects on citizenship engagement.

> H2: The positive relationship between Internet use and civic participation (H2–1) and opinion expression (H2–2) will be contingent on individuals' levels of political interest.

Socio-Geographic Context: Cross-Level Interactions

As communication scholars have argued, citizenship engagement is a multilevel phenomenon that needs to be examined not only by individual-level but also contextual-level factors (Friedland & McLeod, 1999; Kim & Ball-Rokeach, 2006a). On the one hand, the contextual variables could impact individuals' engagement; on the other hand, the importance of individual-level factors on engagement is dependent on contextual factors. Unsatisfied with the long-standing character-istics of overly narrow individualism in communication research, scholars have called for creating multilevel or cross-level research by paying more attention to the influence of various types of social systems, including families, communities, organizations, and countries (e.g., Price, Ritchie, & Eulau, 1991; Slater, Snyder, & Hayes, 2006). With increased access to multilevel data and the development of multilevel modeling and analytical techniques, scholars have conducted cross-level analysis on the influence of media on engagement, theoretically and empiri-cally, nationally and internationally.

For example, Kang and Kwak (2003) examine the interaction effects of resi-dential stability (as a contextual factor) and local media use (as an individual-level factor) on the variations in individuals' civic participation. They find that the use of local TV news is more likely to lead to community participation among those living in a neighborhood with lower residential mobility, while time spent watching TV tends to be negatively related to civic engagement among those whose residence in a community is shorter. From a communication infrastructure theory perspective, which treats the media (including the Internet) embedded in the community communication action context, Kim and Ball-Rokeach (2006a) examined how individuals' civic engagement is influenced by two multilevel components of the communication infrastructure—an integrated connectedness to a storytelling network (ICSN) at the individual-level and the residential context focusing on ethnic heterogeneity and residential stability. Their data show that the relative importance of ICSN for the civic participa-tion is significantly higher in unstable or ethnically heterogeneous areas than in stable or ethnically homogeneous areas. Apart from studies focusing on the moderation influence of community characteristics in the context of the United States, some other studies assess the Internet's impact on democratization with a cross-national comparative approach. They find that the democratizing effects of the Internet are contingent upon several contextual factors at the national level, including the existing level of democracy in a country (Groshek, 2009) and mean educational attainment (Howard, 2009). With multilevel data gathered across 28 countries, Nisbet and his colleagues (Nisbet, Stoycheff, & Pearce, 2012) find that the positive relationship between individual Internet use and citizen commitment to democratic governance is moderated by greater democratization and Internet penetration in each country.

This multilevel perspective is especially important for scholars to examine the influence of the Internet on citizenship engagement in China. China is not only a large country in terms of geography but also very diverse in economic and social development. As Sun (2010) argues, three decades of economic reforms have not eradicated the traditional three basic inequalities (*san da cha bie*) of Chi-nese society—between the rural and the urban, between workers and peasants, and between manual labor and intellectual labor. Instead, they have given rise to even more dramatic disparities between north and south, east and west, coast and inland, and rural and urban. Based on geographic and social diversity, there are also vast inequalities in terms of media/communication development and political culture across different regions or locales. As a result of this social-spatial stratification, there are actually "many Chinas" within the entity that is often referred to as a singular entity. Thus, rather than treating China as a spatial concept, scholars (e.g., Sun, 2010, 2012) have called for "a geographic turn" in Chinese communication research that emphasizes deconstructing and exploring China as consisting of many regions, provinces, and localities, and paying attention to the vast difference across locations. Zhao (2008) also argues that place and location are crucial factors in the political economy of the Chinese media. Both Sun (2010) and Zhao (2008) suggest examining individual, social strata, and regional variations in terms of new media access and influence on Chinese society.

In spite of the great theoretical significance of locale-specific effects of media and Internet use, there are a limited number of quantitative studies (e.g., Chan & Zhou, 2011; Lei, 2011) on the relationship between the Internet and engagement that practically treat China as singular entity or only focus on a single locale inside China. An exception is a study by Pan and associates (2012). Although their analysis shows that the effects of Internet use on individual engagement varies across locations, it doesn't specify which contextual factors are responsible for this difference and how individual and contextual factors interact with each other. So we still do not know how the effects of the Internet are influenced by contextual factors.

This chapter will focus on two contextual factors—Internet penetration and the aggregate level of political interest—in order to examine the cross-level interaction effects on citizenship engagement. The first factor is the Internet penetration of different geographic units. As the "communication infrastructure perspective" suggests (Jung, Qiu, & Kim, 2001; Kim & Ball-Rokeach, 2006b), Internet penetration, along with other infrastructure components, can produce area-level resources for citizens to engage in expressive behaviors or civic activities. It not only encourages individuals to adopt the Internet but also allows citizens to access more pluralistic content that increases citizen demand for democracy (Nisbet et al., 2012). Based on these arguments, we may test if area-level Internet penetration can produce a positive contextual influence on individuals' citizenship engagement. Furthermore, because higher Internet penetration makes it easier for netizens to find peers to exchange information and opinions and engage in discussion of public affairs together, especially regarding local public affairs as well as community issues, I speculate a dynamic relationship between aggregate-level Internet penetration and individual-level Internet use. Earlier empirical studies in other social contexts have shown that Internet penetration moderates the relationship between Internet use and citizen demand for democracy (Groshek, 2009; Nisbet et al., 2012). China has proved to be a society with a significant degree of heterogeneity across different regions in Internet penetration. For example, according to the newest CNNIC statistics (CNNIC, 2013), at the provincial level, the highest Internet penetration rate is 72.2%, for Beijing, while the lowest is 28.5%, for Jiangxi. Since there are no previous empirical studies that examine the contextual influence of Internet penetration on engagement in China, I propose the following research questions:

RQ1: Will aggregate-level Internet penetration be positively related to individual-level civic participation (RQ1–1) and opinion expression (RQ1–2)?

RQ2: Will aggregate-level Internet penetration moderate the relationship between individual Internet use and civic participation (RQ2–1) and opinion expression (RQ2–2)?

The second factor to be examined is the aggregate level of political interest. Here I aggregate individual-level political interest to construct the aggregate level of political interest to represent an important dimension of political culture across different regions or locales. As Almond and Verba (1963) posit, countries are different from each other in terms of their political culture, among which political interest is an important component. In the Chinese context, studies have shown that different regions or locations are heterogeneous in terms of their average level of political interest (e.g., Zhong & Hu, 2013), such as Beijing (as an example of higher levels of political interest) versus Shanghai (which has lower levels of political interest compared to Beijing). The aggregate level of political interest may have a contextual influence on engagement because of the following logics: first, the average political interest may produce an atmosphere to encourage people to participate in expressive and civic activities; second, the higher aggregate level of political interest may facilitate interpersonal communication, informational flow, and opinion exchanges among local citizens; third, in a locale where most of the people have interest in politics or public affairs, netizens will have greater enthusiasm to discuss politics or public affairs online, which allows them to access more content to facilitate their engagement. So, in this study I will explore whether this contextual factor has a direct effect on individual citizenship engagement and whether it has a cross-level interaction effect on the relation between individual Internet use and engagement.

RQ3: Will aggregate level of political interest be positively related to individual-level civic participation (RQ3–1) and opinion expression (RQ3–2)?

RQ4: Will aggregate level of political interest moderate the relationship between the individual Internet use and civic participation (RQ4–1) and opinion expression (RQ4–2)?

Methods

Data

The data analyzed came from a nationwide sample survey conducted between July 15 and October 23, 2010. In each of the 31 provinces (including five autonomous regions and four municipalities) of China, a sample of 1,200 to 1,300 was drawn via a multistage cluster sampling procedure.[3] A qualified national audience research company recruited and trained interviewers to conduct face-to-face interviews. Each interview took, on average, about 61 minutes to complete. The final dataset contains 37,279 complete interviews. The overall response rates were at 62% (in provincial capital cities) and 69% (in other cities or towns) following WAPOR's recommended equation.[4] Each respondent was also located in a socio-geographic unit within each province (or autonomous region or municipality), which was defined operationally, in this study, as the "county-level" (*xian ji*) unit in the official administrative hierarchy. Six hundred twenty-four socio-geographic units were identified via this procedure. Each of the 624 units has as few as 24 (in rural counties) and as many as 736 (in all the urban districts of the four municipalities) individual respondents, with the median being 28.

Measures

The key dependent and independent variables were measured as follows:

Civic Participation. A set of 15 questions asked the respondents whether they had participated in each of the voluntary activities in the past 12 months (0 = no; 1 = yes). The items included gatherings of schoolmate groups, gatherings of amateur hobby groups, meetings of homeowner associations, activities of voluntary organizations, offline gatherings of online groups, and so on. Each respondent's civic participation score is the sum of these activities in which he or she had participated (α = .723). Because four of the 15 items were inapplicable to nonusers of the Internet (such as online fan groups), the index score was divided by 15 for Internet users and 11 for nonusers so that the resulting scale was comparable for the two groups. After that, the 0–1 scale was multiplied by 10 (M = 1.66; SD = 2.00) for ease of interpretation.

Opinion Expression. This dependent variable was measured by asking the respondents to report how often (0 = never; 5 = very often) they expressed their views on a topic, issue, or social problem: in one's own blogs; in posts on online discussion forums; by sending or distributing short text messages via cell phones; by contacting newspapers, radio, or TV stations; by contacting a government agency; by filing petitions to a relevant business; by talking about it among friends. Due to low frequencies in most of these items, they were recoded into 0 (never) and 1 (at least occasionally). A sum across the items was used as an index of opinion expression (α = .872). Because two of the items were about expressive activities on the Internet, the index score was divided by 7 for Internet users and 5 for nonusers so that the resulting scale was comparable for the two groups. After that, the 0–1 scale was multiplied by 10 (M = 2.98; SD = 3.28) for the ease of interpretation.

Internet Use. Respondents were first asked days per week they typically use the Internet, including access to the Internet via a computer or cell phone. With this variable, it was observed that 35.5% of the respondents in the whole sample reported using the Internet.

Political Interest. Respondents were asked to indicate how much they agreed (1 = strongly disagree; 5 = strongly agree) with each of the following statements: "I'm very much interested in politics and public affairs"; "I often think about issues facing the country"; and "I'm very much concerned with the local government's policies." An index of political interest was then created by averaging across three items (M = 3.01; SD = 1.07; α = .784).

Two Major Contextual Variables—Internet Penetration and Average Political Interest. Internet penetration was measured by calculating the proportion of the sample respondents who used the Internet at every county-level unit. Each of the 624 units has as low as 0% and as high as 77% for Internet adoption rate, with the median being 39.8%. Based on the measurement of individual political interest as explained above, the aggregate level of political interest was constructed by calculating the mean of the individual-level political interest at every county-level unit, which revealed a lowest value as 1.40 and a highest one as 4.74, with the median being 3.04.

The control variables included the following:

Demographic Variables. Based on the existing literature on influential factors for engagement, we included 12 socio-demographic variables in this study: sex, age, education (years of schooling), personal monthly income, marital status, holding a professional job, holding a managerial job, being a worker, being a peasant, being a Communist Party member, being a cadre, and number of electronic or other modern household items (all 16 items, including car, air conditioning, refrigerator, microwave oven, piano, vacuum cleaner, motorcycle, etc.) owned.

Internal Political Efficacy and External Political Efficacy. The questionnaire included six questions on a 5-point scale (1 = strongly disagree; 5 = strongly agree) measuring political efficacy, which were adapted from existing sources, such as the American National Election Studies (Craig, Niemi, & Silver, 1990). A factor analysis of these items yielded two clear-cut factors. Indices of internal and external political efficacy were created by averaging the scores of the three items for each factor. The three items measuring *internal efficacy* (M = 2.87; SD = .94; α = .671) were as follows: "Every citizen including me can have an impact on government's policies and behavior"; "I have a pretty clear understanding of the problems that need to be addressed via the government policies"; and "I have the ability to offer constructive opinions on government's policies and behaviors." The items (all reversely coded) making up the *external efficacy* index (M = 2.58; SD = .99; α = .804) were the following: "Government officials of various levels basically won't care what ordinary citizens think"; "Whatever ordinary citizens do, it'd have little impact on government's policies and behaviors"; and "Nowadays, officials of all levels basically only care about their own interests rather than the interests of ordinary people."

Traditional Media Use. For newspaper, radio, and TV news use, respondents were asked how closely (1 = almost no; 5 = very closely) they paid attention to international, national, and local news, respectively. Taking an average across the three frequency items led to an index of *newspaper news exposure* ($M = 3.49$; $SD = 1.07$; $\alpha = .749$), *radio news exposure* ($M = 3.20$; $SD = 1.21$; $\alpha = .834$), and *TV news exposure* ($M = 3.73$; $SD = .97$; $\alpha = .746$).

Other Aggregate-Level Variables. Based on the sociological resource model of citizen engagement, several other aggregate-level variables were created to account for variations among the 624 locales. These include the following: (1) eco-geographic region (1 = West; 2 = Northeast; 3 = Central; and 4 = East), and (2) for each unit, the proportion of the sample respondents who had urban resident status and who were Han nationality, as well as average in personal monthly income.

Statistical Analysis

We estimated a series of linear regression multilevel models (Raudenbush & Bryk, 2002) examining the relationship among individual Internet use, contextual factors, and engagement ($N = 37,279$; $J = 624$). All these models were random-intercept and random-slope full models, which allowed us to assess the independent influences of individual-level variables (individual-level fixed-effect parameters), contextual variables (aggregate-level fixed-effect parameters), and individual-level interaction terms between political interest and Internet use (individual-level interaction effects parameter), as well as cross-level interaction terms among Internet penetration and aggregate-level political interest and individual Internet use (cross-level interaction parameters). Since the sample size was quite large, we set $p \leq .01$ (rather than $p \leq .001$) as the criteria for the statistical significance tests.

Results

Before testing the hypotheses and answering the research questions, it is necessary to describe a general pattern of the civic participation and expressive behaviors in China. The results show that 60.4% of respondents have engaged in at least one form of civic activity, and 66.0% of them have expressed an opinion via at least one communication channel. Among 15 civic voluntary activities, the most popular one is gatherings of schoolmate groups or clansmen associations, with 35.2% having participated in the past 12 months. Among seven expressive activities, discussing social issues with friends is most popular, with 62.8% of respondents having done so.

The Independent Influence of Internet Use on Engagement

The first major hypothesis was whether Internet use has a significant effect on citizenship engagement in the Chinese context (H1). As shown in Table 1.1, after controlling for other individual-level as well as aggregate-level covariates,

TABLE 1.1 Multilevel Regression Models Predicting Citizenship Engagement (Restricted Maximum Likelihood Estimates, $N = 37,279$; $J = 624$)

	Civic Participation	Opinion Expression
Individual-level fixed effects		
Intercept (mean engagement)	.949**	1.998**
Demographic variables		
Sex (male)	−.070*	.055
Age	−.013**	−.037**
Years of schooling	.039**	.070**
Personal monthly income (*yuan*)	.010**	.012**
Single	.340**	.502**
Professional job	.370**	.269**
Managerial job	.164	−.009
Workers	.046	−.120
Farming job	.013	.007
Party membership	.510**	.113
Cadres	−.025	−.020
Modern appliances owned (0–16)	.082**	.056**
Psychological variables		
Internal political efficacy	.096**	.140**
External political efficacy	.047**	.029
Political interest	.152**	.292**
Media use variables		
Newspaper news exposure	.084**	.046**
Radio news exposure	.060**	.083**
TV news exposure	−.015	−.030
Internet use (1 = yes; 0 = no)	.641**	1.469**
Aggregate-level fixed effects		
Eastern region (vs. Western)	−.490**	−.158
Central region (vs. Western)	−.286**	.077
Northeastern region (vs. Western)	−.294*	−.200
Rural area	.123	−.100
% Han nationality	−.623**	−.576*
Average personal monthly income	.008	.007
Internet penetration	.681*	−.136
Average political interest	.102	.482**
Individual-level interaction effects		
Political interest × Internet use	.104**	.139**

(Continued)

TABLE 1.1 (Continued)

	Civic Participation	Opinion Expression
Cross-level interaction effects		
Internet penetration × Internet use	−.310	.224
Average political interest × Internet use	.345**	.261
Random effects		
Intercepts	.292**	.872**
Internet use	.194**	.679*
Internet use & intercepts	.049	−.045
Individual-level residuals	2.867**	7.538**
LR test (vs. the OLS regression, χ^2, df = 5)	1812.01**	1831.03**
LR test (vs. random intercept model, χ^2; df = 4)	106.37**	96.10**

Note: the table shows, for the fixed effect part, the unstandardized regression coefficients from the final random coefficient models and, for the random effect part, the variance of the random slope and intercept as well as the covariance among them. All of the variables are grand-mean centered.

*$p \leq .01$
**$p \leq .001$

the average slopes for both civic participation and opinion expression are still significant (coefficient = .641 for civic participation and = 1.469 for opinion expression; $p < .001$ in both cases). Hypothesis 1, that Internet use in China is a significant factor in citizenship engagement, is thus confirmed.

At the same time, as the resource model suggests (Brady, Verba, & Schlozman, 1995), the results show that younger people, single people, more educated people, and those with a higher social status (more rich, having a professional job, owning more modern appliances) are more likely to engage in both expressive and civic activities. Interestingly, Communist Party members and females are more likely to participate in civic activities, but this is not true for opinion expression. Consistent with those findings in democracies (e.g., Almond & Verba, 1963; McLeod, Scheufele, & Moy, 1999), psychological variables including political interest are proven to be powerful predictors for engagement. Newspaper and radio news exposure are found to be positively related to engagement, while TV news exposure is not significantly related to engagement.

Political Interest as an Individual-Level Moderator

Hypothesis 2 predicted that political interest was a significant moderator to enhance the positive effect of Internet use on citizenship engagement. To examine this issue, we tested whether or not the interaction term of Political interest × Internet use was significant after controlling for Internet use, political interest, and other variables. The results show that the interaction term is significantly related to both civic participation and opinion expression ($p < .001$), which lends support to both H2–1 and H2–2. That is, the impact of the Internet on citizenship engagement in China is contingent on the existing level of individuals' political interest, such that the relationship appears to be more robust for those with greater levels of self-reported interest in politics and local public affairs.

The Influences of Contextual Factors

I then ask whether either the level of Internet penetration (RQ1) or the average in political interest (RQ3) as area-level contextual factors has an independent effect on individual-level engagement. The results (Table 1.1) show that, after controlling for all other variables, Internet penetration still significantly influences individual-level civic participation (coefficient = .681; $p < .01$), although it has no significant relation to individual-level opinion expression. At the same time, aggregate-level political interest is a significant factor for individual-level opinion expression (coefficient = .482; $p < .001$) without having a significant influence on individual-level civic participation.

After testing for the direct effects of the two contextual factors in engagement, we also explored RQ2 and RQ4, which ask whether aggregate-level Internet penetration and political interest moderate the relationship between individual Internet use and citizenship engagement. The results presented in Table 1.1 show that although cross-level interaction effects of Internet penetration are not found, the aggregate level of political interest significantly moderates the relationship between Internet use and civic participation (coefficient = .345; $p < .001$). The slope coefficient (or the strength of effect) of Internet use for civic participation in areas where people have more interest in politics is higher than that in areas where people tend to be politically apathetic. In other words, the importance of Internet use in facilitating civic participation in the Chinese context is contingent on the contextual factor of average political interest. This area-level factor thus not only has a direct effect on individual engagement but also influences the size of the effects of individual Internet use on engagement.

In terms of the influences of other contextual-level factors, the results show that compared with people from other regions, those from the Western region are more likely to engage in civic activities. The residents living in areas with lower percentages of Han nationality tend to express their opinions and participate in civic activities more actively.

Conclusion

This study employs a nationwide random survey data set in order to empirically examine whether the Internet in China has democratizing effects on citizenship engagement and how these relations vary according to some individual-level and contextual-level factors. Our study finds that, after controlling for other variables, Internet use is still significantly related to both civic participation and opinion expression, such that Internet users tend to engage in politics and public affairs more actively compared to Internet nonusers. Since this finding comes from nationally representative data and represents an average effect across different locations, we have more confidence about the positive role of the Internet in facilitating citizens' engagement in Chinese social transformation.

Furthermore, this study also shows that the positive effect of the Internet on citizenship engagement in China is not universal but conditional. At the individual level, it follows the "psychological approach" argument to test whether or not individual political interest moderates the relationship between Internet use and engagement and finally confirms it. At the contextual level, I find that Internet penetration positively relates to individual civic engagement and the average in political interest has a positive impact on individual opinion expression. Although the cross-level interaction effects of Internet penetration and individual Internet use are not found, I do find that the aggregate level of political interest moderates the relationship between individual Internet use and civic participation.

The above findings have several theoretical implications. First, the interaction effects of individual political interest and Internet use demonstrate that the democratizing effects of the Internet in China depend on citizens' existing political interest. It seems that different individuals have differential gains from the Internet in facilitating their engagement in politics and public affairs such that the positive impacts of Internet use are indeed stronger for those who may already be predisposed to engage in these behaviors. In this sense, these data sound a note of caution that, in the Chinese context where average engagement levels are still low, Internet use may also be acting to increase existing gaps in participation.

The second theoretical implication concerns our examination of direct and indirect contextual effects on citizenship engagement. Internet penetration is a significant factor for civic participation even when individual factors were held constant. This finding illustrates that higher Internet penetration may produce a better communication infrastructure and communication action context to encourage citizens to engage in various types of formal and informal civic activities. However, higher Internet penetration does not show cross-level interaction effects with individual Internet use to facilitate engagement. This finding demonstrates that Internet users in areas with higher Internet penetration will not show significant differences in terms of their engagement from those living in areas with lower Internet penetration. That is, although both individual-level and aggregate-level Internet use have positive influences on engagement, they will not produce interaction effects.

In contrast, the aggregate level of political interest is found to not only have a direct impact on opinion expression but also have cross-level interaction with

Internet use to facilitate civic participation. Thus, Internet users living in areas with a higher average political interest will be more likely to participate in civic activities than those living in areas with a lower average political interest. Comparing these two contextual factors, we find that local political culture (political interest as an example) is more important for citizenship engagement than new media technology itself. Whether or not people have higher interest in participating and whether or not the locale has a better atmosphere to encourage participation both play a more crucial role in facilitating engagement, directly and indirectly. It should also be noted that the aggregate level of political interest moderates the effects of Internet use on civic participation but not on opinion expression. This may reflect the fact that, compared with opinion expression, civic participation (e.g., engagement in voluntary associations) requires more collective support and mutual encouragement.

This study contributes to the existing literature in three important ways. First, the results empirically support the optimistic view about the positive effects of the Internet in China. Second, it explicates the contingent effects of political interest at the individual level, which lends support to the "psychological approach." Third, it shows significant cross-location variations not only in mean levels of citizen engagement but also the effect levels of Internet use, in which the aggregate level of political interest plays a greater role. The latter part is particularly important in understanding that such cross-level interactions would yield great theory-refining insights into how the Internet is changing Chinese politics and society.

The current chapter also suggests directions for future research. First, this study uses aggregated values of individual data as a proxy for Internet infrastructure and political culture. We may try to find more efficient census data in future studies. Second, although I examine the two contextual factors of Internet penetration and average political interest based on existing literature and theoretical arguments, the results show that only the aggregate level of political interest has cross-level interaction effects with Internet use on civic participation. This suggests that there are several other contextual factors that future studies should examine. This exploration, I believe, will not only contribute to the study of the democratizing effects of the Internet but also to many other studies on the differential effects of new media technologies in Chinese society.

Notes

1. This chapter is supported by the Chinese national "211" Project, "Audiences in the New Technological Environment" (#211XK02) and the National Social Science Foundation Project, "The Influence of Social Media on Public Opinion in Transitional China" (#13CXW021).
2. Of the effects, 16% are negative, and the rest of 7% of all effects are not reported with their directions.
3. The sample design varies slightly between the four provincial municipalities and the 27 provinces (including five "ethnic minority autonomous regions"). In each of the

four municipalities (Beijing, Shanghai, Tianjin, and Chongqing), the county-level units in the urban district and the county-level units outside of the urban district form two clusters. In the first cluster, 72 residential or village committees were selected; in each, 10 households were selected; from the second cluster, 30 residential or village committees were selected and from each, 13 to 15 households were selected. From each of the selected households, a randomly selected adult was interviewed. In each of the 27 provinces or autonomous regions, three clusters of county-level units are differentiated: those in the provincial capital city, those in the region-level cities, and those in counties. Within each cluster, the same multistage random selection procedure was used. The design called for 36 residential or village committees in each provincial capital city, 10 such primary sampling units from region-level cities, and 15 from counties or county-level cities; from each of the primary sampling units, 15 to 30 households were selected. With this design, the probabilities of selection vary across the county-level units. A sample weight in the inverse to the probability of selection was thus constructed and used to weight the sample. In the implementation, the sampling design was adjusted for practical considerations (e.g., inaccessibility of certain areas due to the lack of modern transportation, political sensitivity, and ethnic and linguistic barriers). The sample sizes among the 31 provincial units range from 899 in Tibet to 1,246 in Shanxi province, with an average sample size of 1,202.

4. The WAPOR equation is $PR = SI / (SI + NR + \alpha U)$, where PR is the response rate, SI is the number of successful interviews, NR is the number of eligible but no-interviews, U is the number of unknown eligibility and no-interviews, and α is the estimated proportion of unknown eligible cases that are actually eligible.

References

Almond, G., & Verba, S. (1963). *The civic culture.* Boston: Little, Brown.

Bimber, B. (2003). *Information and American democracy: Technology in the evolution of political power.* New York: Cambridge University Press.

Boulianne, S. (2009). Does Internet use affect engagement? A meta-analysis of research. *Political Communication, 26*(2), 193–211.

Brady, H. E., Verba, S., & Schlozman, K. L. (1995). Beyond SES: A resource model of political participation. *American Political Science Review, 89*(2), 271–294.

Cai, Y. (2004). Managed participation in China. *Political Science Quarterly, 119*(3), 425–451.

Chan, J. M., & Zhou, B. H. (2011). Expressive behaviors across discursive spaces and issue types. *Asian Journal of Communication, 21*(2), 150–166.

CNNIC (China Internet Network Information Center). (2013). *31th statistical report on Internet development in China.* Retrieved from http://www1.cnnic.cn/IDR/Report Downloads/201302/P020130221391269963814.pdf

Craig, S. C., Niemi, R. G., & Silver, G. E. (1990). Political efficacy and trust: A report on the NES Pilot Study items. *Political Behavior, 12*(3), 289–314.

Delli Carpini, M. X., Cook, F. L., & Jacobs, L. R. (2004). Public deliberation, discursive participation, and citizen engagement: A review of the empirical literature. *Annual Review of Political Science, 7*, 315–344.

Friedland, L. A., & McLeod, J. M. (1999). Community integration and mass media: A reconsideration. In D. Demers & K. Viswanath (Eds.), *Mass media, social control, and social change: A macrosocial perspective* (pp. 197–226). Ames: Iowa State University Press.

Goldman, M. (2005). *From comrade to citizen: The struggle for political rights in China.* Cambridge, MA: Harvard University Press.

Groshek, J. (2009). The democratic effects of the Internet, 1994–2003: A cross-national inquiry of 152 countries. *International Communication Gazette, 71*(3), 115–136.

Hao, X., & Li, Z. (2001). New media technologies: Challenges to China's media system. *Mass Communication Research, 69*(4), 95–111.

Howard, P. (2009). *The digital origins dictatorship and democracy: Information technology and political Islam.* Oxford: Oxford University Press.

Jung, J. Y., Qiu, J. L., & Kim, Y. C. (2001). Internet connectedness and inequality beyond the "divide." *Communication Research, 28*(4), 507–535.

Kang, N., & Kwak, N. (2003). A multilevel approach to civic participation: Individual length of residence, neighborhood residential stability, and their interaction effects with media use. *Communication Research, 30*(1), 80–106.

Kim, Y. C., & Ball-Rokeach, S. J. (2006a). Community storytelling network, neighborhood context, and civic engagement: A multilevel approach. *Human Communication Research, 32*(4), 411–439.

Kim, Y. C., & Ball-Rokeach, S. J. (2006b). Civic engagement from a communication infrastructure perspective. *Communication Theory, 16*(2), 173–197.

Lei, Y. (2011). The political consequences of the rise of the Internet: Political beliefs and practices of Chinese netizens. *Political Communication, 28*(3), 291–322.

Lieberthal, K. (2004). *Governing China: From revolution to reform* (2nd ed.). New York: Norton.

McLeod, J. M., Scheufele, D. A., & Moy, P. (1999). Community, communication, and participation: The role of mass media and interpersonal discussion in local political participation. *Political Communication, 16*, 315–336.

McLeod, J. M., Scheufele, D. A., Moy, P., Horowitz, E. M., Holbert, R. L., Zhang, W., . . . Zubric, J. (1999). Understanding deliberation: The effects of discussion networks on participation in a public forum. *Communication Research, 26*(6), 743–774.

Morozov, E. (2011). *The net delusion—The dark side of Internet freedom.* New York: Public Affairs.

Nisbet, E. C., Stoycheff, E., & Pearce, K. E. (2012). Internet use and democratic demands: A multinational, multilevel model of internet use and citizen attitudes about democracy. *Journal of Communication, 62*(2), 249–265.

Pan, Z., Jing, G., Liu, Y., Yan, W., & Zheng, J. (2012, June). *Digital divide and Internet use in China: Can the Internet facilitate citizenship engagement?* Paper presented at the World Association for Public Opinion Research (WAPOR) Annual Conference, Hong Kong.

Price, V., Ritchie, L. D., & Eulau, H. (Eds.). (1991). Micro-macro issues in communication research [Special issue]. *Communication Research, 18*(2).

Putnam, R. D. (2000). *Bowling alone: The collapse and revival of American community.* New York: Touchstone.

Raudenbush, S. W., & Bryk, A. S. (2002). *Hierarchical linear models: Applications and data analysis methods.* Thousand Oaks, CA: Sage.

Rosen, S. (2010). Is the Internet a positive force in the development of civil society, a public sphere, and democratization in China? *International Journal of Communication, 10*, 509–516.

Shah, D., Cho, J., Eveland, W. P., Jr., & Kwak, N. (2005). Information and expression in a digital age: Modeling Internet effects on civic participation. *Communication Research, 32*, 531–565.

Shah, D., Schmierbach, M., Hawkins, J., Espino, R., & Donavan, J. (2002). Nonrecursive models of Internet use and community engagement: Questioning whether time spent online erodes social capital. *Journalism and Mass Communication Quarterly, 79*, 964–987.

Shi, T. J. (1997). *Political participation in Beijing.* Cambridge, MA: Harvard University Press.

Slater, M. D., Snyder, L., & Hayes, A. F. (Eds.). (2006). Thinking and modeling at multiple levels: The potential contribution of multilevel modeling to communication theory and research [Special issue]. *Human Communication Research, 32*(4).

Sohmen, P. (2001). Taming the dragon: China's efforts to regulate the Internet. *Stanford Journal of East Asian Affairs, 1*(1), 17–26.

Sun, W. (2010). Scaling Chinese media: A geographic turn to future research. *International Journal of Communication, 4*(4), 537–543.

Sun, W. (2012). Rescaling media in China: The formations of local, provincial, and regional media cultures. *Chinese Journal of Communication, 5*(1), 10–15.

Sunstein, C. (2001). *Republic.com.* Princeton, NJ: Princeton University Press.

Verba, S., Schlozman, K. L., & Brady, H. E. (1995). *Voice and equality: Civic voluntarism in American politics.* Cambridge, MA: Harvard University Press.

Wang, S. (2008). The impact of political culture and social structure on political participation. *Qinghuahua University Journal, 4*, 95–112.

Weber, L. M., Loumakis, A., & Bergman, J. (2003). Who participates and why?: An analysis of citizens on the Internet and the mass public. *Social Science Computer Review, 21*(1), 26–42.

Xenos, M., & Moy, P. (2007). Direct and differential effects of the Internet on political and civic engagement. *Journal of Communication, 57*(4), 704–718.

Yang, G. (2003). The co-evolution of the Internet and civil society in China. *Asian Survey, 43*(3), 405–422.

Yang, G. (2009). *The power of the Internet in China: Citizen activism online.* New York: Columbia University Press.

Zhao, Y. (2008). *Communication in China: Political economy, power, and conflict.* Lanham, MA: Rowman & Littlefield.

Zheng, Y. (2008). *Technological empowerment: The Internet, state, and society in China.* Stanford, CA: Stanford University Press.

Zhong, Y., & Hu, W. (2013). Mass political interest in urban China: An empirical study. *China: An International Journal, 11*(3), 87–103.

Zhou, B. H. (2008). Web 2.0 information and expression: A survey study in Shanghai of China. *Journalism & Communication Research, 4*, 75–82.

2

NETWORKED ANTI-CORRUPTION

Actors, Styles, and Mechanisms

Jia Dai, Fanxu Zeng, and Xin Yu

After taking power in late 2012, Chinese president Xi Jinping has been trying to unwind a culture of bribery and graft that has hurt the government's legitimacy and jeopardized economic growth. Aiming to restrict power "by the cage of regulations,"[1] and targeted at both "flies and tigers," the anti-corruption campaign is growing into one of the broadest in China's modern history, snaring thousands of business executives and political officials alike. Western scholars have commented that this is the most ambitious anti-corruption campaign since the Mao era.[2] According to the Party's disciplinary commission, there were 23,000 cases of corruption under investigation, and approximately 182,000 officers were disciplined in 2013, 13% more than in 2012.[3]

In the meantime, the public's anger over the brazen corruption displayed by officials' extravagance seems to have hit a boiling point, and Internet exposure of cases of corruption is becoming increasingly passionate and turbulent. We define this phenomenon as an online anti-corruption campaign, in which random Internet exposure of individual government officials' malversation, such as bribery-taking, causes social impulses toward criticism and impeachment that result in the downfall of the accused official. Exposure of an official's degenerate private life usually enters the public discursive space and induces issue advocacy, with netizens questioning the source of corruption and the abuse of power and discussing what administrative design should be implemented in order to monitor and discipline those in power.

Looking closely at 10 recent high-profile online anti-corruption cases, this chapter attempts to analyze the process and mechanisms of the networked complaint. It aims to identify actors who use social media to expose corruption and abuse, styles of discourses, and the mechanisms that form the networked power that contribute to the downfall of corrupted officials. The main argument is that the connections and interplays among multiple actors, as well as the multilay-ered discourse patterns, constitute, although lacking of specific organization, a powerful network that helps random online exposures become centrally placed and well-attended sites of civic conversation, thus promoting the anti-corruption process that would not have been realized through normal political channels.

Literature Review

The Online Anti-corruption Campaign

When it comes to the question of how the Internet advances anti-corruption campaigns, there is a difference between the Western and Chinese perspectives. Western perspectives of online anti-corruption mainly focus on the influence of e-government on enhancing government transparency (Andersen, 2009; Shim & Eom, 2008). In the Western view, the online anti-corruption is government-led and based on the existing rule of law and procedures; it is rarely realized by external driving forces (Wen, 2013). Regarding the relationship between online media and anti-corruption, studies show that the effects of Internet adoption on corruption reduction are statistically significant, although not too substantial (Lio, Liu, & Ou, 2011); information flow on the Internet increases the aware-ness of corruption, thus inhibiting potential bribery and rent-seeking (Goel, Nelson, & Naretta, 2012); and the Internet can report, save, and disseminate information of corruption in a cost-effective manner. Anonymity reduces the risk of exposure, and corruption pending exposure online that remains unsolved will face great pressure from civil society (Garcia-Murillo & MacInnes, 2009).

We define Internet anti-corruption in China as a process in which the Internet exposure of individual government officials' wrongdoings causes social impulses toward criticism and impeachment—or administrative investigation—that result in the downfall of the accused official. It often has two modes: top-down or bottom-up. The top-down mode is similar to that seen in the Western countries, which is led by the government, from top to bottom. Compared to the existing procedures in Western countries, its uniqueness lies in the fact that, to a large extent, it depends on the power of government to decide who to eradicate, in what way, and whether or not releasing news of its achievements will help ease public anger. Andrew Wedeman, a political science professor at Georgia State University comments, "if the regime wants to go after someone, they go after people. They arrest, they convict and they imprison a substantial number of officials every year."[4] The drawback of such a power-driven model is that it may firmly perform anti-corruption authority, but it is also likely to hide the corruption itself. As Wedeman states, "the Communist Party concentrates such power in the hands of officials that they are in a position to engage in corruption and cover it up at the same time."

A more common pattern is to form a campaign to fight corruption from the bottom-up through online exposure and condemnation of corruption, using the power of surveillance and regulation. This mode creates a force from outside the system and may break the inherent administrative procedures (Wen, 2013). Therefore, this is considered to be an external constraint to the political power. Although the Party Discipline and Supervision Committees have established their own reporting channels to accept reports of corruption leads at different levels, both online and offline, it has limited effect. On one hand, there is the fear of trouble caused by the disclosure of personal information; on the other, the fact that whistleblowers rarely get the government's response to the report also discourages exposure.

Comparatively, anti-corruption through online media such as forums, micro-blogging, and other platforms has the following advantages: first, low cost and convenience improves the probability of corruption being monitored; second, the crowd-sourcing mechanism increases the chance of evidence gathering and visibility expansion, creating deterrence for the corrupt ones (Ren & Du, 2007); and third, public anger over rampant corruption gives greater pressure to advance timely investigations and punishment (Du & Ren, 2011).

The Blurring Boundary Between the Public and Private

The bottom-up anti-corruption campaign often presents the logic of publicizing the private. Namely, details of corrupted officials' private lives are exposed through the Internet; be it wearing luxury watches or having an affair with female subordinates, these discretions evolve into public discussion about the abuse of power—thus, a private issue becomes a public one. This logic has pros and cons: private issues moved from the private sector into the public sphere may expand the publicness of an issue and be conducive to policy change or correction, but it may also cause intrusion of privacy and trample the human rights of those being accused.

This trend of publicizing the private gets more complicated in the Chinese context. While in the Western perspective, the public sphere is independent of the private sphere, and the maintenance of the private sphere depends on the protection of privacy rights, a clear division between the two does not exist in China (Hu, 2009). In the Chinese context, "publicness" emphasizes the public good—namely, universal human well-being or universal equality—which promotes the spirit of public service or selfless actions undertaken for the common good (Chen, 2006). In order to achieve the common good, violation of privacy rights is reasonable and moral, and therefore should be tolerated. Accordingly, the importance of the reasoning that usually characterizes the public sphere can be outweighed by the values and moral judgment emphasized in the private sphere.

Media further blur the boundary between the public and private. Cyber vigilantism, or "human flesh search," describes how Internet media have been appropriated by netizens in order to hunt for the personal information of social deviants or corrupt officials to restore public morality (Cheong & Gong, 2010; Gao &

Stanyer, 2014; Herold, 2011). Social shaming, monitoring, and revenge are normal forms of criticizing administrative and legal injustices (Cheung, 2009a, 2009b).

Regarding how the mechanism of the boundary between the private and public gets blurred, Castells's (2009) concept of "switchers" in network society provides an explanation. Contrary to "programmers" of a network who have the "network-making power" to achieve certain goals, switchers are those functioning against this power. They have "the ability to connect and ensure the cooperation of different networks by sharing common goals and combining resources, while fending off competition from other networks by setting up strategic cooperation" (Castells, 2009, p. 45). In other words, the switchers hold control of the points connecting various strategic networks. Bringing private issues into public view, switchers are able to produce and diffuse agendas and discourses that may otherwise be constrained within the boundary of the private. In order to understand anti-corruption as a resistant form of programming, then, one must explore how new code is introduced into the network and what kind of switching potential is blocked in order to suppress structural domination.

Styles of Anti-corruption Discourses

Along with the blurring boundary between the private and public are multilayered styles of discourse, working independently or collaboratively, in the service of switchers' purposes. Borrowing from Bakardjieva's (2012) theoretical summary of the approaches taken by citizens in political involvement—the deliberative, the radical, and everyday life—we identify the discourse styles taken by actors to enhance public awareness on issues of corruption.

The deliberative. The deliberative style is defined as a rhetorical style assembled or organized for deliberation; it is a process of equal, free, and rational message exchange working toward consensus or agreement on a solution to a problem (Bohman, 1996; Cohen, 1989; Habermas, 1991). The capability of "advancement of claims, presentation of evidence, consideration of counterfactual data" (Ryfe, 2002) and reasoning and criticizing is essential to the deliberative style, and public reason, accordingly, should govern citizens' discourse in the political realm (Rawls, 1993).

However, social pluralism and "unavoidable social complexity" often fail to guarantee a fair and diverse context for speech (Habermas, 1991; Rawls, 1993). Individualized interests and needs may harm the public interest (Sunstein, 2001; Tewksbury, 2005; Webster & Lin, 2002; Webster & Phalen, 1997), and new media have the "potential to create and sustain insulated enclaves of intolerance predicated on little more than personal illusion, rumor, and politically motivated innuendo" (MacDougall, 2005, p. 575). This is especially so in an undemocratic society that has entered the new media era. In China, for example, besides the information control that screens the unpleasant political critique (MacKinnon, 2008, 2009), the Internet's intrinsic characteristics of unrestraint, decentralization, and anonymity arouses a carnival metaphor that highlights the character of lightness, wildness, and ambivalence of online communication (Herold & Marolt, 2011; Yang, 2012). Cases of symbolic violence resulted from social distrust and disrespect are commonly seen in the cyber space (Cheung, 2009a, 2009b; Cheong & Gong, 2010).

In this regard, many argue that the nondeliberative character of Internet communication should be examined and its meaning to public life be reconsidered. A range of newer literature on the public sphere has undermined the traditional notion of enlightenment "reason" and has illustrated the function of radical rhetoric in issue debate and social movements.

The radical. Scholars have demonstrated how dissidents have made the rise of spectacular action a cause for public attention and concern (McCurdy, 2009). Concepts such as the counter public (Brouwer, 2006; Fraser, 1992; Siapera, 2004; Wimmer, 2005), alternative Internet (Atton, 2004, 2006), subactivism (Bakardjieva, 2009), and radical media (Downing, Villarreal, Gil, & Stein, 2001) are found in discourses of radical political positions as alternatives to mainstream political perspectives. Different from the deliberative democracy theory that emphasizes consensus-building and rule of majority (Cohen, 1989; Fishkin, 2009; Fishkin & Laslett, 2003; Gutmann & Thompson, 2002), the theory of radical democracy respects differences that resist consensus and contends that oppressive power relations should be renegotiated and altered (Dahlberg, 2007; Laclau & Mouffe, 1985; Mouffe, 2005). Therefore, the radical creates an "agonistic" public sphere in which politics is associated with power and exclusion (Dahlberg & Siapera, 2007).

Apart from the apparent feature of conflicts and challenges against the mainstream, radical communication style is moralistic in character, as it examines conflicts that lead to pain and suffering (Deluca, 1999; Schwarze, 2006). On one hand, by amplifying the moral and emotional dimensions of social problems, it can overcome public indifference and activate a sense of urgency. Thus media content inscribed with great human interest and dramatic conflict normally gains more visibility. On the other hand, the infusion of moral gravity and pathos may cause sensational effects that undermine rational discussion.

The radical gesture doesn't necessarily help to form a discernible identity (Hands, 2007) among the dissidents and protesters, nor does it promote their goals in an organized manner. This is especially so in undemocratic China, where tolerance of resistance and protests is limited and organized social movements are normally prohibited. Netizens, therefore, are used to acting as atomized individuals, and their initiatives often seem to be contingent and sporadic. They come around when a topic of interest rises and disperse when the agenda temporarily comes to a close. More importantly, they usually start to voice themselves out of regard to personal issues in everyday life.

The everyday life. Studies have documented that political involvement can be realized in the routines of everyday lives. Dahlgren (2003) emphasizes the importance of understanding democracy from the perspective of a "civic culture" anchored in daily life, which focuses attention on values, norms, practices, and frames of reference. Similarly, the notion of "cultural citizenship" (Hermes & Dahlgren, 2006; Rosaldo, 1994) and "flexible citizenship" (Ong, 1999) also sketches out a framework for studying the intersection between cultural citizenship and private life. Hanisch proposed in interpreting women's liberation movements in 1970 that "the personal is political" (Hanisch, 1970). With the inner logic of social campaigns shifting from collective action to connective action, and the organizational and expressive patterns of social movements becoming more personal, the life world and daily dealings of individual persons also bear democratic potentials (Bennett & Segerberg, 2012). Some of the necessary conditions for a functioning democracy exist—aside the public sphere—at the level of lived experience, resources, and subjective dispositions (Dahlgren, 2003).

Convergence of the Three Styles

Fagerjord (2003) proposes a theory of rhetorical convergence, emphasizing how different rhetorical styles are combined into complex texts and thus "complicate significance and reader selections and processes of symbiosis" (p. 134). First, differences of media platforms lead to differences in communication style. A deliberative campaign fits media with a larger capacity and longer circulation time, while radical discourse can more easily take advantage of the speed of Internet communication (e.g., viral communication). Content based on the experiences of everyday life is more suitable to social media that maintains real-world social connections. Second, the fact that targeted audiences—be they policy makers, active contributors, or future leaders—are scattered across all media outlets demonstrates that a campaign must flexibly use different media and diverse discourses to promote its concerns and standpoint. In this regard, rhetorical convergence resembles what Jenkins (2006) describes as "transmedia storytelling," the strategy of which is to make complex information and rhetoric fit into various media features and enhances communication across media.

Based on the above literature review, this study explores the mechanisms forming networked anti-corruption, with specific attention to the actors and their communication styles. Specifically, we ask the following:

RQ1: Who are the actors, and how do they function as programmers/switchers of the network?

RQ2: What are the manifestations of distinctive communication styles?

Method

Anti-corruption Cases

Networked anti-corruption is defined as the supervision of officials' behavior and constraint of power by the public, realized through connected Internet communication.

We developed a case study on 10 select anti-corruption cases (Table 2.1), which took place between 2008 and 2012. They are considered the most significant cases by the Caixin.com,[5] which is deemed as the new benchmark for Chinese media (Canaves & Feng, 2010). One common feature of the cases is that they each started from the exposure of the daily behaviors or lifestyle of an official, usually shocking and outrageous, leading to revelations of more details of corruption. Exposure is then followed by netizens' criticism, institutional investigation, and, eventually, the downfall of the accused officials.

TABLE 2.1 Ten Anti-corruption Cases Studied

Official	Title	Internet Exposure	Punishment
Cai Bin (2012)	The Panyu Branch Political Commissar of Guangzhou City Management Comprehensive Law Enforcement Bureau	Having 21 house properties under his own and family members' names	Bribery-taking; 11 years in prison
Fang Daguo (2012)	Party Standing Committee member and political commissar of Armed Forces Department of the Guangzhou Yuexiu District	Insulted and beat an air attendant in dispute regarding where to put his carry-on baggage	Removed from position and investigated
Yang Dacai (2012)	Chief Secretary of Production Safety Supervision Bureau of Shaanxi	Wearing luxury watches such as Vacheron and Omega	Bribery-taking; 14 years in prison
Duan Yizhong (2012)	Inspector from the Bureau of Quality and Technical Supervision in Guangxi Zhuang Autonomous Region	Pornography of Duan with female subordinates	Bribery-taking; first trial, sentenced to 10 years in prison
Yang Cunhu (2012)	Jingle County party secretary, Shanxi Province	Daughter freeloading 100,000 RMB in 5 years	Removed from position
Zhou Jiezhong (2011)	Liaocheng City, Shandong Province, retired president of hospital	Pornography with various women	Detained and interrogated
Chen Yachun (2010)	Vice Mayor of Maoming, Guangdong	Lives a life of depravity and corruption	Investigated
Han Feng (2010)	Laibin, Guangxi Province, Tobacco Monopoly Bureau, chief bureau	Sex diary	First trial, sentenced 13 years in prison

(Continued)

TABLE 2.1 (Continued)

Official	Title	Internet Exposure	Punishment
Zhou Jiugeng (2009)	Director of the Housing Management Department of the provincial capital Nanjing's Jiangning District	Consuming expensive cigarettes and wearing luxury watches	First trial, sentenced to 11 years in prison
He Zhi (2008)	Hunan Zhuzhou City Grain Bureau Party Secretary	Selling public property to private businessman at a low price	Bribery-taking; embezzlement of public funds and state-owned assets; abusing power; first trial, sentenced to 20 years in prison

The cases discussed here are remarkable for four reasons. First, these were unique occasions in recent Chinese history when suspicion and criticism arising from civic grassroots was attended to and effectively brought down the accused. Second, they are bottom-up campaigns rooted in broad public interest and the long existing distrust toward the Party's administration, rather than top-down party politics and power manipulations; thus they represent the authenticity and spontaneity of actions taken by average citizens. Third, unlike other online civic engagement that bears the character of being sporadic and accidental, these anti-corruption cases appear to be relatively intense and frequent and are formed as serialized efforts. Finally, these cases created dynamic networks composed by a variety of actors, media spaces, and discourse styles, which make them interesting objects of analysis that offer a view into the connected forces and relations that produced concrete outcomes.

Demarcating the Boundaries and Collecting Data

Due to the fact that some of the cases are still ongoing, and discussion about them is fast-growing and swiftly shifting, the unit of analysis used in this study is the "Web storm" (Schneider & Foot, 2005), which reflects inter-actor and inter-site activity over a relatively brief period of time. In most of the cases, a corruption scandal resulted in a Web storm wherein actors worked in a network distributing texts, graphics, and links intensively for several days or weeks.

We first organized the main thread of each case and made judgments based on what material was important among enormous, diverse, and competing social constructions of the cases all vying for attention in a cacophony of networks. Coverage generated from both new and traditional media during the period of active debate were traced and analyzed with special attention to their mutual connections and references. In particular, the "nodes" (key points that switched the discussion from private to public, including important individuals or events) on the unfolding story chain were located, and the related texts and graphs were analyzed. Second, media items were singled out for in-depth analysis based on the prominence (mostly retweeted or cross-posted) they had acquired in public discussion.

Results

Actors connected in exposing, disseminating, and updating the information of corruption contributed to the eventual downfall of the accused. Specifically, whistleblowers functioned as programmers, and the netizens who joined later on functioned as switchers of the networked discussion.

Whistleblowers as Programmers

The whistleblower is the first person or organization that breaks the news or releases the information that aims to arouse social concern and attention. They are the programmers of the network in the sense that they are aware of the life world of the one being exposed and provide many details not known to outsiders. They define the problem and make moral or technical judgment; they also determine the way to enter the problem into public view.

Motives behind the exposures vary. Some exposures are interest-based, and the goal of programming lies in protecting jeopardized individual rights. For instance, in the case of He Zhi, who was the Grain Bureau Party Secretary of Zhuzhou, Hunan, the anonymous whistleblower was an employee of a local mall, which is a public property. When He sold the mall to private hands for a surprisingly low price, employees protested and were threatened with being fired. Reporting the sneaky trading to the public thus became a strategy to address the crisis.

Another common motive is revenge. Chen Yachun, Vice Mayor of Maoming, Guangdong, was exposed by a woman who had had a sexual relationship with him but later found out that he was married and was cheating on his wife. She not only claimed that the Vice Mayor is a "big liar and rogue" but also pointed out his bribery-taking from local businessman.[6] Likewise, the whistleblower in the case of Han Feng's sexual relations with a female subordinate was the subordinate's husband, who exposed his wife's sex diary out of anger and shame.

Another motive is to critique the morals of those who offended social taboos or hurt the public's feelings. When exposing the Deputy Secretary for Quality Supervision Bureau of Guangxi Zhuang Autonomous Region Duan Yizhong's pornography, for instance, the anonymous netizen called to "please take a look at this representative of people who sneaked into the Party cadres—how he spent taxpayers' money on extravagant life, and what he had done in the leadership."[7]

The functions of programmers vary across cases. The cases oriented toward the protection of rights bear obvious tendencies of using the Internet to combat public corruption directly. In He Zhi's case, the exposure was posted on the local government Web site. Subsequent investigation followed, with real-name reporters of corruption and local Discipline Committees joining in. In the end, local media labeled the case as "the first case of online anti-corruption in Hunan province" (Wen, 2008). Therefore, the development of the networked discussion strictly followed the whistleblower's programming.

In other cases, however, whistleblowers aimed solely to direct public attention to disgraceful private affairs, rather than on issues of corruption. But they often sparked investigations of corrupt officials, due, in part, to various netizens joining the network and functioning as switchers during the development of the discussion.

Netizens as Switchers

Updaters appeared in the development of the cases to amend or supplement the initial information that was exposed. The ongoing emergence of new information continued to alter aspects of the case, as well as the focus of public interest, in a way that can be described as "switchers in relay."

For example, in Zhou Jiugeng's case, Zhou initially aroused critiques because he intended to punish real estate developers' mark-down sales, thus irritating members of the public who could not afford housing. Angry netizens mobilized human flesh searches on him the next day, and three days later, another post showed a photo of him consuming expensive cigarettes. Netizens passionately joined this search, checking the price of the cigarettes and questioning his consumption of high-end brands. Thus, the switching process was generated through a range of topics, from the public instance of housing prices to the private topic of a luxury lifestyle.

There were yet more new codes introduced into the network. Soon after, netizens exposed that Zhou's nepotism had benefited family members, including his brother and son, in the real estate market. Critiques about his personal life, therefore, extended to his family, then further to his abuse of power, which eventually pointed to Zhou's corruption (Figure 2.1).

Similarly, in Yang Dacai's case, many netizens joined in contributing to the downfall of Yang, the Chief Secretary of Production Safety Supervision Bureau of Shaanxi. Yang's case started with a photo posted on Sina Weibo, the Chinese version of Twitter, showing him smiling at a traffic accident scene that killed 36 people. His callousness toward the victims ignited public anger. The next day, a series of photos showing him wearing five different luxury watches

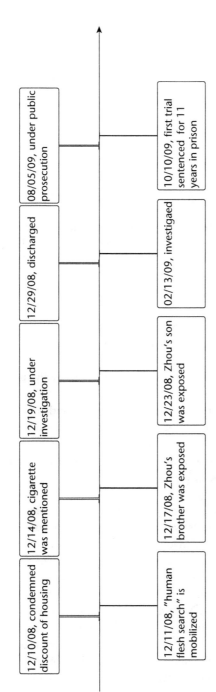

FIGURE 2.1 Switchers in Relay (Zhou Jiugeng's Case)

went viral on Weibo. The following day, a luxury brand expert stood up and confirmed that Yang's watches, glasses, and belts were all real luxury brands. Regardless of Yang's self-defense, more photos surfaced on Weibo showing him wearing luxury watches in addition to the five that he admitted in his defense. Eventually, 11 pricy watches worn by Yang in various public appearances were exposed, which led to the investigation of his bribery-taking and the eventual sentence of 14 years in prison.

Multiple switchers' participation in relaying information unfolded the cases in a more comprehensive and detailed way, with the accuracy of information verified at each phase and depth of corruption revealed.

Defenders' Counter-Switch

While switchers appeared in relay to introduce new codes into the network of discussion, they faced defenders who acted to counter-switch the discussion so as to limit it to the offenders' private lives. For example, In Chen, Yachuan's case, the exposure didn't arouse attention at the very beginning; rather, it experienced many deletions and refutes:

> September 6, 2010: the exposure posted at local online forums, soon deleted.
> October 6, 2010: another post claiming to provide sex video as evidence, which aroused enormous repost and media reports.
> October 24, 2010: Pornography of Chen, allegedly, posted at the Yahoo forum, then deleted.
> October 25, 2010: Chen's secretary denied the authenticity of the pornography, and claimed that the exposure had been reported to both the public security bureau and the municipal government.
> October 26, 2010: one of the local business owners who allegedly had bribed Chen denied the bribery allegations.

Regardless of defenders' counter-switch, the discussion kept fermenting as more netizens join in the network. For example, while posts in the Yahoo forum were deleted, posts in the Maopu forum remained and had 159,574 views and 6,766 replies, which finally triggered uproar online. The government was then forced to respond and investigate further into the cases.

The same occurred in Yang Dacai's case. Under pressure from widespread criticism on the Internet, Yang defended himself in a Weibo post, in which he explained that his smile was to comfort the anxiety of the rescue team and that he bought only five watches with his savings from his legitimate income over the past 10 years. Yet, the spinning effort could not beat the public's muckraking effort. With more photos showing him wearing more luxury watches and the investigation begun, the bribery-taking charges against him were eventually confirmed.

New Media as Gatekeepers

Although online exposure was started by whistleblowers, to what extent this information is visible to audiences depends on the gatekeepers who control the media platforms. The high visibility of Zhou Jiugeng's consumption of expensive cigarettes, for instance, was made possible by an editor of the Tianya bulletin board system, who made it into a headline. Within one day, there were more than 70,000 hits and nearly 2,000 comments. Interestingly, the intense discussion on the expensive cigarettes made the editor suspicious of an advertising spin because he was aware of the fact that the cigarette factory had targeted advertisement to local government cadres. The editor then conducted a survey among netizens to check if this was actually commercial hype. These efforts minimized the potential harm of unverifiable news while increasing the prominence of the exposure.[8]

Gatekeeping mechanisms also functioned in other cases. In the case in which a Party Standing Committee member of the Guangzhou Yuexiu District, Fang Daguo, beat an airline attendant on the plane, inaccurate information such as Fang's official title, the flight number, and details about the quarrel and fight was corrected by discussants who joined later on, including journalists and students who were on site.

The Multiple Roles of Traditional Media

Researchers have documented cases in which hot-topic issues starting online were amplified and extensively distributed by traditional media, resulting in a wide range of social influences (Bennett, 2003; Dahlgren, 2009; Farrell & Drezner, 2008; Kahn & Kellner, 2004). Traditional media presents multiple roles in these cases.

First, they are the whistleblowers themselves. Yang Cunhu, the party secretary of Jingle County, Shaanxi Province, has a daughter, then a college student, who was freeloading 5 years' salary from a local institution under his supervision. This was exposed by the *Economic Observer*, one of the top three newspapers in China focused on economics.

Second, media functioned as visibility amplifiers because they helped to confirm core facts in the chaos of various discourses and highlight the significance of cases in the overall anti-corruption campaign. In He Zhi's case, for instance, local newspaper *Changsha Evening News* reported that He is the first bureau-level cadre in Zhuzhou city who had been investigated. Later, many local media joined the report on the trial results and named the case as the first case of online anti-corruption. The prominent attribution helped to highlight the case and make the public aware of it.

Third, media are also agenda-setters in refining topics and advancing discussion and critiques. In cases such as Chen Yachun and Duan Yizhong, journalists conducted interviews with the accused officials and pressed them to respond to the public's critiques. For instance, Chinese Central TV produced a news program discussing Yang Dacai's case. Convening experts in luxury brands consumption, public management, and lawyers, this program advanced the discussion from mere critiques of the corrupt officials to detailing the procedures and reasons for inspection of them, as well as exploring the institutional design of publicizing officials' property.

Style of Discourse

Everyday life. One common feature of the anti-corruption cases is that exposure started from the personal and private sector. Actors, especially the whistleblowers, encountered social injustices in their daily life, be it the humiliation brought by a wife having an affair or the loss of a job because of public property sold inexpensively to private owners. Rather than behaving like activists who aim to improve the public good or to enhance information transparency or social justice, they chose to act in a particular instance to vent personal anger or ridicule, aiming to pull down the shameful officials. Therefore, the most significant rhetoric style is intuitive everyday life talk, as one netizen commented on the Yang Dacai case:

> We don't understand why he laughed in front of the disaster that made people suffer, and we're deeply sick of his brazen smile. He even laughed by the bus burned into skeleton, by the 36 burned bodies not even turned cold yet, with his hands clasped behind his back and his belly sticking out, laughed so happily. What was he laughing at? Many people were killed in the incident, even if he doesn't need to show tears, he should at least have kept the due respect to the precious lives lost.[9]

The most obvious tactic is to use "hidden text"—euphemisms and satire. Studies (Esarey & Xiao, 2008) have registered the cases in which netizens' use of political satire, implicit criticism, or explicit but guarded criticism has effectively and safely addressed politically sensitive issues. For example, Yang's case was ridiculed by netizens: "I'm afraid officials will have to dress up like beggars from now on. They have to send their money abroad since they dare not to spend their money in China"; "I suggest that officials dress like [they did] in [the] Qing dynasty, restore the standard imperial apparel, then everyone is safe."[10]

Radical. Whether it is exposure out of rights protection, revenge, or moral criticism of a violation of a social taboo, discussion of the cases is full of emotion and radical gestures. The whistleblower of the case of Vice Mayor Chen Yachun depicted him as a "big liar, rogue, and big criminal." The husband who exposed the adultery of his wife and the Tobacco Monopoly Bureau chief Han Feng used a screamer for his BBS post: "Wife, bureau chief Han asks you to have sex with him." There was also the emotional claim that he wanted to "hack him" and "let him taste the agony of losing wife and family!"

The use of a "human flesh search engine" further exacerbates radical communication. Based on massive human collaboration, it identifies and exposes targets that have aroused netizens' wrath. The ruthless exposure of personal information such as home addresses and information about a spouse and children interrupts the targeted person's life. With the absence of legislative enactment to protect personal information, privacy protection in cyberspace is very fragile for average people, not to mention the disgraced and corrupt officials.

Deliberative. Of course, the exposure of corrupt officials is also accompanied by rational criticism, since many have seen the systematic and institutional roots of the corruption. Journalists, public intellectuals, and eyewitnesses try to look beyond private life and explore the locus of the problem and solution. Entanglements of private affairs, therefore, surpassed the scope of the private sector and were interpreted as public issues that have brought political concerns.

Zhou Jiugeng's consumption of luxury cigarettes and his nepotism benefitting family members, for instance, caused many to ask whose interests the government should be pursuing—those of the real estate developers or average citizens. It also brought forth a demand to disclose an official's assets. After all, as an expert of luxury brands in the Yang Dacai case commented, "online anti-corruption is only a supplement to institutional anti-corruption, and if cadres do not open their property record, distrust would only increase; and without institutional anti-corruption to consolidate the prevention and punishment of corruption, online anti-corruption will become meaningless" (Hou, 2012).

Also remarkable is netizens' reflections on the behavior and qualities of the exposure itself. Concerns ranged from the authenticity of exposed information, to the level of the public's rationality, to the apprehension that a more important agenda was being ignored with major attention on the human flesh search action.

Conclusion and Discussion

Examining the Web discussion of 10 high-profile cases of online anti-corruption, this study identifies the model of effective construction of a dynamic network, in which infiltration of bottom-up condemnation of corrupted officials entered into the discursive space marshaled by multiple actors with their strategic use of switching topics and discourses across different media. The main argument is that the connections and interplays among multiple actors, media spaces, and discursive styles constitute, although lacking of specific organization, a networked power by which random exposure of personal affairs effectively invites well-attended civic conversations and actions in the public sphere. The exposure of the life world of those accused, when spotlighted under public view and expanded and switched into discussion on constraining the abuse of power and demanding institutional change, eventually causes boundaries between the private and the public to blur.

The cases of online anti-corruption in China were examined in detail because of their symbolic and historic significance for Chinese civil society and the Chinese mediasphere. They represented the rare occasions in which the energy of subactivism accumulated through everyday and informal networks found access to the public view and achieved concrete goals. The affordances provided by online communities proved to be instrumental in the process: actors demonstrated their capacity to act as both programmers and switchers. New media joined with traditional media to form a mediasphere where different styles of discourse were presented to cause the downfall of the corrupt officials. In the intersections of these various spaces, new roles and opportunities arise for differently positioned actors of civil society. Effective civic expression and action involves creative navigation and visibility across these strands.

This study proposes a perspective on the democratic potential of the Internet that casts light on facets of democracy located outside of the more often discussed concept of the public sphere; namely, toward changes unfolding in the life world that involve lived experience, resources, and subjective dispositions at its core. If the bourgeois public sphere in the Habermasian sense is based on the alienation of man from his private life world, then the cases presented here imply that advancement of public issues may also rely upon the link between a man and his private life. The fact that issues originated from the life world can trigger discussion in the public sphere, therefore, extends the understanding of the public sphere in an era in which new media has made the infiltration of one's personal life into the public sector significantly more prominent.

With the existence of the switching function realized by cyber vigilantism, we see how the established programs or the original agenda of a debated issue evolve along various switching points and thus strengthen the public opinion. The findings of this study enrich our understanding of Castell's concept of the "space of flows," the material organization of time-sharing social practices that work through flows (Castells, 2004, p. 147). The competition of the material organization between the programmers and switchers has changed the direction of the information and opinion flows, and by doing so it loosens the established boundary between the public and private.

In summary, switching between the private and public should be viewed as a double-edged sword. On one hand, publicizing the private can set up flags and invite investigation into a corrupt official; it may also incur intrusion of privacy for average citizens. At each switching point, what really matters is whether the switcher can provide solid and accurate information serving his own interest. The complex situation in the Chinese cyberspace is characterized by opaque and asymmetric information (the government being reluctant to release unpleasant news), as well as heavy censorship (MacKinnon, 2008, 2009), making the analysis of switchers' functions theoretically necessary and practically important. When top-down systemic reformation is beyond expectations for the time being, then leveling up private issues to the public and leveraging power from the bottom up is certainly appealing.

The major limitation of networked anti-corruption efforts is that they lack rule of law and institutionalized procedure. First, they are contingent upon the determination and force of the government in fighting corruption, as well as the power struggle within the political system. For instance, the relatively effective networked anti-corruption scenario doesn't seem to be applicable in cases involving corrupted national leaders, who are depicted as "tigers" in the current anti-corruption movement. Rather than the bottom-up exposure, the tigers are usually uncovered from top-down Party cleaning and in most of the cases entangled with political purges. After all, private life details of the national leaders is not likely to be witnessed by average netizens, and the disclosure of them has to be dependent upon the institutional power.

Second, anti-corruption is often accompanied by violence, violation of privacy, and lack of respect to human rights (Cheong, & Gong, 2010; Gao & Stanyer, 2014; Herold, 2011). As a result, irrational behavior such as personal attacks and slander occur frequently, which is not conducive to the formation of democratic deliberation in the Chinese digital public sphere.

In addition, because of the anonymity of Internet speech, anti-corruption actions can be manipulative and deceptive tools of malicious attacks (Wang, 2010), or psychological catharses of social injustice, resulting in polarized speech (Le & Yang, 2010; Liu & Xie, 2014), violations of reputation and privacy, or defamation actions against others (Quan & Wang, 2013). To overcome these limitations, online networked anti-corruption efforts must collaborate with, and be supported by, institutional anti-corruption campaigns.

Notes

1. President Xi Jinping's speech at the second meeting of the 18th plenary session of the Central Commission for Discipline Inspection.
2. Comment by Anthony Saich, a professor at Harvard University's John F. Kennedy School of Government. Retrieved from http://www.bloomberg.com/news/2014–03–03/china-s-xi-broadens-graft-crackdown-to-boost-influence.html.
3. Xinhua News, "No exclusion area—2014 new expectations of anti-corruption," February 28, 2014. Retrieved from http://news.xinhuanet.com/2014–02/28/c_12620 6840.htm.
4. Andrew Wedeman interview, "How real is China's anti-corruption campaign?" By Celia Hatton, September 4, 2013, BBC News, Beijing. Retrieved from http://www. bbc.com/news/world-asia-china-23945616.
5. Caixin.com, "Officials sacked because of Internet exposure." Retrieved from http://china.caixin.com/2012–10–15/100447044.html.
6. Post on Maopu. Retrieved from http://dzh.mop.com/whbm/20101023/0/S3l3g5Ic 0bd638lz.shtml.
7. Post on Baidu tieba. Retrieved from http://tieba.baidu.com/p/1350197683?pn=1.
8. Evening News, "Investigation on the case of Zhou, Jiugeng," February 13, 2009. Retrieved from http://news.sina.com.cn/o/2009–02–11/123315145654s.shtml.

9. Zhejiang Online-Qianjiang Evening News, "Shaanxi Administration of Work Safety Secretary smile at accident scene, and photos wearing luxury watches exposed online," August 28, 2012. Retrieved from http://news.qq.com/a/20120828/000605. htm.
10. Netizen comments from Tianya BBS, 9/22/2012. Retrieved from http://bbs.tianya. cn/post-free-2782136-1.shtml.

References

Andersen, T. B. (2009). E-government as an anti-corruption strategy. *Information Economics and Policy, 21*(3), 201–210.

Atton, C. (2004). *An alternative Internet*. Edinburgh: Edinburgh University Press. doi:10.3366/edinburgh/9780748617692.001.0001

Atton, C. (2006). Far-right media on the Internet: Culture, discourse and power. *New Media & Society, 8*(4), 573–587. doi:10.1177/1461444806065653

Bakardjieva, M. (2009). Subactivism: Lifeworld and politics in the age of the Internet. *The Information Society, 25*(2), 91–104. doi:10.1080/01972240802701627

Bakardjieva, M. (2012). Reconfiguring the mediapolis: New media and civic agency, *New Media & Society, 14*(1), 63–79. doi:10.1177/1461444811410398

Bennett, W. L. (2003). New media power: The Internet and global activism. In N. Couldry & J. Currans (Eds.), *Contesting media power* (pp. 171–177). Lanham, MD: Rowman and Littlefield.

Bennett, W. L., & Segerberg, A. (2012). The logic of connective action: Digital media and the personalization of contentious politics. *Information, Communication & Society, 15*(5), 739–768. doi:10.1080/1369118X.2012.670661

Bohman, J. (1996). *Public deliberation: Pluralism, complexity, and democracy*. Cambridge, MA: MIT Press.

Brouwer, D. C. (2006). Communication as counterpublic. In G. J. Shepherd, J. John, & T. Striphas (Eds.), *Communication as perspectives on theory* (pp. 171–177). London: Sage. doi:10.4135/9781483329055.n22

Canaves, S., & Feng, S. (2010, January 7). Hu Shuli's new magazine venture. *Wall Street Journal*. Retrieved from http://blogs.wsj.com/chinarealtime/2010/01/07/hu-shulis-new-magazine-venture/

Castells, M. (2004). An introduction to the information age. In F. Webster, R. Blom, E. Karvonen, H. Melin, K. Nordenstreng, & E. Puoskari (Eds.), *The Information Society Reader* (pp. 138–149). New York: Routledge.

Castells, M. (2009). *Communication power*. Oxford: Oxford University Press.

Chen, R. (2006). *Gonggong yishi yu Zhongguo wenhua* [*Public Awareness and Chinese Culture*]. Beijing: New Star Press.

Cheong, P., & Gong, J. (2010). Cyber vigilantism, transmedia collective intelligence, and civic participation. *Chinese Journal of Communication, 3*, 471–487. doi:10.1080/175447 50.2010.516580

Cheung, A. (2009a). China Internet going wild: Cyber-hunting versus privacy protection. *Computer Law and Security Review, 25*(3), 275–279.

Cheung, A. (2009b). A study of cyber-violence and Internet service providers' liability: Lessons from China. *Pacific Rim Law and Policy Journal, 18*, 323–346.

Cohen, J. (1989). Deliberation and democratic legitimacy. In A. Hamlin & P. Pettit (Eds.), *The good polity: Normative analysis of the state* (pp. 17–34). Oxford: Basil Blackwell.

Dahlberg, L. (2007). Rethinking the fragmentation of cyberpublic: From consensus to contestation. *New Media & Society, 9*(5), 827–847. doi:10.1177/1461444807081228

Dahlberg, L., & Siapera, E. (2007). *Radical democracy and the Internet: Interrogating theory and practice.* New York: Palgrave Macmillan. doi:10.1057/9780230592469

Dahlgren, P. (2003). Reconfiguring civic culture in the new media milieu. In J. Corner & D. Pels (Eds.), *Media and the restyling of politics: Consumerism, celebrity and cynicism* (pp. 151–170). London: Sage.

Dahlgren, P. (2009). *Media and political engagement: Citizens, communication and democracy.* Cambridge: Cambridge University Press.

Deluca, K. M. (1999). *Image politics: The new rhetoric of environmental activism.* Mahwah, NJ: Guilford Press.

Downing, J., Villarreal, F., Gil, G., & Stein, L. (2001). *Radical media: Rebellious communication and social movements.* Thousand Oaks, CA: Sage.

Du, Z., & Ren, J. (2011). Woguo wangluo fanfu tedian yu qushi de shizheng yanjiu [Empirical research on network characteristics and trends of corruption]. *Henan Shehui Kexue, 19*(2), 47–52.

Esarey, A., & Xiao, Q. (2008). Political expression in the Chinese blogosphere: Below the radar. *Asian Survey, 48*(5), 752–772. doi:10.1525/AS.2008.48.5.752

Fagerjord, A. (2003). *Rhetorical convergence: Earlier media influence on web media form* (Doctoral dissertation, University of Oslo). Retrieved from http://folk.uio.no/andersfa/downloads/RhetoricalConvergenceCh1.pdf

Farrell, H., & Drezner, D. (2008). The power and politics of blogs. *Public Choice, 134,* 15–30. doi:10.1007/s11127-007-9198-1

Fishkin, J. (2009). *When the people speak: Deliberative democracy and public consultation.* New York: Oxford University Press.

Fishkin, J., & Laslett, P. (Eds.). (2003). *Debating deliberative democracy.* Oxford: Blackwell. doi:10.1002/9780470690734

Fraser, N. (1992). Rethinking the public sphere: A contribution to the critique of actually existing democracy. In C. Calhoun (Ed.), *Habermas and the public sphere* (pp. 109–142). Cambridge, MA: MIT Press.

Gao, L., & Stanyer, J. (2014). Hunting corrupt officials online: The human flesh search engine and the search for justice in China. *Information, Communication & Society, 17*(7), 814–829. doi:10.1080/1369118X.2013.836553

Garcia-Murillo, M., & MacInnes, I. (2009). A policy game in a virtual world. In R. E. Ferdig (Ed.), *Handbook of research on effective electronic gaming in education* (pp. 489–507). doi:10.4018/978-1-59904-808-6.ch028

Goel, R. K., Nelson, M. A., & Naretta, M. A. (2012). The Internet as an indicator of corruption awareness. *European Journal of Political Economy, 28,* 64–75. doi:10.1016/j.ejpoleco.2011.08.003

Gutmann, A., & Thompson, D. (2002). *Why deliberative democracy?* Princeton, NJ: Princeton University Press.

Habermas, J. (1991). *The structural transformation of the public sphere: An inquiry into a category of bourgeois society.* Cambridge, MA: MIT Press.

Hands, J. (2007). Between agonistic and deliberative politics: Towards a radical e-democracy. In L. Dahlberg & E. Siapera (Eds.), *Radical democracy and the Internet: Interrogating theory and practice* (pp. 89–107). New York: Palgrave Macmillan.

Hanisch, C. (1970). The personal is political. In S. Firestone & A. Koedt (Eds.), *Notes from the second year: Women's liberation* (pp. 204–205). New York: Redstockings.

Hermes, J., & Dahlgren, P. (2006). Cultural studies and citizenship. *European Journal of Cultural Studies, 9*(3), 259–265. doi:10.1177/1367549406066072

Herold, D. K. (2011). Human flesh search engines, carnivalesque riots as components of a "Chinese democracy." In D. K. Herold & P. Marolt (Eds.), *Online society in China: Creating, celebrating, and instrumentalising the online carnival* (pp. 127–145). New York: Routledge.

Herold, D. K., & Marolt, P. (Eds.). (2011). *Online society in China: Creating, celebrating, and instrumentalising the online carnival.* New York: Routledge.

Hou, W. (2012, September 25). 27 days: Looking back at the public opinion evolution in the downfall of the "smiling brother." *Procuratorial Daily.* Retrieved from http://fanfu. people.com.cn/n/2013/0924/c64371–23011570.html

Hu, Y. (2009). Gongsi lingyu yu Zhongguo shehui. *Dangdai Zhongguo Yanjiu, 2.* Retrieved from http://www.modernchinastudies.org/us/issues/past-issues/104-mcs-2009-issue-2/1091–2012–01–05–15–35–41.html

Jenkins, H. (2006). *Convergence culture: Where old and new media collide.* New York: New York University Press.

Kahn, R., & Kellner, D. (2004). New media and Internet activism: From the "battle of Seattle" to blogging. *New Media & Society, 6*(1), 87–95.

Laclau, E., & Mouffe, C. (1985). *Hegemony and socialist strategy: Towards a radical democratic politics.* Verso: London.

Le, Y., & Yang, B. (2010). Wangluo jihua xianxiang yanji: jiayu sige zhongwen BBS luntan de neirong fenxi [Exploring Online Polarization Phenomenon: Content Analysis of Four Major Chinese BBS Forums]. *Qingnian Yanjiu, 2010*(2), 1–12.

Lio, M., Liu, M., & Ou, Y. (2011). Can the Internet reduce corruption? A cross-country study based on dynamic panel data models. *Government Information Quarterly, 28,* 47–53. doi:10.1016/j.giq.2010.01.005

Liu, Y., & Xie, Y. (2014). Wangluo fanfu yuqing shijian de xingcheng yu yanbian jizhi yanjiu [Formation and evolution mechanism of online anti-corruption]. *Xiandai Chuanbo, 4,* 69–74.

MacDougall, R. (2005). Identity, electronic ethos, and blogs: A technologic analysis of symbolic exchange on the new news medium. *American Behavioral Scientist, 49*(4), 575–599. doi:10.1177/0002764205280922

MacKinnon, R. (2008). Blogs and China correspondence: Lessons about global information flows. *Chinese Journal of Communication, 1*(2), 242–257.

MacKinnon, R. (2009). China's censorship 2.0: How companies censor bloggers. *First Monday, 14*(2). doi:10.5210/fm.v14i2.2378

McCurdy, P. (2009). *"I predict a riot"—mediation and political contention: Dissent!'s media practices at the 2005 Gleneagles G8 Summit* (Doctoral dissertation, London School of Economics and Political Science). Retrieved from http://etheses.lse.ac.uk/5

Mouffe, C. (2005). *On the political.* New York: Routledge.

Ong, A. (1999). *Flexible citizenship: The cultural logics of transnationality.* Durham, NC: Duke University Press.

Quan, L., & Wang, R. (2013). Minzhong canyu wangluo fanfu xinli yanjiu [Psychology of the public in anti-corruption participation]. *Xuexi Luntan, 3,* 58–60.

Rawls, J. (1993). *Political liberalism.* New York: Columbia University Press.

Ren, J., & Du, Z. (2007). Wangluo xiaoying cuisheng fanfu xin qixiang [Anti-corruption spawned by the Internet]. *Renmin Luntan, 7,* 20–21.

Rosaldo, R. (1994). Cultural citizenship and educational democracy. *Cultural Anthropology, 9*(3), 402--411.

Ryfe, D. M. (2002). The practice of deliberative democracy: A study of 16 deliberative organizations. *Political Communication, 19*(3), 359--377. doi:10.1080/01957470290055547X

Schneider, S. M., & Foot, K. (2005). Web sphere analysis: An approach to studying online action. In C. Hine (Ed.), *Virtual methods: Issues in social science research on the internet* (pp. 157–170). Oxford: Berg.

Schwarze, S. (2006). Environmental melodrama. *Quarterly Journal of Speech, 92*(3), 239–261.

Shim, D. C., & Eom, T. H. (2008). E-government and anti-corruption: Empirical analysis of international data. *International Journal of Public Administration, 31*(3), 298–316. doi:10.1080/01900690701590553

Siapera, E. (2004). Asylum politics, the Internet and the public sphere: The case of UK refugee support group online. *Javnost—The Public, 11*(1), 79–100.

Sunstein, C. (2001). *Republic.com.* Princeton, NJ: Princeton University Press.

Tewksbury, D. (2005). The seeds of audience fragmentation: Specialization in the use of online news sites. *Journal of Broadcasting & Electronic Media, 49*(3), 332–348. doi:10.1207/s15506878jobem4903_5

Wang, J. (2010). Wangluo jiandu [Internet monitoring]. *Fazhi yu Shehui, 5,* 178–180.

Webster, J. G., & Lin, S. F. (2002). The Internet audience: Web use as mass behavior. *Journal of Broadcasting & Electronic Media, 46*(1), 1–12.

Webster, J. G., & Phalen, P. F. (1997). *The mass audience: Rediscovering the dominant model.* Mahwah, NJ: Lawrence Erlbaum Associates.

Wen, F. (2008, October 7). Netizen's report brings the first case of anti-corruption in Hunan. *Legal Weekly.* Retrieved from http://news.eastday.com/c/20081007/u1a3903733.html

Wen, H. (2013). Wangluo fanfu: Shizheng anli yu neizai jili [Online anti-corruption: Empirical cases and inner mechanism]. *Shehui Kexue, 10,* 17–27.

Wimmer, J. (2005). Counter-public sphere and the revival of the European public sphere. *Javnost—The Public, 12*(2), 93–110.

Yang, G. (2012). Lightness, wildness, and ambivalence: China and new media studies. *New Media & Society, 14*(1), 170–179.

3

MEMETIC ENGAGEMENT AS MIDDLE PATH RESISTANCE

Contesting Mainland Chinese Immigration and Social Cohesion

Pauline Hope Cheong and Yashu Chen

A rising area of interest on the affordances of digital and social media is the creation and spread of online memes. Memes refer to cultural ideas, symbols, or practices in which dissemination generates imitations and reproductions that do not have to be exact in order to reinforce beliefs and spur thought contagion in society (Blackmore, 2000). Memes are network building and bridging units of social information transmission (Dawkins, 1989). As online interactants consume, produce, and share alternative or unorthodox texts, the potential of online memes to catalyze and facilitate social change has significant meaning for civic participation and the challenges and restructuring of state authority relations (Cheong & Gong, 2010; Cheong & Lundry, 2012).

In light of the corporeal and symbolic expansion of Chinese presence globally, this chapter examines the key online memes that have emerged in relation to the intensification of mainland Chinese immigration or the "mainland invasion." Singapore and Hong Kong have traditionally been migrant states and share a postcolonial heritage with a Chinese ethnic majority. However, recent social protests have emerged to contest the influx of Chinese mainlanders, even as immigration policy (or the lack thereof) supports migration of these *zhongguo xinyimin* to boost the finance, real estate, tourism, and retail industries. A slew of controversial anti–Mainland China memes have been transmitted. This prompts a systemic investigation of their spread and evolution as well as the sociocultural implications of these newer participatory forms of citizen engagement where increasing numbers of citizens are using their personal online and social media networks to communicate and mobilize. This form of lay engagement facilitated by the "connective action" of personal online networks differs from traditional organization-led collective action (Bennett & Segerberg, 2012).

This chapter discusses the processes and forms of memetic engagement, where online interactants cocreate and circulate memes in transmedia and online–offline ways, highlighting networked practices of meme circulation and (re)appropriation across contemporary convergence culture. We argue that memetic engagement can function as middle ground resistance (Scott, 1985) enacted by subordinate classes to effect opposition in strongly regulated societies because civilians can rarely engage in effective open rebellion but can retaliate in prosaic and constant struggles. Drawing from two case studies, this chapter demonstrates how memetic engagement may help lay persons respond to class conflicts even as their governments strategically restructure their authority to contend with alternative narratives and contentious polity. Additionally, this chapter will further understanding in how the personalization of politics via online communication plays out within Chinese societies, and under what differing conditions and capacities, for comparative analyses on public civic engagement.

Memetic Engagement: The Rise of Chinese Digital Creatives

In recent years, there has been intense public debate about immigration, class, and social cohesion in Singapore and Hong Kong. Attention to this set of interrelated issues has been focused around changing patterns of immigration, income inequalities, and unprecedented breakdowns in social services affecting healthcare, housing, education, and transportation. With the national birthrate below its replacement level, Singapore has seen a steep intake of foreigners with an addition of 1 million foreigners since 2005. Its most recent government policy paper on population said it expected its population to increase by 30% to between 6.5 to 6.9 million by 2030, with foreigners making up close to half of that number (Prime Minister's Office, 2013). Hong Kong is a special administrative region of China, with a different economic, political, and legal system (Holiday & Wong, 2003). From 1997 to 2012, 760,000 Mainland Chinese migrated to Hong Kong (Lau, 2013). Moreover, since the Individual Visit Scheme began in 2003, thousands of mainland tourists have visited Hong Kong. In 2011, 28 million Mainland Chinese tourists travelled to Hong Kong, with 34.9 million a year later; a significantly high number given Hong Kong's resident population of 7 million (Hong Kong Tourism Board, 2013; Lai, 2012).

Additionally, there has been a growing preoccupation in these cities, along with other societies worldwide, with the possible dangers of immigration to social cohesion represented by growing polarization between the global capitalist class (which includes many new immigrants) and the gradually slimming middle classes of locals (Cheong, Edwards, Goulbourne, & Solomos, 2007). The Gini coefficient of inequality has risen significantly in Singapore and Hong Kong, whose wealth gaps are currently among the highest globally (Hong Kong Statistical Society, n.d.).

Notably, rising numbers of citizens have mounted demonstrations to voice their opposition to the resurgent discourse on immigration, which frames new immigrants from China as "foreign talent" or as "capital" needed to sustain Asian economic prosperity. Their remonstrance presents a plea to authorities to scale back immigration and limit foreigner access to public goods and services; access that is seen as a right of natural-born citizens but nonetheless has recently come under siege in light of rising inflation, corporatization, and overcrowding.

Underpinning these expressed alarms is the notion of class, since many *xiny-imin* are perceived to be economically privileged, yet culturally inferior (marked by their unfamiliarity and disrespect for local laws, customs, and languages). In Singapore, new mainlanders have been implicated in high-profile cases as perpetrators of physical violence (e.g., drivers involved in road fatalities), verbal abuse (e.g., hurling insults at locals), and threats to the local community (e.g., Chinese family curtailing their neighbors from cooking aromatic local foods) (Mahtani, 2012). Similarly, in Hong Kong, class dynamics are operant in the case of the "Chinese Locust," where mainlanders are portrayed as rapacious consumers and opportunistic pregnant mothers. Under the Immigration Ordinance, children born in Hong Kong gain citizenship, with access to benefits unavailable to their mainland-born counterparts, benefits such as superior medical care, free education, and visa-free travel to many countries (Chu, 2012).

Of interest here is the increasingly visible, vigorous, and mediated expression of these class dynamics alongside recent social protests. Both countries do not enjoy unfettered press freedom, and reports produced by international agencies such as Freedom House and Reporters Without Borders show a decline in the freedom of information, although Hong Kong traditionally has a more outspoken and free media. Yet both countries enjoy one of the highest Internet usage rates worldwide, making them fertile ground in which to examine meme engagement.

We attend to digital meme communication given the recent popularity and capacity to provide understanding of lay resistance and civic engagement. Broadly, memetic engagement for purposes of political commentary and activism involves the creation, circulation, transmediation, remix, and reappropriation of striking cultural ideas and symbols and their derivatives across multiple communication platforms. Digital media convergence affords citizens the ability to collaboratively construct and share previously inaccessible information as they archive, tag, and reticulate news (Goode, 2009). In the process, online users simultaneously act as producers, distributors, and critics. In some contexts, this implies an increased agency in what has hitherto been lay persons' limited capacity to communicate about civic and political affairs.

Under these circumstances, it is significant to understand how memetic engagement may alter the current episteme, including how people come to understand and interpret current events. The construction of "truth" is contested alongside rumors and misinformation, particularly in an information vacuum or censorship amidst heightened social anxieties (Bernardi, Cheong, Lundry, & Ruston, 2012). Consequently, the (re)circulation of memes can function as media "viral codes" (Rushkoff, 1996) to influence a society's agenda or cultivate resistance to its dominant discourse. As activist Andrew Boyd argued, "truth is a virus," and "social movements cannot live by meme alone. Yet memes are clearly powerful- both analytically and operationally. A vital movement requires a hot and happening meme" (p. 378).

Historically, alternative interpretations of the social order have been performed "backstage" by marginalized populations to critique authority (Goffman, 1959) and entertaining "carnivalesque play" to satirize elite norms (Bakhtin, 1993). Jokes and humorous texts have challenged official news of national disasters (Oring, 2010) and public strategic communication on international security (Goodall, Cheong, Fleischer, & Corman, 2012). Digital media use today potentially extends the scope and impact of oppositionist activities as jocular digital remixes, and dramatic video mash-ups constitute varying (re)presentations of the "truth" (Meikle, 2008) to affect how lay people perceive and remember political authorities (Lessig, 2008). Silva and Garcia (2012), for instance, argued that the spread of the "Downfall meme" on YouTube mash-ups, which featured the portrayal (and reproach) of Hitler, critiqued political systems worldwide when meme-making addressed politicians' abuse of power, greed, and corruption.

Against this background, we propose that memetic engagement functions as middle ground resistance (Scott, 1985) enacted by online participants embedded in highly regulated contexts because civilians can rarely engage in effective open rebellion without reprisal but they can retaliate in prosaic and constant struggles to their minimum disadvantage. In contexts where open criticism is met with disapproval or punishment, the average citizen is in a weak position vis-à-vis the ruling authority. Thus, middle ground resistance practices represent "weapons of the weak" (Scott, 1985) to help civilians articulate their critique of power, while enjoying a measure of impunity.

Emerging from James Scott's ethnographic research in Malaysia, middle ground resistance had been conceptualized to understand quotidian tactics practiced by rice farmers when faced with the then "new green revolution." Refusing to accept official definitions of power and marginalization by wealthy land owners, peasants engaged in experimental and inventive practices like humor and mockery, grumbling and slander, rumor mongering, character assassination, and sabotage. Strikingly, Scott's analysis of the guises of peasant ideological struggle under conditions of social stress and inequality reveals certain features in common with contemporary mediated activism. They require little or no coordination, make use of implicit understanding and informal networks, practice safety in anonymity, and often represent a form of self-help and typically avoid any direct clash with authority, making middle ground resistance a compelling frame and equally applicable to understand memetic engagement directed toward oppositional goals (Cheong & Lundry, 2012).

As we will illustrate, in a climate of heightened social anxiety, memetic engagement can conceivably help citizens protest against mainstream media representations and express their dissent on government policy. Examination of anti–Mainland Chinese memes permits us to observe emerging dimensions of proletariat participation as the current episteme is altered by the sharing of unorthodox texts amid tensions in immigration and class in Singapore and Hong Kong. As forms of resistance and cultural protest reflect the conditions and constraints under which they are generated, our inquiry is grounded in case studies.

Examining Memetic Engagement Associated With Mainland Chinese Migration

As case studies provide rich contextual details to understand the processes and causes underlying contemporary events within their real-life contexts (Yin, 2009), we selected the two cases below based on an information-orientation selection (Flyvbjerg, 2006) to yield maximum heuristic content. Following the method recommended by Shifman and Thelwall (2009) to conduct Web memetics, adapted to the specifics of our contexts and research objectives, we gathered as many URLs of pages mentioning the memes as possible, using a combination of search engine queries in English and Chinese on Google and Baidu. This helped to "assess the Web presence of the memes, and the URL list is used for subsequent analysis" (Shifman & Thelwall, 2009). Data was then collected on YouTube, in Chinese and English, using keywords "Singapore Ferrari car crash" and "Hong Kong locusts" mentioned in the titles or "About" sections of the videos.

We followed the links directed to "suggested videos." Videos were organized by ranking view counts with the "Filter" tab on YouTube to identify the top videos for data analysis. We then created lists of data where titles, URLs, dates, number of views, comments, and shares of videos were entered into a database ($N = 400$). We also employed the Google and LexisNexis search engines to source other iterations of the meme, across platforms and through following hyperlinks that reflect the archival and Web-like nature of digital records. These searches also allowed us to identify the earliest appearance of each meme and trace a timeline of its evolution. When no new derivatives were found, and after analyzing variations of repeated material, collection stopped after more than 200 hours of ethnographic observations of textual, audio, and visual content in newspapers, Web sites, public forums, and social media sites. The researchers reviewed the data mainly in Chinese and English, and in the vernacular dialects known as "Singlish" (pidgin mix of English, Malay, and Hokkien) and Cantonese. Attention was paid to qualitatively assessing the revised and additive nature of each meme engagement, and observations on altered versions were recorded in our database. Given this chapter's length, we focused our discussion on the top 20 videos and key derivatives in print, blogs, microblogs, online forums, and open groups on social media including Facebook, Renren, Tianya, Sina blogs, Netease blogs, and Sina Weibo (N = 1000). Mainland Chinese/mainlanders are used as shorthand descriptors to differentiate between Singaporean Chinese/ Singaporean and Hong Kong Chinese/Hong Konger. When citing quotations, we have reproduced the original meaning of the content as faithfully as possible when the primary language was not English.

The "Ferrari Crash" Meme of a Feckless Mainland Chinese Migrant

The Ferrari crash meme of a feckless Mainland Chinese migrant is related to and arguably catalyzed by the spread of Singapore's first viral video. This amateur video is especially noteworthy since it first surfaced on the internet, rather than as breaking news on the state's strongly managed media. The 29-second video, which was uploaded by a user called "TheMockymocky" on Monday, May 14, 2012, shows a speeding Ferrari after running a red light colliding head-on into the side of a cab, sending both vehicles flying through the air (TheMockymocky, 2012). The brief yet highly dramatic video clip was uploaded on YouTube two days after the accident, which was recorded by the video camera of a fellow cab driver who was two car lengths behind the taxi that was hit as it moved off slowly after the traffic light turned green at a junction (Anonymous, 2012a).

The driver was identified in the local newspapers the next day as 31-year-old Chinese businessman Ma Chi, a financial investor from Sichuan who had relocated to Singapore with his wife and child four years prior and who was in the midst of applying for permanent residency. Ma Chi was instantaneously killed in the car accident while the Singaporean taxi driver and his Japanese passenger died later in the hospital. Two additional people—a Malay motorcyclist and the female passenger in the Ferrari—were also injured.

This crash promptly drew irate responses, and the Ferrari crash quickly became a meme and recurrent topic of blog posts, status updates, tweets, photoshopped images, and video mash-ups. The amateur video went viral with 2.4 million views on YouTube in the first 5 days and subsequently hit more than five million views. The video also drew 3,597 comments, 2,308 likes, and 3,845 shares. This number of views is high in a nation of about 5.3 million residents. Even more remarkable is the total tally of the top 20 YouTube videos searched in English and Chinese related to this content: there were 14 million views, more than 9,000 comments, 4,000 likes, and 6,000 shares.

Sharing and recirculation of the meme took place publicly on YouTube where comments made on the original video included vulgar and derogatory pronouncements on Ma Chi. Numerous comments denounced Ma Chi as being typical of all mainlanders, who were ascribed reckless and dishonorable motivations ("worst drivers in the world"), on top of being "barbarian" lawbreakers. Many comments appeared to be made or voiced from the standpoint of

Singaporean Chinese, some eager to direct misgivings toward new mainlanders and differentiate themselves from the "ungrateful migrants" allowed into the country. Antiforeigner sentiments based on class practices were rampant, as evident, for example, in a comment by "goonersify" that said, "All these f* Chinese nationals do is bring their anti-social behavior here. Spitting everywhere and shouting on their mobile phones among other things. I'm a Chinese Singaporean and even I can't stand them." And "YouuTubeKinG" wrote, "I'm Singaporean Chinese and we are civilized and conscience unlike China Chinese today. In the past, our forefathers aka descendants also came down from China to Singapore. As our forefathers grew families, they taught us character values, hygiene, manners and show compassion . . . China people are zombies."

Interestingly, we also observed how comments on the same YouTube platform voiced from the standpoints of overseas Chinese in Hong Kong and Toronto mentioned similar negative stereotypes and encouraged mutual solidarity to block the entry of Mainland Chinese. For instance, "terrymanwai" wrote, "We Hong Konger and Singaporean should unite together to maintain our 'core value.' We should let the western people know that our real Chinese are different from those communist educated Chinese in China! They speak noisy . . . like showing off big brand, cheating, dirty, always say patriotic but emigrate." In response to this comment, "88daruma" wrote, "Agree with Terry! Mainland Chinese are NOT Chinese period. Another Mainland Ching recent killed some poor Hong Kong driver by speeding in Sai Kung. We now watch very carefully for these cars coming cross border to Hong Kong. They break the law and leave very quickly." Strongly worded comments like these reflect the rage that some diverse overseas Chinese have toward mainland migrants, illustrating how the Ferrari crash meme served as a portal for some to express criticism at their respective government's open immigration policies to Chinese nationals.

The Ferrari crash video was quickly copied, generating multiple identical mirror videos with different URLs. Several videos containing the original footage were released but were altered by the addition of photos showing the crash wreckage and also included subtitles and commentary (for example, in the second most popular YouTube video [IZ Reloaded, 2012], it was pointed out that Ma Chi's flamboyant red shoes matched the red color of his sports car).

The relative longevity of the Ferrari crash meme after the accident could be partly attributed to the bland and fairly positive mainstream media portrayal of Ma Chi. The breaking news story in the main English newspaper, the *Straits Times*, was a brief write-up, headlined "2 dead, 3 injured in three-way Bugis crash" (Siau, 2012). The 371-word article described Mr. Ma as "generous with donations to the [immigrant group] association and to the needy," and a "hard-working, righteous and loving father and husband." In addition, headlines on Chinese media described Ma Chi as a "young and capable," "tall and handsome" successful entrepreneur who was "not a heavy drinker" preferring "tea" over alcoholic drinks ("PRC Ferrari," 2012). In contrast, little attention addressed the suspicious circumstances of his accident (for example, why was he in the car with a lady who was not his pregnant wife at 4 a.m.? Initial eyewitness accounts also said he reeked of alcohol, yet mainstream news reported that no traces of alcohol were found in his blood and urine). This seeming disjuncture and lack of information transparency prompted a series of "human flesh searches" that ensued when netizens took it upon themselves to act as "vigilantes" and collectively investigate the socio-demographic information of deviant personalities (Cheong & Gong, 2010) to determine Ma Chi's background. It seemed particularly suspicious that a young person in his early thirties could offer to drive a "limited edition" luxury car (worth US$1.4 million).

In the midst of the information vacuum on Mr. Ma and the accident, online interactants spread rumors that tainted Ma Chi as a "spoilt, rich brat" or scion of a prominent family (Peh, 2012) gained traction, including one widely circulated rumor that claimed he was the son of a fugitive Chinese mafia boss ("PRC netizens," 2012). These rumors were not officially verified. Other blogs also mentioned postings by Chinese netizens that alleged that Ma Chi was involved in the money laundering of millions in Hong Kong (Iron Bowl, 2012). Another rumor labeled him as the son of a high-ranking official, Ma Kai, and pictures of Ma Kai's wife (Tan, 2012), who resembles the image of Ma Chi's mother as shown in Singapore media reports, surfaced (this speculation was later disputed). In addition, "conflicting information" was found on the "mystery female passenger" (Anonymous, 2012b). Online interactants speculated about the relationship he had with his young female passenger, who was described by mainstream news as a recent graduate of a hospitality course, but other accounts have painted her as a scantily dressed *ah lian* (pejorative term for shallow, materialistic, sexually loose Chinese girl), believed to be working at a well-known nightclub. Overall, these alternative accounts appear to render Ma Chi as a corrupt and lawless representative of the *fu er dai* (rich second generation) who flaunt their wealth with impunity.

Meme sharing and transmission further propagated online where this meme evolved over time with personalized ideas, images, and messages in social media platforms. For example, a mock Facebook profile page for Ma Chi was created, characterizing him as a restless soul "in Hell" (Mahtani, 2012). A handful of readers commenting on the satirical page praised its unidentified creator and posted anti–Mainland Chinese comments. After the Facebook account was banned, a Twitter parody account with the username "mrmachimachi" was set up ostensibly by Mr. Ma Chi, whose bio read, "I currently reside in Hell. Burn me some love." The first tweet, on May 18, 2012, read, "Just checked in, Hell seems like a pretty dark place," and subsequent tweets featured updates on his interactions with Satan and other dead celebrities, from global pop stars to a previous Singaporean President. In another instance on the site "Singaporememe. blogspot.com," a graphic poster was created that headlined in bold capitals "You Deserved it!" against the background image of the mangled Ferrari. The seven deadly sins were printed across the image and subtitles read "SIN CITY, where Wealth and Social Status triumph over morals."

After the crash, the amateur video and its derivatives were taken up by a number of international news agencies, facilitating the global spread of the meme. Reports highlighted the accident but linked it specifically to foreigner resentment in Singapore. For instance, a report by *Agence France-Presse* (Anonymous, 2012c) was entitled "Ferrari Crash Fuels Singaporean Anti-Foreign Sentiment," a Bloomberg story headline read "Ferrari Deaths Fuel Anti-Foreigner Anger as Singapore Votes" (Adam & Tan, 2012), a *Wall Street Journal* article was titled "Ferrari Crash Foments Antiforeigner Feelings in Singapore" (Mahtani, 2012), and an article by the *New York Times* was titled "In Singapore, Vitrol against Chinese Newcomers" (Jacobs, 2012). These articles highlighted the growing public resentment, particularly toward Chinese nationals ushered in by liberal visa policies to boost growth by immigration. These reports and other commentaries written by local bloggers weeks and even months after the accident referenced the Ferrari crash and other issues in transportation breakdowns, housing inflation, and unemployment to explain this uncommon wave of hostility and defend the alleged "xenophobia" expressed by native Singaporeans (Seeing through, 2012; Okulski, 2012).

The "Locust" Meme of the Animalistic Mainland Chinese National

The locust meme involving the animalistic portrayals of Mainland Chinese nationals as rapacious consumers in Hong Kong surfaced in January 2011, arguably ignited by the viral video named "Locust World," which portrayed new mainlanders as locusts and presented critiques lobbed against the Chinese Communist Party (CCP) and the Chinese government. The 258-second video, which was created by three online users of the Musical Channel of the Hong Kong Golden forum online and uploaded by one of the online users, named ChinglishVlogs, was itself an amateur mash-up of video clips, photos, and adapted lyrics, mimicking the form of a music video and based on a classic Cantonese song (ChinglishVlogs, 2011). Specifically, the music video highlighted various frantic and maniacal behaviors of Mainland Chinese, including their border crossings to give birth in Hong Kong hospitals and grabbing imported milk powder (perceived to be of higher quality than those found in China). The video also featured many socially inappropriate behaviors of Mainland Chinese, including eating in the subway, relieving their bowels indiscriminately, smoking in public venues, and abusing officials of the Hong Kong government. Critique was also directed at the Chinese government, as seen for instance, in the lyrics that said, "the nation [China] cheats and steals," "the statement that 'China is a powerful country' is a trap to brainwash Hong Kongers," and "the nation assimilates us with Mandarin Chinese." Throughout the video, it seemed that concerns were raised about the future of Hong Kongers because of the influx of mainlanders and the growing dominance of the CCP and the Chinese government.

The "Locust World" music video spread virally and has had over two million views. It also received extraordinarily high exposure with 35,000 comments and 40,000 likes. Viewers commented on the original video of "Locust World" in Chinese, Cantonese, and English on YouTube. Comments included vulgar attacks, fierce arguments, and dissatisfaction. Strikingly, some comments disparaged Mainland Chinese as a *wumao* (literally means five pennies, a derogatory label for a member of the CCP), mainland "dogs" or "pigs," and pests of a country that is powerful yet culturally inferior to Hong Kong. Many comments raised objections to the entry of mainlanders, as exemplified by this comment by "TheMyHK": "Mainland Chinese grab milk powder, what can our babies eat? Mainland Chinese speculate on property, how can we afford an apartment? Mainland Chinese drive up prices of commodities, how can we support ourselves?" Furthermore, comments also highlighted the perceived threat of erosion to the Hong Kong identity. For example, "mslovehk1" said, "I have never been a Chinese in my life. We are Hong Kongers. Hong Kongers should support the independence of Hong Kong. We must build the wonderful future for our next generation." And "khl14" wrote, "I will never become a Chinese. I firmly deny the Chinese identity. I am a Hong Konger." Numerous comments also labeled the CCP as "authoritarian" ("like Hitler"), and some expressed an eagerness to eliminate the CCP ("Overthrow CCP").

Notably, we also found self-identified overseas Chinese from Macau and Taiwan who commented on the music video, voicing similar anti-mainland sentiments. For example, "Yan131452008" wrote, "I am a Macanese and support Hong Kong. Let us eradicate 'locusts'!" Another comment made by a Macanese, who identified as "dylan96117," said, "F* Mainland Chinese! The situation of Macau is also not good. So many Mainland Chinese come to Macau every day to purchase milk powder, spit, dump rubbish, and give birth to babies. F*! As a Macanese, I will support you (Hong Kongers)." Voices from the standpoints of overseas Chinese in Taiwan implicitly showed the dissatisfaction with Mainland Chinese and resentment toward the Chinese government. For instance, "bj8888jb" wrote, "Taiwan would rather be governed by Japan! Taiwan wants independence!" Another comment, made by "131321a," stated, "I felt like crying when Taiwan carried out the Individual Visit Scheme for Mainland Chinese. I think Taiwan would become another Hong Kong if we implemented this policy at the national level. Please do not stain Taiwan, okay?"

The animalistic portrayal of Mainland Chinese as locusts rapidly became a meme, igniting its travel as a symbolic idea and image in discussions and debates on ethics, race, social problems, and politics online and offline, in Hong Kong and China. It has since been copied and featured as a key motif in videos, photoshopped images, full-page advertisements, and blogs.

Specifically, imitation and adaptation of the "Locust World" video swiftly generated numerous similarly titled but varied videos. These highly circulated mash-ups mostly employed the same background music but were modified with different titles, subtitles, pictures, and video clips portraying Mainland Chinese as locusts, exhibiting a varied array of inappropriate behaviors. There were also other mash-ups that utilized different songs, pictures, subtitles, and/or video clips. Memetic engagement also appeared to deepen the narrative of Mainland Chinese as locusts, since several videos added lengthy commentaries explicating the choice of the locust symbol and its good fit as a derogatory mascot for the Mainland Chinese.

Moreover, memetic engagement involved performative and embodied actions when several small-scale citizen resistance tactics were enacted, filmed, and then circulated. For instance, a top circulated video created by *Apple Daily* documented how several Hong Kong students sang "Locust World" in front of Mainland Chinese in shopping areas and even publicly humiliated a woman who sat on the street by questioning whether she was educated or not. Another video, entitled "Crowd outside the door of D&G [Dolce & Gabbana] curses upon seeing 'Locust' tourist bus," featured how a crowd of almost 100 Hong Kongers responded to an event initiated on Facebook by cursing loudly and taking photos when a bus ferrying Mainland Chinese tourists approached a luxury goods store (Anonymous, 2012d; Chen, 2012). In yet another example of online-offline meme engagement, a video entitled "Hong Kong mothers are angry and mainland mothers are locusts" featured multiple Hong Kong pregnant women responding to a call on Facebook for a sit-down demonstration in the iconic Victoria Park and protested with hand-held signs with slogans like "Local pregnant women are angry," and "It is time for us to say 'No,'" with images of pregnant women and babies (Appleactionews, 2011).

Memetic engagement also proceeded with personal appropriation of older media forms into the genre of online music videos, drawing upon material reflecting the mounting historical tensions between China and Hong Kong. In one video, which garnered more than 175,000 views, a 12-second segment of an old Hong Kong movie was used to show the disruptive and outlandish behaviors of Mainland Chinese on the subway, such as pushing others and toying with the handrails, and the reactions from two Hong Kong passengers who expressed ridicule and resentment toward them (Tayman, 2012). Another music video utilized a 3-second segment of an outdated television commercial on pesticides and added a voiceover with subtitles to convey the parallel urgency of eliminating Mainland Chinese like household pests (Littlesteak, 2011).

Besides mimicry and reappropriation of the locust meme on online videos, lay engagement with the locust meme was enacted via transmediation of the meme in various print and social networking sites. In February of 2012, Hong Kongers published a full-page color advertisement titled "Hong Kong has endured enough" on *Apple Daily*, one of Hong Kong's best-selling newspapers.

The advertisement directly referenced the locust meme by portraying a giant locust perched atop a mountain looking at Hong Kong's skyline, and the tagline pointedly decried the border-crossing and "instant citizenship" activities by Mainland Chinese with the rhetorical question, "Are you willing for Hong Kong to spend one million dollars every 18 minutes to raise children born to mainland parents?" This controversial advertisement was created after monies were raised via an online fund-raising campaign on Facebook and the Hong Kong Golden Forum (Anonymous, 2012e).

In addition, some Hong Kongers appropriated Facebook with 3.7 million users in Hong Kong (Figueroa, 2012) to create new groups and pages to critique mainlanders. For instance, a Facebook group with more than 116,000 likes named "Opposing mainland pregnant women coming to Hong Kong to give birth" described that its community would "regularly hold activities like demonstrations, sit-ins and rallies" to "claim back interests of local pregnant women, moms, women, children and local citizens." Furthermore, the group will "always be against all policies regarding new immigrants." To express their dissatisfaction, members of these groups have posted events, news, videos, and photoshopped images about prohibiting pregnant Mainland Chinese from entering Hong Kong, satirizing the uncivilized behaviors of Mainland Chinese and commenting on Mainland China's history and policies including issues related to human rights violations.

The locust meme ad was promptly circulated in many popular mainland digital and social media including Tianya Forums and Netease blogs. The ad stirred up dissatisfactions and outbursts of anger among Mainland Chinese interactants. One online user of Tianya Forum wrote, "Hong Kongers always carp at Mainland Chinese. When they come to Mainland China, they show their displeasure with everything to stress how they are superior to Mainland Chinese," and, "I suggest that Chinese government cut off supplies of fresh water to Hong Kong. This will remind them that Mainland China is the mother of Hong Kong. What ungratefulness!" (Yuebeiwang, 2012). Another Tianya Forum post referenced other meme derivatives of the "Hong Kong had endured enough" poster and said, "Why do we curse each other instead of correcting our mistakes? Why do some Mainland Chinese only curse Hong Kongers? Why do some Hong Kongers not dissuade them?" to show his anger toward internecine struggles implied by the ad and derivatives such as "Shanghai has endured enough" and "Beijing has endured enough" (Honghu, 2012). One popular blog article with about a 100,000 views titled "The Hong Kongers who have endured enough display their ugliness" said, "those Hong Kongers who usually praise themselves for being civilized seem to target all Mainland Chinese . . . I want to ask some Hong Kongers, what do you mean by doing this? Are you Chinese?" (Diguoliangmin, 2012).

To respond to "Hong Kongers have endured enough," some online users created a colored advertisement titled "Mainland Chinese have tolerated enough" and uploaded it onto microblogs. The ad showed a son sitting on his father's shoulders and read, "Because you are the son, Daddy would give you 210 billion as a gift each year," and "We cannot allow the ignorant son to sit on our shoulders any more. We should suspend supplies of power, water and food to the son." Online users in Mainland China and Hong Kong experienced a tit-for-tat and largely intensified the conflict between two areas (Anonymous, 2012e).

The locust meme gained traction worldwide as the locust ad was taken up in international press stories. For instance, a report by the *New York Times* wrote that "Angry Hong Kongers have taken to calling mainland visitors 'locusts'" (LaFraniere, 2012). And an article from CNN carried the headlined, "Hong Kong Newspaper Rails against Chinese 'Invasion'" (Lai, 2012). Additionally, a report by BBC News was titled "Hong Kong Advert Calls Chinese Mainlanders 'Locusts'" (Anonymous, 2012f). These news stories by international news organizations highlighted Hong Kongers' cultural gulf with their mainland counterparts and their fears that their distinctive postcolonial culture would be eroded by new mainland sojourners and migrants.

Conclusion

Tensions over immigration and anti-foreigner sentiments pose a formidable social as well as political challenge for civil societies and governments worldwide, as authorities endeavor to balance economic and community needs, and address concerns for social cohesion. Traditional research on political communication in Western-style democracies has focused on rational discourse and participatory action led by powerful institutions, but newer forms of citizen engagement are emerging via critical discourse shared on personalized networks online (Bennett & Segerberg, 2012), including the viral sharing of emotional and satirical audio and video content. This chapter discussed the various forms of memetic engagement as pathways for citizens' political participation to share critical discourse centered on the negative portrayal of Mainland Chinese migrants in response to the recent swell of Mainland Chinese migration to Singapore and Hong Kong.

In information environments that could be characterized as being moderately to strongly regulated, memetic engagement serves as middle ground resistance (Scott, 1985) enacted by online users as they participate in creating, remixing, and widespread recycling of alternative news. By collaboratively (re)constructing and spreading information and images related to the Ferrari crash and the locust, the actions of netizens resisting mainland immigration can arguably be characterized as a form of "eloquent" political action that "doesn't look like politics" (Duncombe, 2002) as new multimedia texts challenge official immigration policies and perspectives put forth by government and mainstream media outlets. Particularly in contexts of limited press freedom and erstwhile political apathy, memetic engagement allows a participative, prolonged, and potentially more profound social discussion about sensitive issues as citizens share pointed comments online and collaborate to uncover "the truth" under conditions of information vacuums, censorship, or perceived propaganda. In this sense, memetic engagement helps facilitate a restructuring of state authority relations as citizens' communications scale up to affect public opinion and political action (in contexts where they can publicly organize a demonstration or when their critiques are taken up by ruling authorities in the longer term). It is notable, for instance, that the locust meme was associated with the passing of a two-can limit on exports of milk formula law (it restricts travelers from taking more than 1.8 kilograms of infant milk powder out of Hong Kong) in 2013 (e.g., Hannon, 2013). At the time of writing, the most recent protests against the influx of Mainland Chinese in Hong Kong also involved protestors waving placards describing mainland shoppers as locusts (Shadbolt, 2014).

Although YouTube videos are often seen as trivial entertainment, findings here illustrate how raw amateur footage points to the perceived inadequacies of social and political systems and, in this sense, serve to empower citizens to voice critiques of governing authorities. Prior analyses have proposed that YouTube memes have "six common features: focus on ordinary people, flawed masculinity, humor, simplicity, repetitiveness and whimsical content" (Shifman, 2011). The present analysis highlights two other striking features: shock and stock.

The Ferrari crash had registered a high shock value as it featured how the horrific surprise of a seemingly bizarre car collision physically and literally spun out of control. "Locust World" conveyed shock value through its portrayal of mainland newcomers as crass, stock characters. Both memes also involved the jarring dehumanization of mainland nationals, who were ascribed with derogatory attributes. Ma Chi, as a representative of the nouveau riche but corrupt mainlander, is reduced to a spectral ghostly presence while the locust meme dehumanized Mainland Chinese sojourners through discursive labeling and portrayals of them as pests. These elements are paradoxically at once farcical and serious, yet not inconsequential in the contexts examined as citizens collectively sought to investigate Ma Chi's background to incriminate him, and as Hong Kong citizens took to the streets to air their grievances.

Yet, it is important not to overly romanticize these "weapons of the weak" as it is unlikely (and hardly possible to conclude) that memetic engagement will promptly stem Mainland Chinese border crossings. Indeed, while online data can be enduring, some data discussed here were transient and sketchy. For instance, the satirical Facebook account of Ma Chi was shut down, and tweets posted before March 30, 2012, including the original meme about "Hong Kongers have endured enough," are not shown on Sina Weibo.

Furthermore, ground and legal conditions expose the tenuousness of memetic engagement. For instance, the arrest for alleged sedition of the creator of a satirical "Demon-cratic" comic strip in Singapore (Loh, 2013) points to the local constrains that may chill lay memetic engagement. As Silva and Garcia (2012) observed in their analysis of the "Downfall meme," "humorists, in particular cartoonists, play a game of tug-of-war with those in power, a very imbalanced game at times, with serious consequences" (p. 107). Indeed, tug-of-war-like power dynamics influence the civic opportunities and conditions for memetic engagement, which differ from situation to situation. Here, digital media use enabled connective action of personalized content sharing across personal networks, in lieu of trusted organizations to front and orchestrate collective action in the contentious politics surrounding immigration. Concatenate online-offline meme engagement, however, was witnessed in Hong Kong but not in Singapore, where there are stricter laws against illegal public assembly. Therefore the discussion here is instructive for understanding the wider civic and cultural significance of memetic engagement to critique and contest governing authorities as well as addresses some of its pragmatic limitations to effect social change.

Moreover, this chapter adds to our understanding of the global dynamics and artful nature of citizen prosumption. Although both memes discussed here have specific local origins, their significance resonated with online interactants worldwide. Yet as Ang and Pothen (2011) observed in their analysis of "racism" toward Indian migrants in Australia, "instant and pervasive communicative connectivity does not necessarily encourage greater cross-cultural exchange, mutual understanding, and intercultural dialogue. Instead, it tends to solidify nationalist bias and stereotypes" (p. 140). Related to this, memetic engagement here involved heated invective to highlight a heightened nationalist divide, illustrating the diversity and imbrications between varied peoples of Chinese ethnic descent. Our analyses found that some locals in Singapore and Hong Kong discursively distanced themselves from their Chinese counterparts with the insistence that they are "not Chinese" or "not PRC" and spurred the creation of new labels for mainlanders like "China-ese," "Cheena" (Singlish for a very Chinese influenced person, usually fresh from China), and mainland "Chings." This critical discourse highlights how "the rise of Greater China" is neither a monolithic bloc nor a cohesive clique (evidenced in, for example, the numerous comments on social media that conflated different Chinese societies as one country). As there were thousands of comments on the online videos (e.g., more than 35,000 comments on the "Locust World" video), in-depth content analyses were not conducted on these comments here. Future research could address in more detail the rich diversity in the expression (and possible contradictions) of multiple Chinese identities, backgrounds, and cross-cultural adaptations. This could also encompass an investigation in online interactants' construction and diffusion of "counter" memes to invalidate negative stereotypes and promote cross-cultural understanding associated with challenging sociopolitical developments in Asia and beyond.

References

Adam, S., & Tan, A. (2012, May 24). Ferrari deaths fuel anti-foreigner anger as Singapore votes. *Bloomberg*. Retrieved from http://www.bloomberg.com/news/2012–05–25/ferrari-deaths-fuel-anti-foreigner-anger-before-singapore-poll.html

Ang, I., & Pothen, N. (2011). The transnational communication of "racism": Media, migration and the shaping of international relations. In T. Kuhn (Ed), *Matters of communication: Political, cultural and technological challenges to communication theorizing* (pp. 125–144). New York: Hampton Press.

Anonymous. (2012a, May 15). Video of Ferrari crash shows speed of high-impact collision. *Yahoo! News Singapore*. Retrieved from https://sg.news.yahoo.com/video-of-ferrari-crash-shows-speed-of-high-impact-collision-.html

Anonymous. (2012b, May 14). Who's the mystery female passenger in horror Ferrari crash? *AsiaOne*. Retrieved from http://news.asiaone.com/News/Latest%2BNews/Singapore/Story/A1Story20120514–345800.html

Anonymous. (2012c, May 15). Ferrari crash fuels Singapore anti-foreign sentiment. AFP News. Retrieved from https://sg.news.yahoo.com/ferrari-crash-fuels-singapore-anti-foreign-sentiment-193659157.html

Anonymous. (2012d, January 11). Why D&G enraged Hong Kongers. *Tencent News*. Retrieved from http://view.news.qq.com/zt2012/dg/index.htm

Anonymous. (2012e, February 7). The conflict between Mainland China and Hong Kong: Who should self-introspect, "locusts" or "dogs." *Fenghuang News*. Retrieved from http://news.ifeng.com/opinion/special/huangchongyugou/

Anonymous. (2012f, February 1). Hong Kong advert calls Chinese mainlanders locusts." *BBC News China*. Retrieved from http://www.bbc.co.uk/news/world-asia-china-16828134

Appleactionews. (2011, August 28). Hong Kong moms are angry: Mainland moms are locusts [Video file]. Retrieved from https://www.youtube.com/watch?v=8hAi9pzh6Eo

Bakhtin, M. M. (1993). *Rabelais and his world* (Hélène Iswolsky, Trans.). Bloomington: Indiana University Press.

Bennett, W. L., & Segerberg, A. (2012). The logic of connective action: Digital media and the personalization of contentious politics. *Information, Communication & Society, 15*(5), 739–768. doi:10.1080/1369118X.2012.670661

Bernardi, D., Cheong, P. H., Lundry, C., & Ruston, S. (2012) *Narrative landmines: Rumors, Islamist extremism, and the struggle for strategic influence.* New Brunswick, NJ: Rutgers University Press.

Blackmore, S. (2000). The meme machine. New York: Oxford University Press.

Chen, W. Z. (2012, January 8). A crowd of people loudly cursed f* when seeing bus ferrying locusts [Video file]. Retrieved from: https://www.youtube.com/watch?v=Nq-k85_T010

Cheong, P. H., Edwards, R., Goulbourne, H., & Solomos, J. (2007). Immigration, social cohesion and social capital: A critical review. *Critical Society Policy, 27*(1), 24–49. doi:10.1177/0261018307072206

Cheong, P. H., & Gong, J. (2010). Cyber vigilantism, transmedia collective intelligence, and civic participation. *Chinese Journal of Communication, 3*(4), 471–487. doi:10.1080/17544750.2010.516580

Cheong, P. H., & Lundry, C. (2012). Prosumption, transmediation and resistance: Terrorism and man-hunting in Southeast Asia. *American Behavioral Scientist, 56*(4), 488–510. doi:10.1177/0002764211429365

ChinglishVlogs. (2011, February 27). Locust world [Video file]. Retrieved from https://www.youtube.com/watch?v=aWZFgkJNxDM

Chu, K. (2012, February 20). Tensions grow over "mainlanders" giving birth in Hong Kong. *USA TODAY*. Retrieved from http://usatoday30.usatoday.com/news/world/story/2012–02-14/chinese-mainland-pregnant-women-hong-kong/53159886/1

Dawkins, R. (1989). *The selfish gene*. Oxford: Oxford University Press.

Diguoliangmin. (2012, February 2). Those Hong Kongers who have "endured enough" just show their ugliness [Web log post]. Retrieved from http://mogewen3761.blog.163.com/blog/static/767184201212103413372/

Duncombe, S. (2002). *Cultural resistance reader.* New York: Verso.

Figueroa, B. (2012, May 4). Connecting the citizens of Hong Kong via social media. Retrieved from http://www.brandingpersonality.com/connecting-the-citizens-of-hong-kong-via-social-media/

Flyvbjerg, B. (2006). Five misunderstandings about case-study research. *Qualitative Inquiry, 12*(2), 219–245. doi:10.1177/1077800405284363

Goffman, E. (1959). *The presentation of self in everyday life.* Garden City, NY: Doubleday.

Goodall, H. L., Cheong, P. H., Fleischer, K., & Corman, S. (2012). Rhetorical charms: The promise and pitfalls of humor and ridicule as strategies to counter extremist narratives. *Perspectives on Terrorism, 6*(1). Retrieved from http://www.terrorismanalysts.com/pt/index.php/pot/issue/view/33

Goode, L. (2009). Social news, citizen journalism and democracy. *New Media Society, 11*(8), 1287–1305. doi:10.1177/1461444809341393

Hannon, J. (2013). 45 arrested in Hong Kong on charges of smuggling baby milk formula. *Los Angeles Times.* Retrieved from http://articles.latimes.com/2013/mar/04/world/la-fg-wn-china-baby-food-20130304

Holiday, I., & Wong, L. (2003). Social policy under one country, two systems: Institutional dynamics in China and Hong Kong since 1997. *Public Administration Review, 63*(3), 269–282. doi:10.1111/1540-6210.00289

Honghu. (2012, February 18). Hong Kongers have had enough? Chinese should be those who have endured enough [Web log post]. Retrieved from http://bbs.tianya.cn/post-free-2389326-1.shtml

Hong Kong Statistical Society. (n.d.). Mainland arrivals and baby boom in Hong Kong. Retrieved from http://www.hkss.org.hk/SPC/2010–11/AwardPDF/10–11S-2nd.pdf

Hong Kong Tourism Board. (2013). Tourism performance in 2012. Retrieved from http://www.tourism.gov.hk/english/statistics/statistics_perform.html

Iron Bowl. (2012, May 14). Ma Chi—Ferrari driver that killed cabbie in Singapore [Web log post]. Retrieved from http://robinlow.blogspot.com/2012/05/ma-chi-ferrari-driver-that-killed.html

IZ Reloaded. (2012, May 14). Singapore Ferrari taxi crash footage [Video file]. Retrieved from https://www.youtube.com/watch?v=oZG1HgOyFkU

Jacobs, A. (2012, July 26). In Singapore, vitriol against Chinese newcomers. *New York Times.* Retrieved from http://www.nytimes.com/2012/07/27/world/asia/in-singapore-vitriol-against-newcomers-from-mainland-china.html

LaFraniere, S. (2012, February 22). Mainland Chinese flock to Hong Kong to give birth. *New York Times.* Retrieved from http://www.nytimes.com/2012/02/23/world/asia/mainland-chinese-flock-to-hong-kong-to-have-babies.html?pagewanted=all&_r=0

Lai, A. (2012, February 7). Hong Kong newspaper ad rails against Chinese "invasion." *CNN.* Retrieved from http://www.cnn.com/2012/02/01/world/asia/locust-mainlander-ad

Lau, S. (2013, March 21). Mainland Chinese migrants since 1997 now make up 10pc of Hong Kong population. *South China Morning Post.* Retrieved from http://www.scmp.com/news/hongkong/article/1195642/mainland-chinese-migrants-1997-now-make-10pc-hong-kong-population

Lessig, L. (2008). *Remix: Making art and commerce thrive in the hybrid economy.* London: Penguin Group.

Littlesteak. (2011, March 5). Seventeen [Video file]. Retrieved from https://www.youtube.com/watch?v=goPl1GdO3ao

Loh, A. (2013, April 23). S'pore cartoonist arrested for alleged sedition. *Yahoo! News Singapore.* Retrieved from http://sg.news.yahoo.com/blogs/singaporescene/pore-cartoonist-arrested-alleged-sedition-143415161.html

Mahtani, S. (2012, May 25). Ferrari crash foments antiforeigner feelings in Singapore. *Wall Street Journal.* Retrieved from http://online.wsj.com/article/SB10001424052702304707604577423880540657976.html

Meikle, G. (2008). Whacking Bush: Tactical media as play. In M. Boler (Ed.), *Digital media and democracy: Tactics in hard times* (pp. 367–382). Cambridge, MA: MIT Press.

Okulski, T. (2012, May 16). WATCH: An absolutely horrifying Ferrari crash in Singapore leaves 3 dead. *Business Insider.* Retrieved from: http://www.businessinsider.com/watch-an-absolutely-horrifying-ferrari-crash-in-singapore-leaves-3-dead-2012-5

Oring, E. (2010). *Jokes and their relations.* Lexington: University Press of Kentucky.

Peh, S. H. (2012, May 16). Chinese netizens slam driver as "spoilt brat." *Straits Times.* Retrieved from http://singaporeseen.stomp.com.sg/singaporeseen/this-urban-jungle/netizens-in-china-slam-ferrari-driver-as-spoilt-rich-brat-whos-a-disgrace

PRC Ferrari driver sped to beat red lights causing fatal accident in Bugis and killing Singaporean lady [Web log post]. (2012, May 13). Retrieved from http://temasektimes.wordpress.com/2012/05/13/prc-ferrari-driver-sped-to-beat-red-Xlights-causing-fatal-accident-in-bugis/

PRC netizens speculate that Ma Chi may be linked to a fugitive mafia boss from Chongqing [Web log post]. (2012, May 16). Retrieved from http://temasektimes.wordpress.com/2012/05/16/prc-netizens-speculate-that-ma-chi-may-be-linked-to-a-fugitive-mafia-boss-from-chongqing/

Prime Minister's Office. (2013). A sustainable population for a dynamic Singapore. Retrieved from http://202.157.171.46/whitepaper/downloads/population-white-paper.pdf

Rushkoff, D. (1996). *Media virus: Hidden agendas in popular culture.* New York: Ballantine.

Scott, J. (1985). *Weapons of the weak: Everyday forms of peasant resistance.* New Haven, CT: Yale University Press.

Seeing through colored lenses: How Singaporeans view the SMRT strike [Web log post]. (2012, December 8). Retrieved from http://singaporearmchaircritic.wordpress.com/2012/12/08/seeing-through-colored-lenses-how-singaporeans-view-the-smrt-strike/

Shadbolt, P. (2014, March 7). Hong Kong protests take aim at "locust" shoppers from mainland China. *CNN.* Retrieved from http://www.cnn.com/2014/03/07/world/asia/hong-kong-china-visitors-controversy/

Shifman, L. (2011). An anatomy of a YouTube meme. *New Media & Society, 14*(2), 187–203. doi:10.1177/1461444811412160

Shifman, L., & Thelwall, M. (2009). Assessing global diffusion with Web memetics: The spread and evolution of a popular joke. *Journal of the American Society for Information Science and Technology, 60*(12), 2567–2576. doi:10.1002/asi.21185

Siau, M. E. (2012, May 13). 2 dead, 3 injured in three-way Bugis crash. *Straits Times.* Retrieved from http://www.stcars.sg/guides-articles/motoring-news/2-dead-3-injured-in-three-way-bugis-crash/a/65211

Silva, P. D., & Garcia, J. L. (2012). YouTubers as satirists: Humor and remix in online video. *Journal of Democracy and Open Government, 4*(1), 89–114.

Tan, K. (2012, May 19). Could Ferrari driver in Singapore crash be son of state Councilor Ma Kai? [Web log post]. Retrieved from http://shanghaiist.com/2012/05/19/ferrari-driver-singapore-ma-kai.php

Tayman, N. (2012, January 22). Locusts [Video file]. Retrieved from https://www.youtube.com/watch?v=Ls0t8R1dI-8

TheMockymocky. (2012, May 14). Singapore tragic accident video—warning, graphic (Ferrari / taxi) [Video file]. Retrieved from http://www.youtube.com/watch?v=8Jf AaOABk4g

Yin, R. K. (2009). *Case study research: Design and methods* (4th Ed.). Thousand Oaks, CA: Sage.

Yuebeiwang. (2012, February 3). Respond to Hong Kongers have "endured enough" [Web log post]. Retrieved from http://bbs.tianya.cn/post-feeling-2085520–1.shtml

4

ENGAGING GOVERNMENT FOR ENVIRONMENTAL COLLECTIVE ACTION

Political Implications of ICTs in Rural China

Rong Wang

With the rapid development of Internet applications, researchers are interested in understanding the impact that information and communication technologies (ICTs) impose on both civil society and government. This study examines these overarching questions: in what contexts are social movements more likely to happen when there are enough ICTs to be used? Can we perceive empowering effects of ICTs? Guided by the interaction framework of state and society (Yang, 2009; Zheng, 2007), this study looked into environmental collective action in rural China.

China is rapidly entering the network society (Castells, 2001) as more and more citizens are becoming active users of new ICTs, represented by Internet use both through computer connections and mobile devices. By the end of June 2013, Internet users in China totaled 591 million. With the rapid growth of China's mobile users, the number of mobile Internet users reached 464 million, accounting for 78.51% of all Internet users. These numbers represent a 44.1% rate of Internet penetration in China (CNNIC, 2013).

However, a digital divide between rural and urban populations clearly exists. First, the level of Internet connectivity differs greatly. As of June 2013, the population of Internet users in rural areas only accounted for 27.9% of the total population of Internet users in China (CNNIC, 2013). Second, Internet users in urban areas of China are more likely to connect using a personal desktop or laptop. As of June 2013, 73.6% of urban users accessed the Internet from a personal desktop, 52.4% from a laptop, and 78.4% from a mobile phone. Only 58.5% of rural users accessed the Internet from a personal desktop and 32.4% from a laptop. However, 78.9% of rural users accessed the Internet from mobile phones (CNNIC, 2013). Third, another significant difference lies in patterns of Internet use. Although there is no difference in terms of using the Internet for entertainment and interpersonal communication, rural users are less likely to use the Internet for reading news or seeking information (CNNIC, 2006, 2011). See Table 4.1 for more detail.

Despite the rural–urban digital divide, the penetration rate of information services has improved significantly in rural areas in the past decade. More and more rural residents are using e-commerce trading platforms to get connected directly to market demand. One major driving force of the Internet use in rural China is the growth of mobile subscriptions (Bloomberg Businessweek, 2011).

TABLE 4.1 Differences in Online Activities Among Internet Users in Urban and Rural China

Internet Applications	Internet Users in Urban China	Internet Users in Rural China
Reading online news	81.5%	66.5%
Using search engines	78.4%	65.8%
Listening to music	68.4%	68.9%
Playing online games	47.0%	47.1%
Watching movies or TV series	61.2%	60.9%

Credit: CNNIC, 2006

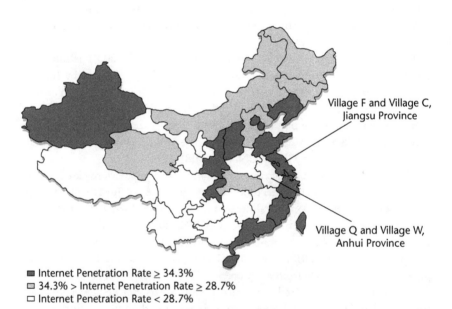

Village F and Village C, Jiangsu Province

Village Q and Village W, Anhui Province

■ Internet Penetration Rate ≥ 34.3%
☐ 34.3% > Internet Penetration Rate ≥ 28.7%
☐ Internet Penetration Rate < 28.7%

FIGURE 4.1 Internet Penetration in Different Provinces of China

Source: CNNIC, 2011

Relying upon interview data collected from four villages (village Q and village W from Anhui province, and village F and village C from Jiangsu province), the researcher conducted four case studies to understand the role of ICTs in organizing and coordinating social support for environmental collective action in rural China and examined how ICTs may impact state-society interaction. This chapter contributes to empirical studies on collective action and environmental movements. First, it provides evidence that ICT-mediated environmental collective action can impact China's liberalization of communicating with the government and expressing citizens' concerns. ICT platforms facilitate engagement for common goals among citizens, local governments, nongovernmental organizations (NGOs), and other social forces, which helps to enhance participants' political trust in the government. Second, the findings show that whether or not ICTs function as tools for collective action depends upon the sociopolitical environment, such as leadership and solidarity among participants and the source of pollution. Third, the findings reveal that environmental collective action in China can be more constructive than disruptive, given that the state is capable engaging with other stakeholders to solve environmental issues. In certain circumstances there are greater levels of engagement and negotiation with the government, rather than governmental control.

ICTs and State-Society Interactions in China

For many years, scholars have considered the relationship between the state and society as dichotomous, while some recent scholarship has stated that certain dimensions of state power have more to do with the capability of the state to work through and with other social actors (Castells, 2009; Zheng, 2007). The state and society mutually define each other (Evans, 1995; Migdal, 2001; Migdal, Kohli, & Shue, 1994).

Zheng (2007) provides an analytical framework to understand the relationship between the state and society, arguing that the Internet moderates this relationship. This framework is composed of four arguments. First, the Internet empowers both the state and civil society. The Internet can facilitate political liberalization and make government more open, transparent, and accountable, thus enhancing the trust society holds in the state. Second, the decentralizing effect of the Internet is enormous and goes beyond the reach of state power. Third, the Internet has created a new infrastructure for the state and society to interact with each other more frequently than before, either through engagement or disengagement. Fourth, the Internet produces a recursive relationship between state and society, which reshapes both the state and society.

The key stakeholders in the state-society interaction framework include party and state organizations, local government, private sectors, and civil society (Yang, 2009; Zheng, 2007). In China, the Internet has played a crucial role in challenging state power, particularly through the engagement of "mass public, civil society, the economy, and the international community" (Zheng, 2007, p. 79). One of the most cited instances of this form of engagement is the Sun Zhigang case,[1] which pushed the state to eliminate the custody and repatriation policy. Journalists, human rights NGOs, and other social actors utilized online forums, e-mail, and other ICT platforms to mobilize support, which contributed to the success of this case, yielding a positive impact on China's political progress (Yang, 2009; Zheng & Wu, 2005).

ICTs can positively impact social change (Qiang, 2011; Yang, 2009). However, the role of ICTs in democratic development should not be overstated. Nothing inherent to the Internet can automatically achieve social change (Lim & Kann, 2008). In the Chinese context, a conflict exists between the government's drive to implement effective policies for rapid ICT development and its agenda to control and manage potential political risks brought by new technologies (Zheng, 2007). The government's tight control over the Internet does not mean suppressing access to cyberspace or an absolute lack of information flow. To some extent, China's ICT policies and regulations allow citizens to participate in online collective action, which is in effect shaping an arena for the state and society to achieve compromise. Yet the effects of ICTs in the state-society interaction framework remain under-examined: How does online collective action occur and what is the role of ICTs?

ICT-Mediated Environmental Collective Action in China

Collective action is defined as actions undertaken by individuals or groups in pursuit of the same collective good (Marwell & Oliver, 1993). ICT-mediated collective action is characterized by self-organizing mechanisms that rely on decentralized networks and the agency of participants. Disorganized social groups that stand in contrast to bureaucratic mechanisms of coordination can succeed in utilizing ICTs to overcome resource limitations and collectively challenge the power of organized interests (Ganesh & Stohl, 2010; Kreiss, 2009). Evidence of ICTs facilitating collective action has been found in antiwar demonstrations and environmental movements (Bennett, Breunig, & Givens, 2008; Chadwick, 2007; Glasbergen, 2010).

Social movements are "collective challenges by people with common purposes and solidarity in sustained interaction with elites, opportunities and authorities" (Tarrow, 1994, pp. 3–4). For collective action to develop into social movement, it requires sustained interaction with power-holders (Pinard, 2011; Tarrow, 1996). ICTs can be effective in creating more opportunities for self-organized collective action through low mobilization costs, high visibility, promotion of collective identities, and creation of community (Garett, 2007; Hampton, Livio, & Goulet, 2010). Although this suggests social movements are more likely to happen when there are enough ICTs to use, Garett (2007) argues that this is too controversial to come to a conclusion. This study investigates in what context social movements are more likely to happen with enough ICTs and whether we can perceive empowering effects of ICTs in China.

Because of the distinct media and policy environment, ICT users in China have developed their own strategies for participating in online collective action (Yang, 2009). Users technically avoid direct confrontation with the government by carefully circumventing censorship and creatively tiptoeing around state-imposed boundaries to free speech. They are engaged in many forms of artful—even playful—evasion to overcome and resist control and express dissent (Yang, 2009).

This research looks into collective action on environmental issues. With the Chinese government's drive toward economic development and industrialization, great concern has arisen regarding environmental preservation. Eleventh and twelfth 5-year plans released by the central government both made strong policy statements about moving toward a greener economy; these statements were expected to shape China's actions toward environmental protection (Hilton, 2011). The Ministry of Environment Protection has reported that rural environmental problems have become increasingly prominent, particularly deteriorating water quality and contributing to soil erosion (MEP, 2012).

Recent years have seen a rise in environmental concern in China, evidenced by the increasing number of environmental NGOs being established. However, the occurrence of environmental collective action does not equal the existence of environmental social movements. Stalley and Yang (2006) pointed out two reasons for this. First, most environmental collective actions are merely spontaneous responses to a local policy or a particular polluting factory. They often fail to survive and broaden beyond an immediate goal, even with help from domestic and international NGOs. Second, these actions tend not to seek influencing policy, focusing instead on apolitical campaigns of enhancing environmental awareness. Ho (2002) presents the same conclusion, finding that environmentalism in China is not contended and lacks the opportunity and immediate urgency to confront policy makers.

The targets and goals of environmental activism in China differ from those of more radical collective action. Environmental activism engages in a more moderate repertoire of collective action, in which members mainly use public forums, study tours, photo exhibits, petition letters, and collective signatures (Yang, 2004). Their engagement is constructive rather than disruptive, seeking to promote public awareness, dialogue, participation, and information dissemination. Environmental activists tend to target business practices and consumer behaviors, without directly challenging government power.

Although environmental collective action began much earlier than the establishment of China's first Environmental Protection Law, in 1979, ICT-mediated environmentalism is a relatively recent phenomenon. The growth of environmentalism in China arose with the spread of the Internet. Participants in environmental action have been fascinated by copying offline styles in cyberspace

(Yang, 2004). Bulletin board systems (BBS) and online forums are the most popular applications, providing new avenues for information sharing and action coordination among participants (Yang, 2009).

Most studies of environmentalism are focused on urban areas, where the Internet is more accessible. Rural-based environmental protests against ill-conceived industrial projects and the embezzlement of pollution prevention funds are seldom examined (see exceptions in Economy, 2004; Jing, 2003; Stalley & Yang, 2006; Yang, 2009). Given the large rural population, it is important to understand environmental activism in rural China. This study examines the following research question:

> RQ1: How have ICTs been used by rural residents to interact with local government on environmental issues and organize environmental collective action?

Liberalization Versus Democratization

To understand the effects of ICT-mediated collective action on social change, two concepts need to be defined: liberalization and democratization. Liberalization is a process of defining and extending rights to effectively protect both individuals and social groups from arbitrary or illegal acts committed by the state or third parties (O'Donnell & Schimitter, 1989). Democratization is a process that requires systematic changes to the power regimes (O'Donnell & Schimitter, 1989). These two processes are not related in a linear or inevitable way (Carothers, 2002; O'Donnell & Schimitter, 1989; Schneider & Schmitter, 2004). The transition from liberalization to democratization consists of a liberalization of autocracy and consolidation of democracy (Schneider & Schmitter, 2004).

These two concepts have been applied to understanding political changes in Asia, Africa, Latin America, and Eastern/Central Europe. Howell (1998) explored the connections among civil society, economic liberalization, and democratization in contemporary China. He argued that in the post-Tiananmen era, the civil society sector might be the potential force of democratization.

Contemporary collective action facilitated by ICTs has provided new sources of information and reduced coordination costs, and thus expanded opportunities for citizens to contribute to political processes (Bimber, Flanagin, & Stohl, 2012). However, Zheng (2007) argues that collective action in China is unable to trigger political democratization, due to its precariousness and dependence on governmental power. ICTs have provided new opportunities for openness, transparency, and political accountability, which would never happen otherwise. Thus, by facilitating Internet-based collective action, ICTs are capable of promoting liberalization. In certain cases, Internet-enabled radical collective action may produce political distrust and even a crisis of confidence in political institutions which may impose negative effects on the state-society interaction (Lee & Zhang, 2013; Zheng, 2002).

Elizabeth Economy has provided an extensive analysis of China's environmental collective action, focusing on its conflicting elements. China's environmentalists, Economy (2004) suggests, could hasten the process of breaking down political barriers that are currently preventing a larger environmental movement by engaging the younger generation. However, environmental protection in China is facing challenges from the following sources: the institutional weakness of State Environmental Protection Administration, problems of the legislative and judicial bodies, the power of financial and planning agencies, the relatively low central investment, and the coordination between the central and local authority (Economy, 2004). Furthermore, she points out that the growth of local economy, proactive government leaders, and higher GDP per capita are conducive to environmental protection. The nature of polluting enterprises (stated owned or private) also affects the success of environmental collective action.

The majority of cases in China's environmental movements do not dissent against political institutions or target radical political changes (Yang, 2009). In certain cases, local governments funded villages to install ICT facilities to raise public awareness of environmental protection, and the government was tolerant of environmental protests as long as they were not too disruptive (Jing, 2003). What remains uncovered is how the ICT-mediated environmental collective action is capable of promoting liberalization. This study examines the following research question:

RQ2: What are the political implications of ICT-mediated environmental collective action in rural China?

Research Design and Method

This study applies a cross-case analysis to mining four case studies in order to answer the research questions through systematic comparison. Cross-case method facilitates the comparison of commonalities and difference in the units of analyses in case studies, such as events, activities, and processes (Khan & Van-Wynsberghe, 2008; Miles & Huberman, 1994). This study relies on in-depth interview data collected from four villages: two in Bengbu Municipality (Anhui Province) and another two in Taizhou Municipality (Jiangsu Province), both in eastern China (Figure 4.1). Anhui is located across the basin of the Yangtze and Huai Rivers. Experiencing a slow development in Internet connectivity, Anhui has a penetration rate lower than the global average level, which was 28.7% in 2010. Jiangsu is located along the east coast of the Yellow Sea, with the Yangtze River passing through its southern parts. Compared to Anhui, Internet connectivity in Jiangsu displays a higher development. As of December 2010, its penetration rate was higher than the global average.

Data was collected from May to July of 2011. Semi-structured interviews were conducted face-to-face in Mandarin Chinese, and the researcher translated the transcripts into English. How rural residents engage with ICTs must be interpreted with reference to their economic, social, and cultural backgrounds, and also with reference to their interaction with other social forces. Therefore, interviews were conducted not only with villagers but also with leaders from villager self-governance committees, local government representatives, local environmental protection bureau (EPB) staff, environmental NGO staff, and one Chinese scholar.

In Bengbu, 22 interviews were completed with villagers from village Q and village W: 10 females and 12 males, most of whom were between 25 and 60 years old. One interview was conducted with the head of W's villager self-governance committee. Three interviews were conducted with staff from a local NGO, which assisted both villages for rights defending. Another interview was conducted with a Chinese communication scholar who led a research project focused on Huai River pollution.

Village Q was chosen because of its success in a long-standing fight against three polluting factories. The story was portrayed in a documentary and became known worldwide through a nomination by a major film award in 2010. Village W was referred to by a local environmental NGO. The pollution in W was still ongoing at the time of research. Villages Q and W were comparable in terms of location and pollution caused by state-owned enterprises.

In Taizhou, 12 interviews were completed with villagers from village F and village C: two females and 10 males. In addition, there were two interviews with villager self-governance committees, two interviews with local EPB staff, and one interview with a local government official in charge of environmental issues. To better understand the environmental protection endeavor in rural Jiangsu, the researcher conducted interviews with representatives from three NGOs.

Village F was selected because of a successful case of environmental collective action, documented in a BBS run by the municipality government. Village C was suggested during the interview with local EPB staff. In village C, there was a successful small-scale environmental collective action in 2010 which involved a small enterprise that was run by a villager and polluted local fisheries. These two villages were different from the two from Anhui: they were facing pollution from small enterprises run by villagers; pollution was handled with satisfying solutions; and environmental collective actions were small and sporadic.

In total, 47 interviews were included for data analysis. All interviewees were informed of the confidentiality and anonymity in advance. They were also informed of how ICTs were defined in this research. On average, each interview lasted for 30 minutes. The interview questions for villagers covered three main topics: (1) villagers' attitudes of using ICTs for environmental collective action; (2) their experience in using ICTs for environmental collective action; and (3) their relationship with local governments during the environmental collective action. Questions designed for other interviewees were focused on attitudes of ICTs, perception of the role of environmental NGOs, environmental protection challenges in rural areas, and perception of the relationship between villagers and the local government.

The data analysis proceeded in several steps. For RQ1, the researcher identified all statements in which the interviewees talked about ICTs explicitly, such as how they felt about using mobile phones to communicate about environmental issues and using the Internet to report pollution to the government. To address RQ2, about the political implications of ICT-mediated collective action, findings were summarized based on perspectives from different social groups. In the end, comparison across the four cases provides a way to better answer the research questions.

Rising Environmentalism and Different Patterns of ICT Use

RQ1 addresses how the villagers use ICTs to communicate with local officials and mobilize supporters for environmental collective action. Generally, respondents' awareness of ICTs' role in organizing events, gathering information, and documenting evidence was low. ICTs were mainly used to disseminate knowledge and information about environmental policies and laws, based on successful and partially successful cases of collective action in three villages. Mobile phones were most frequently used. The expenses of computer and Internet applications were perceived as being high.

According to interviews with government officials and EPB staff, plenty of communication channels are available for villagers to engage with the government regarding environmental issues. These channels include the national environmental protection hotline 12359; the hotline of the Ministry of Environmental Protection, the Department of Environmental Protection at the province, municipality, and county level; mayor's hotlines; government and EPB Web sites; and walk-in reporting to the government and agencies.

Evidence of rising environmentalism among rural residents was clear, given the increasing number of complaints the local EPB received. Recorded by the local EPB of Taixing, there were 160 cases reported from January to May in 2011. Of those cases, 135 were made through phone calls, four by mail, six in person, and 15 through online platforms. One EPB official mentioned that the number of pollution reporting cases started increasing since 2006, and the weekly meetings at the local EPB always emphasized the importance of handling these reports.

Different patterns of ICT use are apparent in the four villages. In general, the respondents' awareness of the role of ICTs in facilitating environmental collective action was low, except for respondents in village Q where the villagers succeeded in a social movement with assistance from external forces such as NGOs and journalists. The external support helped enhance villagers' awareness of environmental protection and utilizing ICTs for environmental protection.

Village Q. Findings from Q showed the dynamics of ICT use by villagers. During the movement, they communicated with officials mainly through face-to-face meetings and sometimes organized protests in front of government buildings. This may have been because of the geographic proximity. Traveling to either district or municipality government buildings takes less than 30 minutes by bike. It also only takes 15 minutes to go to the local EPB. Furthermore, villagers perceived it to be more efficient to talk to officials directly. Sending letters or posting online was perceived as time consuming. Confrontation in person can pressure state representatives for a prompt response. Villagers also acted strategically, including limiting the number of protesters in order to not trigger the government's alert on social instability.

As the movement went on, there was evidence of ICT-enabled communication between villagers and officials, especially when other social groups were involved, such as international and local environmental NGOs and journalists. For example, the villagers at Q used mobile phones to call local officials when they found signs of pollution, either calling their office phones or personal cell phones.

There was also evidence of using ICTs for documenting pollution at Q. Before the local NGO provided assistance, villagers used a camera owned by the movement leader to record pollution. The camera was equipped with basic functions and cost less than 100 RMB (approximately US$16.25). Later on, the local NGO provided villagers a secondhand digital video recorder and a voice recorder. The villagers were able to film important progress of the movement and also record their negotiation with local officials.

Another finding about the use of ICTs at Q shows how villagers accessed the Internet through third parties. One local environmental NGO and one international environmental NGO learned about environmental protection efforts initiated by villagers through a national television program. They sent staff to help villagers gather product information from polluting chemical plants, which was used by villagers as proof to show that their living condition was severely damaged by the pollution. Other third parties include neighbors and environmentalists from other provinces. The movement leader noted:

> In the earlier days, I asked my neighbors who had Internet access at home to find information on the safe distance which chemical factories should be kept away from residential areas. It did not work, because we did not know what keywords to type in. I had no idea what law terms to look into. In the end, a nationally well-known environmentalist from Fujian Province heard about our story from the CCTV program and contacted us. He is more experienced in environmental lawsuits than us. He came to visit us and helped us locate the information. We are still in touch.

The penetration of Internet connectivity at village Q was relatively low. The majority of residents had no direct access to the Internet. Accessing the Internet through third parties is a strategy used by Q villagers for gathering information.

This is consistent with their relatively positive view of the Internet's role in facilitating social movement.

Village W. Findings from village W show evidence of villagers using mobile phones to report pollution to the government. However, ICT use was very limited and remained primarily an individual activity. When informants did not receive feedback from officials, the frustration pushed them back to tolerate the pollution. One villager said:

> I called the nationwide hotline 12359 several times, reporting that one of the chemical factories near our village was discharging waste gas at midnight. It was so noisy that we could not sleep. The receptionist responded that they knew about the pollution and would gradually find the solution. I also tried to call the mayor's hotline but could not get through. I did not call the local EPB, because it would be of no use. The pollution has existed for a long time. If the local EPB was useful, they should have already done something for our village.

Most of the respondents from W stated no experience in using ICTs to report pollution, although they did use ICTs in their daily life. ICTs frequently used by villagers included mobile phones and computers with Internet access, which were mainly used for entertainment and interpersonal communication. One villager reported using the Internet to search for work-related information. Due to low literacy, text messaging was used less often than phone calls.

Villages F and C. Respondents' awareness of using ICTs to report pollution to the government was low. Nearly all of them said that they did not know about the nationwide environmental protection hotlines nor considered it relevant. Most of the respondents mentioned that they were too busy with work to care about environmental protection. Even though most of the respondents were aware of the pollution in the village, nobody wanted to report it to the local government because of perceived risks.

There were exceptions to these types of responses. Unless the pollution had caused serious damages to personal interest, they would stand out to talk to local officials or even circumvent the local level by bringing the issue to a higher-level government. Cases of exception were found in both F and C. In F, three brothers collectively called the environmental protection hotline and reported to the provincial EPB that a local chemical factory caused cancer in their family. In C, a group of fishermen reported on a government BBS that a local meat-producing workshop discharged waste water directly to the river and creek. One officer from the Taixing EPB discussed how these cases could be explained by the village culture:

> Villagers tend to have a low sense of collectivism. They do not consider environmentalism as a public good. They will only take actions to report pollution when their personal interests are violated. Otherwise, they remain silent.

Most of the respondents from C and F said they never heard about anyone reporting pollution and refused to tell further information. This can be explained by the structure of a typical Chinese village, which is closely connected by consanguinity. It is quite common that in one village most of the residents share the same surname. In some cases a village is named after one surname. Most villagers are potentially related from a few generations prior. Social pressure in the local community may explain why the villagers were reluctant to report the pollution or discuss information about the informants. The villager self-governance committee member from C said:

> Reporting pollution was mostly anonymous, as the informants did not want to let the enterprises know who they were. They are neighbors who see each other almost daily. It would be awkward if the informants disclosed their names.

To answer RQ1, different patterns of ICT use were found in rural China for villagers interacting with the government with regard to environmental issues. However, ICTs tended to be used on individual levels. Several challenges prevented villagers from using ICTs for environmental collective action. First, respondents worried about the affordability of ICTs. On average, a villager earns 1,000 RMB every month. Mobile phones and computers cost 300 to 5,000 RMB. Second, low literacy was identified as a barrier for using mobiles and computers. The highest education amongst the respondents was a secondary school diploma. Some respondents did not complete elementary school. Third, limited channels of learning environmental protection policies and laws constrained their ability of using ICT to search for information, communicate with officials, or document evidence. Even though some college students had been organized by NGOs to give villagers free lectures on environmental protection policies and laws, it did not occur on a regular basis.

Political Influences of Environmental Collective Action

RQ2 focused on identifying political influences in the environmental collective actions in rural China. Villagers were asked how they felt about the local government's efficacy in responding to their inquiries about pollution issues, whether they were satisfied with the performance of the local government, and how they perceived their interactions with the government.

Regarding the extent to which the villagers trusted the local government, the respondents from F and C expressed some doubt in the local government's accountability. These respondents had no experience in participating in any environmental collective action, although there were successful cases in their villages. A few villagers noted that although they had no idea who reported the pollution, they heard that the government and local EPB took effective measures to solve the problem. However, more respondents expressed their distrust in local government. One villager said:

> I have heard about people complaining to the township government, but they did not get satisfying answers. I think it may be related to local protectionism the government holds.

In general, villagers from W also held very low trust in the local government's credibility, while villagers from Q had a more balanced view about their relations with the government. A few respondents from W mentioned a collaboration with a nearby village two years ago, in which they sent a petition letter to the provincial government. The letter was signed by most of the villagers, but they never heard anything back. Villagers complained that the committee did not make enough effort and only cared about their own business. The head of W villager self-governance committee said:

> Our committee reported to upper level government many times but it did not work out. Now the committee has no idea what to do. Maybe it is better if villagers use the Internet to report the pollution directly to the provincial or even central government. Through the Internet, it will be easier to disseminate the information. I could not think of other means. It is complicated.

The majority of the respondents from W were not satisfied with the performance of either the local government or its EPB. They suspected that polluting factories were protected by the government since they contributed a lot to government avenues. Only three respondents from W held a relatively positive attitude toward the local government. One of them was the villager who made calls to government hotlines four times. As mentioned earlier, he, however, did not trust the EPB or villager self-governance committee.

Findings from Q showed how the government changed its passive attitude to active engagement during the movement and how its relationship with villagers also experienced positive changes. The movement leader said:

> We should not assume the government is bad. I understand why, at the beginning of our movement, the government was very passive. These three chemical plants contributed many taxes to the local economy. Another reason is that officials are concerned about their careers. They needed to wait and follow instructions from their superiors. The government actually helped our villagers a lot to succeed in our movement. It forced the polluting factories to relocate and our environment improved. I understand it is not easy for the government to take such actions.

Most of the respondents from Q thought highly of their leader, who motivated other villagers to participate and stick to a common goal, helped mobilize support from NGOs and media, and eventually forced the government to take action. However, they were also aware that the government played an important role. One respondent said:

> The factories moved to a chemical industrial park with strict environmental protection requirements. I do not think this relocation happened because of any individual's power. It is the government that imposed pressure to the factories . . . The last day for the relocation, the government cut the electricity and water so the factories could not operate.

So far, villagers from Q were satisfied with the government's performance. However, some issues are still left unsolved. Villagers are not sure if the government can keep its promise in the long run. They expressed concern over the possibility of new factories entering the village. The villagers also wanted the government to promote information transparency of environmental protection, especially information on those factories with high risk of pollution.

To answer RQ2, the successful movement in Q showed that ICT facilitated the mutual engagement between the government and activists, together with social support from NGOs and journalists. Villagers in Q held a more balanced view of the government's accountability and were more aware of information transparency and their rights, supporting the liberalization argument on ICTs' political impact. In other villagers, respondents tended to have distrust in the government and its agencies, possibly due to a lack of experience in participating in environmental collective action or a lack of political interest. To better interpret findings from four villagers, the next section provides a cross-case comparison to identify key factors influencing the use of ICTs for environmental collective action and its political impact.

Comparison Across Four Villages

The interview data had to be interpreted within specific contexts. Villagers' responses were based on their experiences in utilizing ICTs in the social movements. The social movement in Q already succeeded, and most of the respondents participated. However, there was no collective action at W, only ICT use on an individual basis to communicate with local officials, which turned out to be a failure. Villagers, who had no experience in using ICT to express their voice, heard about others' frustrating experiences. The collective actions at F and C were successful or partially successful, although they cannot be considered as social movements. Most of the respondents from F and C had no experience in ICT-enabled environmental collective action; however, they may have been influenced by what happened in the village. Bearing these differences in mind, a comparison of the findings can point to implications on how environmental collective action can take place and what political influences it may have. This comparison is summarized in Table 4.2.

The first difference is *the status of ICT development*. Among the four villages, F and C had the most advanced ICT infrastructure, followed by W, and then Q. Another difference was that only Q had *strong leadership and solidarity* among environmental activists. Although F and C had a few villagers who acted as a team during their negotiation with the local government and polluting enterprises, their actions were not taken in terms of protecting environment as a collective good. The third difference is *the perception of ICTs' role in facilitating villagers' participation in public affairs*. Respondents from Q had the most positive attitude. It is likely the successful movement that made them confident of ICTs' role in organizing and mobilizing supporters, documenting pollution, and gathering information.

The last difference is respondents' *perceived trust in the local government*. The respondents from Q held greater political confidence in how the local government

TABLE 4.2 Comparison of the Four Cases

Factors	Village Q	Village W	Village F	Village C
Location	Bengbu, Anhui	Bengbu, Anhui	Taizhou, Jiangsu	Taizhou, Jiangsu
Nature of polluting enterprises	Private chemical factories	State-owned	Small enterprises run by villagers	Small enterprises run by villagers; private chemical factory
Leadership and solidarity	high	low	low	low
Experience of using ICTs in daily life	high	high	very high	high
Perception of ICTs' role in public participation	***high***	low	low	low
Trust in the local government	***very high***	very low	low	low
Status of ICT development	low	high	very high	very high
Collective action outcome among respondents	very high	NA	NA	NA

Note: Cells in italic and bold font indicate that the responses were from a village where there was collective action.

responded to villagers' environmental protection initiatives and took actions to solve the issues. At F and C, the respondents had some trust in the local government but were suspicious of its political will in helping the local community. The respondents from W held almost no trust in the local government's credibility. These differences indicate that villagers' active engagement in the movement and their frequent interaction with local officials may have improved their perception on the local governments' accountability. The lower trust at F and C can be explained by the fact that so few villagers utilized ICTs for public participation. ICT-enabled environmental collective action at F and C was too sporadic to form a collective force. The low political confidence at W could also be explained by the rare cases of villagers taking initiative to communicate with officials or take actions collectively. Another reason could be the frustrating experience of using ICTs on an individual basis to express their voice to the government.

Based on these findings, this study concludes that the local government is able to engage in environmental protection endeavors initiated by the villagers and work with other stakeholders to solve issues. There was more engagement and negotiation than control at Q, F, and C. ICT use, either through direct or indirect access, contributed to the success of two-way communication between villagers and the local government. At Q, the environmental movement helped villagers gain knowledge about environmental policies and laws, and thus they managed to press the government for better performance in information transparency and openness in decision making. Evidence from these findings shows that environmental collective action has the potential to improve liberalization and the state-society relationships.

Conclusion and Discussion

This chapter examined the use of ICTs by rural residents in China for public participation in environmental issues. Based on interview data from four villages, this study found that although face-to-face meetings with the local officials were favored by villagers, evidence showed that ICTs were used to communicate with the local government and EPB, document instances of pollution, and search for environmental protection related information. Mobile phones were the most frequently used form of ICT. Since Internet connectivity is not as widespread in rural areas, rural environmental activists utilized strategies to access the Internet through third parties.

Several challenges prevented villagers from using ICTs for environmental collective action. Low literacy is a barrier for villagers to use mobile phones for texting or accessing the Internet, as well as to use computers. Other challenges include the perceived expenses of ICT hardware and services, and villagers' limited knowledge about environmental policies and laws.

How villagers viewed their relations with the government yielded interesting findings. Villagers from Q witnessed how the local government changed its attitude during the course of the movement. They agreed that it was the mutual engagement between the state and other social forces that helped enhance their bargaining power with the government and facilitated their success in fighting against polluting factories. At an early stage of the movement, local officials passively ignored villagers' appeals made through face-to-face communication, petition letters, and phone calls. With the help of local and international environmental NGOs, the activists became more skilled in information searching and documentation via direct and indirect ICT access. Under pressure from society and, in particular, mainstream news media, the government joined villagers' initiatives and forced the relocation of polluting factories. Overall the villagers were satisfied with the government's performance. This indicates that ICT-mediated collective action can improve villagers' political trust in the local government.

At F and C, some common patterns are apparent in how villagers perceived the role of ICTs in promoting conversation with the local government, and to what extent they trusted the local government. These two villages shared common environmental concerns caused by small enterprises run by peer villagers. Due to the village culture in China, anonymous reports were delivered to the local government. Even though the government and EPB solved the pollution cases, villagers still doubted its credibility due to social pressures in the local community and villagers' unwillingness to communicate with officials.

Respondents from W held very little trust in the local government. This may be related to the fact that very few people tried to communicate with local officials, although they were aware that the local government should take the responsibility for environmental protection in its administrative regions. Most of the respondents perceived no value in using ICTs to participate in public affairs.

This study found that ICT development status does not correlate to ICT utilization for participation in public affairs, which depends on at least these following factors: awareness of the roles of ICTs in facilitating collective action, citizens' knowledge of policies and laws, literacy, and leadership and solidarity among potential participants. These factors can possibly explain why participation at W remained at the individual level and why villagers failed to unite to protect public goods.

As found in Q, environmental social movements definitely exist in rural China, which took its own course to evolve from individual appeal, to contentious collective action, to sustained civic engagement. The movement succeeded in pressing the government to join villagers' initiatives, with support from NGOs and journalists. Villagers were able to state their rights, collaborate with other social forces, and eventually protect their community rights from illegal behaviors of polluting factories. Key stakeholders from this successful social movement were identified (see Figure 4.2). Findings from the comparison of four villages shows that ICT-mediated collective action helps contribute to the liberalization process in China by improving the relations between the local governments and villagers and by enhancing villagers' need for information transparency.

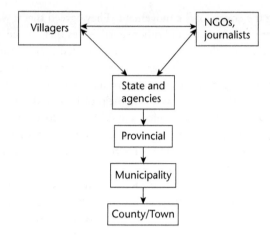

FIGURE 4.2 Key Stakeholders From a Successful Environmental Movement in Rural China

Acknowledgments

The research was supported by grants from the International Development Research Centre (IDRC). The author wants to thank Dr. Evan Due, Dr. Matthew Smith, and Dr. Milagros Rivera for their comments on earlier drafts.

Note

1. The custody and repatriation policy allowed the police (usually in the city) to detain people if they did not have a residence permit or temporary living permit. The police could have also returned them to the place where they could legally live or work (usually rural areas).

References

Bennett, W. L., Breunig, C., & Givens, T. (2008). Communication and political mobilization: Digital media and the organization of anti-Iraq war demonstrations in the U.S. *Political Communication, 25,* 269–289.

Bimber, B., Flanagin, A. J., & Stohl, C. (2012). *Collective action in organizations: Interaction and engagement in an era of technological change.* New York: Cambridge University Press.

Bloomberg Businessweek. (2011). *China mobile users pass 600 million, fueled by rural areas.* Retrieved from http://www.businessweek.com/news/2011–04–21/china-mobile-users-pass-600-million-fueled-by-rural-areas.html

Carothers, T. (2002). The end of the transition paradigm. *Journal of Democracy, 13*(1), 5–21.

Castells, M. (2001). *The Internet galaxy: Reflections on the Internet, business, and society.* Oxford: Oxford University Press.

Castells, M. (2009). *Communication power*. Oxford: Oxford University Press.

Chadwick, A. (2007). Digital network repertoires and organizational hybridity. *Political Communication, 24*, 283–301.

CNNIC. (2006). *Survey report on the Internet usage in Chinese rural area*. Beijing: Author.

CNNIC. (2011). *China Internet Network Information Center Annual Report 2011*. Beijing: Author.

CNNIC. (2013). *Statistical survey report on the Internet development*. Beijing: Author.

Economy, E. C. (2004). *The river runs black: The environmental challenge to China's future*. Ithaca, NY: Cornell University Press.

Evans, P. (1995). *Embedded autonomy: States and industrial transformation*. Princeton, NJ: Princeton University Press.

Ganesh, S., & Stohl, C. (2010). Qualifying engagement: A study of information and communication technology and the global social justice movement in Aotearoa, New Zealand. *Communication Monographs, 77*(1), 51–74.

Garett, R. K. (2007). Protest in an information society: A review of literature on social movements and new ICTs. *Information, Communication & Society, 9*(2), 202–224.

Glasbergen, P. (2010). Global action networks: Agents for collective action. *Global Environmental Change, 20*, 130–141.

Hampton, K. N., Livio, O., & Goulet, L. S. (2010). The social life of wireless urban spaces: internet use, social networks, and the public realm. *Journal of Communication, 60*(4), 701–722.

Hilton, I. (2011). Introduction: the evolving blueprint, in China's green revolution: Energy, environment and the 12th five-year plan. *China Dialogue*. Retrieved from http://www.chinadialogue.net/content/file_en/4255/China_s_green_revolution_ebook_2001.pdf

Ho, P. (2002). Greening without conflict? Environmentalism, NGOs and civil society in China. *Development and Change, 32*(5), 893–921.

Howell, J. (1998). An unholy trinity? Civil society, economic liberalization and democratization in post-Mao China. *Government and Opposition, 33*, 56–80.

Jing, J. (2003). Environmental protests in rural China. In E. J. Perry & M. Selden (Eds.), *Chinese society: Change, conflict and resistance* (pp. 204–222). New York: Routledge.

Khan, S., & VanWynsberghe, R. (2008). Cultivating the under-mined: Cross-case analysis as knowledge mobilization. *Forum: Qualitative Social Research, 9*(1), article 34. Retrieved from http://www.qualitative-research.net/index.php/fqs/article/view/334/729

Kreiss, D. (2009, August). *Institutional context of use of new media in electronic politics: From Howard Dean to Barack Obama*. Paper presented at the American Sociological Association Annual Conference, San Francisco. Retrieved from http://danielkreiss.files.wordpress.com/2010/05/kreiss_instit-contexts.pdf

Lee, C. K., & Zhang, Y. (2013). The power of instability: Unraveling the microfoundations of bargained authoritarianism in China. *American Journal of Sociology, 118*(6), 1475–1508.

Lim, M., & Kann, M. (2008). Politics: Deliberation, mobilization, and networked practices of agitation. In K. Varnelis (Ed.), *Networked publics* (pp. 77–107). Cambridge, MA: MIT Press.

Marwell, G., & Oliver, P. (1993). *The critical mass in collective action: A micro-social theory*. New York: Cambridge University Press.

MEP. (2012). The annual report of Ministry of Environment Protection of the People's Republic of China. Retrieved from http://english.mep.gov.cn/

Migdal, J. S. (2001). *State in society: Studying how states and societies transform and constitute one another*. New York: Cambridge University Press.

Migdal, J. S., Kohli, A., & Shue, V. (Eds.). (1994). *State power and social forces: Domination and transformation in the third world*. New York: Cambridge University Press.

Miles, M. B., & Huberman, A. M. (1994). *Qualitative data analysis: An expanded sourcebook* (2nd ed.). London: Sage.

O'Donnell, G., & Schimitter, P. C. (1989). *Transitions from authoritarian rule: Tentative conclusions about uncertain democracies*. Baltimore: Johns Hopkins University Press.

Pinard, M. (2011). *Motivational dimensions in social movements and contentious collective action*. Montreal: McGill-Queen's University Press.

Qiang, X. (2011). The battle for the Chinese Internet. *Journal of Democracy, 22*(2), 47–61.

Schneider, C. Q., & Schmitter, P. C. (2004). Liberalization, transition and consolidation: Measuring the components of democratization. *Democratization, 11*(5), 59–90.

Stalley, P., & Yang, D. (2006). An emerging environmental movement in China? *China Quarterly, 186*, 333–356.

Tarrow, S. (1994). *Power in movement: Social movements, collective action and politics*. New York: Cambridge University Press.

Tarrow, S. (1996). Social movements in contentious politics: A review article. *The American Political Science Review, 90*(4), 874–883.

Yang, G. (2004). Is there an environmental movement in China? Beware of the "river of anger." *Asia Program Special Report, 124*, 4–8.

Yang, G. (2009). *The power of the internet in China: Citizen activism online*. New York: Columbia University Press.

Zheng, Y. (2002). State rebuilding, popular protest and collective action in China. *Japanese Journal of Political Science, 3*(1), 45–70.

Zheng, Y. (2007). *Technological empowerment: The internet, state, and society in China*. Stanford, CA: Stanford University Press.

Zheng, Y., & Wu, G. (2005). Information technology, public space, and collective action in China. *Comparative Political Studies, 38*(5), 507–536.

5

MOBILE ACTIVISM AND CONTENTIOUS POLITICS IN CONTEMPORARY CHINA

Jun Liu

The rapid proliferation of mobile phones around the world has made this device not only the most common form of electronically mediated communication in everyday life but also an indispensable tool in contentious politics in the past decade (e.g., Allagui & Kuebler, 2011; Castells, Fernandez-Ardevol, Qiu, & Sey, 2007; Ibahrine, 2008; Liu, 2013a; Rafael, 2003). Although studies increasingly recognize the relevance of mobile phones in contentious politics, the research in this area so far is still best described as inchoate. The question that *how—and to what extent*—mobile communication contributes to the organization and mobilization of contentious politics remains largely unspecified. This study aims to fill the void by taking mobile phone uses for contentious activities in China as the case. By scrutinizing three cases in which Chinese people adopted and appropriated their mobile phones as a key means to mobilize protests and drawing upon 33 interviews with participants in these cases, this study demonstrates how people expand the political uses of mobile phones in their struggles against the authorities. More specifically, it delineates the dimensions of mobile communication that operate in the organization and mobilization of contentious politics beyond information dissemination.

I first present a critical review of current studies on mobile phones and contentious politics. Second, given the literature on social ties and mobilization in social movement studies, I propose to investigate how mobile communication embeds the dynamics of *guanxi*, a key concept involved in the intricate social ties constituting Chinese culture, and further influences the process of mobilization. Third, I specify the method, including case selection, data collection, and analysis methods. Fourth, I interrogate how mobile phone uses contribute to the organization and mobilization of protests. Fifth, I conclude with a discussion of the relevance of mobile phones to the mobilization of contentious politics in China and suggest a more nuanced and sophisticated research agenda to understand the role of mobile phones in contentious politics.

Mobile Phones and Contentious Politics Across the Global: A Review

The emerging role of mobile phones in the organization and mobilization of contentious politics has attracted considerable attention around the world (e.g., Castells et al., 2007; Liu, 2013b; Qiu, 2008a; Rheingold, 2008; Suárez, 2006). Rheingold (2002), as early as in 2002, underlined the emergence of the "smart mob" in virtue of the proliferation of mobile technologies that dramatically amplify people's organizational capability for political activism. In the following decade, the pervasive adoption of the mobile phone as a crucial means of recruitment and mobilization for protests around the globe established this device as an indispensable resource in political activism and contentious politics.

Although studies have recognized the importance of mobile phones as means of mobilization in contention situations (Castells et al., 2007, pp. 185–213; Ibahrine, 2008; Qiu, 2008a; Rheingold, 2008; Suárez, 2006), the contribution from mobile phone uses to the mechanism of organization and mobilization of contentious activities remains largely unclear and even highly contested. A large proportion of studies have expounded the technological affordances of mobile phones—just to mention a few: widespread accessibility, decentralized diffusion of information, low communication cost, high message credibility, and asynchronous communication—for mobilization (Castells et al., 2007, p. 188; Hermanns, 2008; Rafael, 2003; Rheingold, 2008; Suárez, 2006). Nevertheless, so far there is not necessarily any *causal* explanation between these affordances and the mechanism of mobile phone–facilitated political mobilization. Additionally, some studies attribute the legitimation of mobilization initiatives via mobile phones to certain *external forces* beyond mobile communication.[1] Put differently, the efficiency of mobilization by mobile communication lies not in the mobile phone per se but in external factors such as the context (e.g., Rafael, 2003, p. 415) or intermedia dynamics (e.g., Qiu, 2008a). Others, on the contrary, emphasize the embedment of existing social networks via mobile communication as an *internal* force on recruitment and mobilization for contentious politics (e.g., Allagui & Kuebler, 2011; Howard & Hussain, 2011, pp. 36, 39). Here, instead, it is the mobile interaction that embodies the key driving force—the embedment of existing social ties and networks—for mobilization *without* relying on outside elements. What, thereby, is the contribution from mobile communication to the mobilization of contentious activities? Understanding the specific dimensions of mobile communication that contribute to political mobilization will be an important step toward ascertaining the theoretical mechanism underlying the effect of mobile communication on political activism.

This study aims to provide some preliminary answers to this question by taking mobile phone–mediated political activism ("mobile activism" hereafter)[2] in China as the case. As the largest mobile phone powerhouse in the world today, China reached over 1.1 billion mobile phone users by the end of July 2013

(Xinhua, 2013). The rapid prevalence and wide use of mobile phones, as in other parts of the world, have expanded the potential of this device from a device for interpersonal communication to, increasingly, a tool to breach government censorship (e.g., Latham, 2007), satirize authoritarian rules (e.g., He, 2008), and organize a wide range of contentious activities including large-scale demonstrations and protests (Liu, 2013a; Weber, 2011). Regarding studies on mobile communication and its political implications in China, some scholars examine the way mobile phones empower "vulnerable groups"; in particular, rural-to-urban migrants (Qiu, 2008b; Wallis, 2013, pp. 169–175). Others take mobile phone–facilitated protests as examples to explicate the contribution of mobile phones to civil society (e.g., Weber, 2011). Nevertheless, none of these studies touches upon mobile communication and the mechanism of mobilization. As an emerging yet rarely touched upon topic in both communication studies and China studies, mobile activism in China offers cases worthy of closer examination for illustrating and understanding the role of mobile phones in contentious politics.

Mobile Communication, Social Ties, and Contentious Mobilization: A Research Agenda

To gain a better understanding of the role of mobile communication in contentious mobilization, it is necessary to draw lessons from at least two perspectives as follows: first, the contribution of existing social ties to efforts of mobilization and, second, mobile phone–mediated social cohesion.

Social ties have been seen as a basic but relevant recruitment agent before the mobile phone became affordable and accessible (e.g., Diani & McAdam, 2003; Tilly, 1978). As social movement studies demonstrated, such ties integrate "networks of trust" (Tilly, 2005), identify shared individual preferences and perceptions (McAdam, 1988; Passy, 2003), engender movement identity (Friedman & McAdam, 1992), and exercise social control during movement actions (Snow, Louis, Zurcher, & Ekland-Olson, 1980). Although communication technology provides the possibility of organizing collective action across geographical, cultural, ideological, and issue boundaries, social ties within extant activist networks still strongly influence effective mobilization. Diani (2000), for instance, emphasizes the existing bonds and solidarities in virtual networks that are necessary for effective mobilization to evaluate the capability of communication technology to expand or create new cohesive networks from existing strong ties and trust. Bennett (2003) also demonstrates the relevance of personal network ties to individual activists who wish to *activate* their political resources and to overcome vulnerabilities of network politics, such as loosely structured networks and weak ties. In short, the function of communication technology in mobilization still depends on existing social ties that generate the mechanisms accounting for its mobilizing affect.

Meanwhile, as studies persuasively argue, mobile communication engenders mediated ritual interaction and strengthens social cohesion within the family and the peer group (Ling, 2004, 2008; Ling & Yttri, 2002). In the context of China, in particular, it is necessary to specify the word *guanxi*. *Guanxi* connotes pervasive social ties among parties that make up a social network in Chinese society (Gold, Guthrie, & Wank, 2002). Beyond its literal translations as "relation" or "personal connections," *guanxi* implies intangible emotional attachments (e.g., trust and reliability) and ethical obligations established by reciprocity between two or more individuals (Christensen & Levinson, 2003, p. 573; Gold et al., 2002, p. 4). The establishment, maintenance, and application of *guanxi* accordingly enable individuals to look for help from the social resources of their *guanxi* networks, or Bourdieu's concept of "social capital": "The aggregate of the actual or potential resources which are linked to possession of a durable network of more or less institutionalized relationships of mutual acquaintance and recognition" (1986, p. 246).[3]

Encapsulating every aspect of Chinese society, *guanxi* has also penetrated mobile interactions (e.g., Chu, Fortunati, Law, & Yang, 2012; Wallis, 2013). Liu (2013b) proposes the concept of a "*guanxi*-embedded mobile social network," in which *guanxi* has been incorporated into both mobile communication and interpersonal networks in the wake of the increasing popularity of mobile devices and the huge rise of phone use in maintaining social ties and relations in Chinese society. Meanwhile, as several studies have identified, in contemporary contentions in China, social ties–based mobilization has become a crucial means of organization (Shan & Jiang, 2009; Shi & Cai, 2006). The research question thereby asks:

> How does mobile communication, embedding the dynamics of guanxi as social ties, influence the mechanism of political mobilization in China?

Additionally, as Deng and O'Brien (2013) elucidate, social ties can also be employed by the authorities to generate "relational repression" in order to demobilize protesters during contentions in contemporary China. *What, thereby, is the element that contributes to political mobilization through mobile communication beyond social ties?*

Methods

As exploratory research, this study employs the multiple-case study design to investigate mobile phone uses for the mobilization of contentious activities in China. Interrogating "a contemporary phenomenon within its real-life context" (Yin, 2009, p. 18), the multiple-case study design allows for qualifying, synthesizing, and generalizing observations beyond a specific instance. The cases in this study include, chronologically: (1) a two-day anti-paraxylene[4] (hereafter anti-PX) protest in Xiamen, southeast China's Fujian Province, in 2007, in which over 20,000 people had been mobilized primarily by mobile text messages to protest against a chemical factory that they perceived as a threat to their well-being (Xie & Zhao, 2007); (2) a mass incident in Weng'an, southwest China's Guizhou Province, in 2008, in which local residents employed their mobile phones to assemble thousands of people and torched government buildings due to the allegation of a cover-up of a female student's "unusual death" (Yu, 2008); and (3) a three-day taxi strike in Fuzhou, southeast China's Fujian Province, in 2010, in which taxi drivers had largely relied on mobile calls as the primary means to initiate strikes protesting the failure of local government to address the problems of the city's inequitable cab fare structure (Chen et al., 2010; *China Daily*, 2010). These three protests share a common feature: the adoption of mobile phones as a key means to initiate and facilitate protest mobilization. Thus, they provide a basis for identifying and synthesizing how Chinese people employ their mobile phones for mobilizing contentions.

After case selection, this study uses snowball sampling to locate protest participants. As a network-based sampling approach, snowball sampling is well suited for recruiting "hidden populations" that are hard to access using other sampling strategies. In the context of China, the authorities have exerted harsh controls over new media platforms to identify protest participants and stifle potential collective mobilization. To openly recruit protest participants as interviewees is thus difficult to achieve. Instead, sampling through mobile connections on the basis of existing social connection ensures to keep issues (i.e., protest participation) under a low profile and to gain rapport and trust from interviewees. In practice, this study locates participants in protest cases as interviewees by tracking the flow of mobilization messages within their mobile networks.[5] The initial "seeds" for sampling were provided by local journalists or editors, who were contacts of the author. Thirty-five participants were initially recruited.

Next, because of the politically sensitive nature of protest participation in China, the researcher wanted interviewees to participate completely voluntarily. As a result, two of the interviewees withdrew, reducing the sample to 33.[6]

A face-to-face, semi-structured interview guide was designed to investigate how interviewees used their mobile phones and perceived mobile communication in protests through a focused, conversational way between the researcher and the interviewees. Interviewees were asked to specify their mobile phone uses for mobilization and to justify their responses to mobilizing texts or calls and the messages' impact on their practices. In particular, this study focuses on the actual use of mobile phones, instead of the results of the events, in order to grasp the nuanced and detailed influence of mobile communication while avoiding exaggerating its role in contentious politics, as there are too many other contingent factors influencing government decisions to act or adopt a certain plan. Conducted in Chinese, each interview typically lasted around one-and-a-half hours. After data collection, the explanation-building approach and cross-case synthesis methods were employed in order to address the question of *what* is the contribution of mobile communication to the mobilization of contentious activities.

Mobile Communication and Contentious Activities in China: Cases

The Anti-PX Protest in Xiamen

As one of the largest middle-class protests in recent years, the anti-PX protest in Xiamen has become identified with "the power of text messaging" (Xie & Zhao, 2007, p. 16) during a process of remaking a public agenda by text messaging–facilitated demonstrations. Without informing residents, local government started PX production at a petrochemical factory; the factory was later perceived as a health threat by local residents. To keep residents from knowing about and discussing this project, the government prevented the distribution of reports that discussed the PX project, censored related words (e.g., PX) on the internet, and further asserted the negative information about the PX project as "rumor."[7] Against this backdrop, the warning regarding the PX project was diffused largely via text messages, which were also used to urge residents to join a street protest to show their dissatisfaction toward this government practice. One of the most renowned texts that "millions of Xiamen residents forwarded frenziedly around their mobile phones" within three days at the end of May read:

> For the sake of our future generations, take action! Participate among 10,000 people, June 1 at 8 a.m., opposite the municipal government building! Hands tied with yellow ribbons [as a symbol associated with environmental protection]! Pass this message on to all your Xiamen friends!
> *(Lan & Zhang, 2007)*

Although local government noted this mobilization initiative and worked on "stabilizing" local residents, the proliferation of mobile texts calling for protests still resulted in two days of demonstrations with over 20,000 participants. The demonstrations forced local government to halt the construction of the PX project immediately and relocate it six months later.

The Weng'an Mass Incident

Unlike the environmental concern in the anti-PX case, the mass incident in Weng'an was triggered by a female student's "unusual death," which ignited the long-lasting tension between local government and people. Before the unusual death happened, residents had long held deep-rooted dissatisfaction with local authority due to forced demolition and land grabbing by local government, lack of employment, and corrupt government practices (Zhao, Zhou, & Liu, 2008). Moreover, local government and public security agencies had hired mafia-style gangs to stifle public grievances by colluding with these gangs, offering them "protection umbrellas." Consequently, local residents did not have any place to redress their grievances and also suffered from a lack of a sense of security in everyday life (Ding, 2008). The tension between local residents and the government was a ceaseless aggravation.

After the death of the female student, local government declared that the student had committed suicide by leaping into the river. However, her relatives refused to accept the verdict and claimed she had been raped, killed, and then tossed into the river by two male suspects, who were believed to have familial ties with the local public security bureau. The student's family presented a petition for a thorough examination of the corpse to the county's party committee office, but police refused the petition. Tension mounted and claims emerged, stating that the student's relatives had been assaulted by the police. One mobile message read: "Without conducting a full autopsy, the police believed the female student committed suicide by jumping in a river, and they did not take mandatory measures against the suspect and ignored the family's call for a full autopsy" (Buckley, 2008). This ignited the public's anger as the death became intertwined with corrupt government officials, merciless policemen, and perceived injustice across the small county. Mobile texts and calls mobilized almost 10,000 people, who went to the public security bureau where they smashed and burned all the police vehicles parked there and set fire to government buildings.

The Taxi Strikes in Fuzhou

The taxi drivers' strikes in Fuzhou are but one example of the many driver protests that have taken place in China since 2008. Discontent with the controversially rigid manner of enforcing traffic regulations by local police and long-standing concerns including high fuel prices and rising rental fees due to the inaction of local government prompted taxi drivers in over 10 cities to stage strikes, one after another, between 2008 and 2013 by primarily using calls and texts via their mobile phones (*Global Times*, 2013; Huang & Wills, 2011). In Fuzhou, taxi drivers attempted, in the beginning, to address their discontent via local media. Due to censorship from the government, however, local media were not allowed to air taxi drivers' grievances and anger.[8] Then taxi drivers tried to post their discontent on Weibo—China's equivalent of Twitter—seeking a government response and public support. Again, this information was deleted or blocked in a short space of time.[9] On April 23, 2010, in response to an unbearable surge in penalties handed out by the police, thousands of taxi drivers in Fuzhou went on strike, and mobile calls were the key conduit for the mobilization, leaving the city's streets nearly empty (*China Daily*, 2010).

To summarize, although these three cases took places in different types of areas (urban and rural) and involved different groups of people (the middle-class in Xiamen, the rural population in Weng'an, and the taxi drivers, mostly rural-to-urban migrants, in Fuzhou), and the reasons for these events were different (protection of the environment, justice-seeking, and complaints about the inappropriate charges from government), all of them embraced the mobile phone as a crucial means of organizing and facilitating protests.[10] The question now is, how did mobile phone use contribute to the organization and mobilization of these protests?

Findings and Discussions

As studies have already identified, given that mobile devices are easy to use, inexpensive, and make group messaging available, they provide people with a swift and convenient means to distribute mobilization initiatives on a large scale (e.g., Howard & Hussain, 2011; Rheingold, 2008). This instantaneous diffusion allows for the rapid proliferation of mobilization initiatives. This makes it difficult for the authorities to predict when and where the proliferation of a mobilizing message via mobile phones will ensue, and thus to intervene in the outbreak of protests (Rheingold, 2002). Nevertheless, very little is known about *why* people choose to forward mobilizing messages and, more importantly, to follow the call to engage in contentious activities. Drawing on interviews with participants in these protests, this study observes that, beyond rapid diffusion of mobilizing messages, mobile communication generates *a unique mechanism* for the organization and mobilization of protests in China. As a means of interpersonal communication, the mobile phone enables people to activate and accumulate their *guanxi* during the protest mobilization process. Furthermore, given its conversational and expressive affordances (e.g., Reida & Reida, 2010), mobile communication is able to relay people's emotions and experiences, which can be a driving force for protest recruitment and mobilization.

Mobile Communication and the Accumulation of Guanxi for Protest

As the interviews revealed, through mobile interactions, people activated and mobilized their *guanxi* networks for political action. The activation and involvement of *guanxi*, and, more specifically, a strong sense of trustworthiness, reciprocity, and reliability regarding *guanxi* acts as the driving force for both recruitment and participation in protests.

First, with trustworthiness strengthened through *guanxi* networks, information via mobile communication enjoys a high credibility, and this makes people more likely to trust and disseminate further these messages. For instance, in the Weng'an case, people kept on disseminating messages regarding the controversial death of the female student as these messages were coming from their "reliable sources from *guanxi* networks,"[11] even after local government had labeled such messages as "rumors" (Lai, 2011). As one interviewee explained, "It is a matter of mutual trust [toward people from your *guanxi* networks], not verification [of the fact]."[12] Here, the statement demonstrates that the mutual trust in the bilateral relations within *guanxi* gives high credibility to mobile messages. In the Xiamen case, similarly, the interviewees noted that they would trust those messages against the PX project from their mobile social network, even if "the senders do not have enough knowledge about the topic [i.e., the impact of PX plants on the local environment]."[13] Also to note, the high credibility of mobile messages obtained through *guanxi* networks does not mean that people take for granted that the information from their *guanxi* network is *fact*. To be sure, as in the anti-PX case in Xiamen, it is impossible for people with little background knowledge in chemicals to make a judgment regarding the potential effects of PX plants on the local environment. Nevertheless, the trustworthiness from *guanxi* puts aside that fact and highlights the perceived reliability of the person from *guanxi*, or as one respondent argues, "It's better to believe it than not, especially when messages are coming from the people you trust."[14] In this way, given established *guanxi* relationships, high credibility encourages people to follow such messages from their *guanxi* networks and distribute them further via mobile communication.

Second, the reciprocal obligation from *guanxi* shapes the response to mobilizing messages, driving people to engage in protest participation and recruitment as a kind of fulfillment of their obligations on the basis of *guanxi*. In practice, when people receive a mobilizing message via mobile communication, they view such a message as an appeal from their *guanxi* networks and not simply a piece of mobilization information. As one interviewee explained, "it [the message] is more than a piece of information. Because it [the message] is a piece of information from a specific sender, who could be your friend, colleague, relative, and so on from your *guanxi* networks."[15] As that statement demonstrates, the mobile message reminds people of the *guanxi* between senders and themselves, on the one hand, and their duties in their *guanxi* networks, on the other hand. For receivers, whether or not—and how—to respond to the (mobilizing) request in this message from *"a specific sender"* (Ling, 2004, p. 151) depends not just on the information itself but, more importantly, on *guanxi* and the reciprocal obligation in guanxi between communicators. Another interviewee said, "beyond informing you about protest issues, the message actually asks for your participation as a kind of reciprocal help in terms of your *guanxi*."[16] Against this backdrop, for the receiver, the positive response to the request registers the reciprocity in the mutual relationship.

On the contrary, if a person refuses to respond to the appeal from their *guanxi* network, as one interviewee said, "you will probably lose your *guanxi* resource and people will in turn not respond to your request in future, as you have failed to fulfill your role and duty in *guanxi* practice."[17] In this way, it is *guanxi*—reciprocal obligation, in particular—that generates a kind of "pressure" on people about how they respond to and act on the mobilizing message.

In this way, such feelings of duty and obligation, largely self-perceived given the basis of the reciprocal nature of *guanxi*, encourage people to diffuse mobilizing messages within their *guanxi* network as at once a sort of social support and a fulfillment of their duties in *guanxi*. As one interviewee explained, "it [mobilizing your social resource by disseminating messages] is a crucial way to demonstrate that you are a reliable friend, even if it concerns joining a protest [as a politically sensitive issue in China]."[18] Consequently, the proliferation of mobilizing messages expands its influence not only by informing more people but also by recruiting and accumulating more *guanxi* networks and resources in the dissemination practice.

Third, the mutual reliability from *guanxi* also contributes to both the proliferation of mobilizing messages and the recruitment and mobilization process of protests. A large majority of the interviewees noted that they had immediately passed the message on, via their mobile phones, to people in their *guanxi* networks. As several interviewees mentioned, "if the message is important to me, it becomes important to my friends."[19] The text messages calling for demonstrations against the PX project also stated: "Pass this message on to all your Xiamen friends!" It is clear here that, through mobile communication, on the one hand, stable reciprocity and relational reliability among people emerge readily by disseminating messages that they perceive as relevant to those within their *guanxi* network. On the other hand, given the relational reliability in *guanxi*, people mobilize their social network resources as social capital: from *guanxi* contacts to response to the appeal, be it related to mobilization or not, disseminating messages further via their mobile phones. As such, low-cost, convenient, and highly efficient mobile communication leads to the quasi–mass communication of even censored or mobilization messages throughout *guanxi* networks within a short period of time, making it possible for this kind of message to unite as many people as possible, as soon as possible.

To sum up, in the process of mobilization, the mobile phone functions in a sense like neighborhood salons that help aggregate individual preferences into a collective choice through interpersonal, horizontal communication. Embedded in the dynamic of *guanxi*, more specifically, mobile phone–mediated mobilization is more symmetrical (i.e., given its peer-to-peer communicative pattern) and less hierarchical than traditional group mobilization such as that done by political parties or nongovernmental organizations. Put another way, there are no leading roles in the process of mobilization that utilizes *guanxi* to advocate for engagement or participation. Rather, there are only friends, relatives, colleagues, and so on—in short, the people you know and the people with whom you have *guanxi* relationships. Accordingly, mobilization via mobile phones is less like an order and more like an appeal for help from *guanxi* connections. To positively respond to messages and circulate them through one's mobile phone has thus become a crucial way to fulfill one's duty and obligation in social support of *guanxi* practice, which consequently becomes a driving force to simultaneously promote the proliferation of mobilizing calls and recruit more people for protests through mobile networks.

Mobile Communication and the Accumulation of Emotions and Experiences

In addition to the accumulation of *guanxi* through mobile phones, mobile communication connects the individual and his and her emotions and experiences that were previously isolated, articulating these emotions and experiences into collective ones; these, in turn, become a driving force for protest participation and mobilization. In other words, the process of information dissemination via mobile phones for mobilization includes not just a kind of information dissemination itself but also a process of sharing and articulating communicators' feelings, emotions, and experiences. The articulation of feelings and emotions, as social movement studies suggest, functions as an essential component of collective mobilization because it involves shared experiences of empowerment and collective effervescence, which is greatly affective as it inspires the move "from framed emotion to action and from individual to collective" (Flam & King, 2005, p. 4–5; also see Aminzade & McAdam, 2002; Yang, 2000). The articulation of emotions and experience via mobile communication thus galvanizes widespread distrust and anger over official corruption, irresponsibility, inaction, and suppression of the people, pushing more people to participate in protests.

The mobilization process of the taxi strikes in Fuzhou is a case in point. When drivers were calling and talking with each other via their mobile phones regarding the strike issue,

> You can feel the strong emotion and attitude from the other side [of the mobile phone], including the grievance of unfair treatments by the police and the anger over government's inaction. Such feelings resonate with your own experience . . . You know that you are not alone . . . From the tone [of the conversation], you can also recognize people's willingness to engage in the strike. It really empowers the feeling of togetherness [for strike].[20]

As this quotation indicates, beyond the transfer of information, the vocal interaction via mobile phones unfolds and evokes a large degree of feelings and emotions regarding suppression and exclusion, as well as exploitation by the authorities. Such kinds of feelings and emotions allow people to perceive the attitudes from one another on the other side of the call by embodying vocal elements such as voice, tone, pitch, and volume. As people received more calls from their fellow friends and colleagues, they increasingly recognized that their emotions and experiences were resonating among more and more people. The recognition of the resonance and articulation of emotion and experience accordingly engenders cohesion among protest participants.

Besides the vocal interaction, mobile text messages also facilitate the articulation of emotions and experiences. In the Weng'an case, text messages about the cover-up of the female student's unusual death struck a chord, reminding other residents of their bitter experiences under local authority's iron rule. As one interviewee said,

> When we got this information about the event [the cover-up of the student's death and the later neglect of demands from her family from the mobile phone], it just reminded me of our own harsh experiences . . . this event lets us know that both we and her family share a mutual connection because both have been treated poorly by the government. We forwarded this message [via our mobile phones] to let more people know about this event. People then will know that they are not the only ones who suffered from the unfair treatments [by the government].[21]

The above statement observes that people indicated and shared their attitudes toward local authority by disseminating the female student's story through their mobile devices. The spreading of this kind of message resonated, connecting individuals' experiences and gathering them into a collective one. More specifically, when people communicated with each other and forwarded this story, they implicitly told those to whom they sent messages that "this is not just other people's stories or experiences; I also have similar experiences."[22] In turn, once people got more of the same or similar messages via their mobile phones, they got more affirmations from the people in their *guanxi* networks that their feelings and experiences were shared and resonated with more people. In this way, the more people there are involved in mobile communication, the more experiences people share, the more emotional support people get, and the bigger the collective experience becomes. In turn, the articulations of emotion and experience have pushed more people to engage in protests.

In summary, beyond passing on mobilizing messages, mobile communication facilitates a process of emotional expression, accumulation, and mobilization through which people articulate their suppressed experiences, empathize with each other through similar feelings of suffering, and generate cohesion among themselves. Also through mobile communication people recognize that, instead of being separate individuals, they are "networked" (Rainie & Wellman, 2012) individuals enjoying support from their friends and their *guanxi* networks. The feeling of solidarity and empowerment pushes an increasing number of people toward the mobilization call and makes them much more likely to engage in protests.

Conclusion

The past decade has witnessed the increasingly indispensable role the mobile phone plays in collective actions across the globe. Nevertheless, the question of how the mobile phone contributes to and empowers the organization and mobilization of contentious activities remains largely unclear and highly contested. Given the aspects of mobile technologies that favor the organization of collective actions, more importantly, what is the exact mechanism that engages people in contentious situations? As arguments against "technological determinism" have already underlined, technology is only partly the answer to either sociopolitical changes in general or the mobilization process in particular. In practice, it is specific social and cultural contexts that dramatically shape the mobilization process.

As this study demonstrates from the analysis of cases, the mobile phone plays a relevant role in accumulating people's *guanxi* network resources while articulating their experiences and emotions, both of which act as key driving forces for the mobilization of contentious activities in China. More specifically, on the one hand, mediated by mobile phones, the mobilization process is developed around social ties—*guanxi*—in the context of China. Accordingly, this mobilization process gives more weight to credibility, reciprocity, and reliability based on *guanxi* than on abstract principles of sender-receiver in mass communication. Spreading information via mobile phones via a personal approach, mobilization initiatives and even rumors mobilize a key social resource: people within a social network. Through social networks, these efforts draw hundreds or thousands of people together for public protests or mass incidents, creating a cascading effect that inflames public anger, passions, or resistance and makes waves in China's society. This form of mobile phone–facilitated mobilization is largely based upon people's interpersonal communication, which unites individual elements into a coherent whole.

On the other hand, mobile activism articulates a collective experience of suppression, exclusion, and exploitation in China. Mobile communication enables ordinary people to connect and share their individual feelings, emotions, and experiences with each other. The more people who engage in the mobile phone–facilitated communicative sphere, the more suppressed experiences are shared, confirmed, and articulated, and the more people who understand that they are not the only ones who suffer from the bullying, dispossession, and injuries caused by the authorities. In this way, mobile activism is not generated by institutions but is based on personal feelings, experiences, and motivations and articulated via mobile devices; the articulation of experience accordingly achieves the formation of tight-knit groups based on their common experience with the authorities. In this way, the dynamics of mobile activism lie simultaneously in the incorporation of interpersonal, horizontal communication that accumulates people's social ties—*guanxi* in China—and the articulation of social experiences that registers the feelings and emotions of oppression and injustice in everyday lives and consolidates solidarity for contentious activities.

This study contributes to current scholarship of mobile phones and contentious politics from the following two perspectives. First, beyond simply suggesting that *guanxi* as a social network plays a key role in the process of political mobilization, it elaborates on the questions of how *guanxi*, embedded in mobile communication, intervenes in this process and why it matters. As this study elucidates, mobile phone–mediated social ties embody multiple dimensions (i.e., credibility, reciprocity, and reliability) that intervene in the process of mobilization and induce people to become involved in contentious activities. Specifying these dimensions, as Passy notes, gives us "a more complete explanation of the entire process of individual participation" (2003, p. 22). This study thereby suggests that future research in this field may benefit from drawing on lessons from social movement scholars that address the relevance of social ties as a mechanism of mobilization from different aspects, such as network strength, density, and frequency, and salience and centrality. Second, focusing not just on the process of information dissemination but also on the articulation of feelings, emotions, and experiences beyond information dissemination via mobile communication, this study addresses the relevance of the mobile phone as a key and convenient resource for ordinary people to communicate with each other and express their experiences—in particular those unrecognized, suppressed, and marginalized in a repressive context—and make those experiences more visible. With this in mind, the reason that people engage in contentious activities is *more than* social tie–based mobilization. This study reminds us that to better understand the role of mobile phones in the process of political mobilization we should not only look at the use of mobile devices during contentious moments, but also connect their use with the political potential embedded in the actual experience and routine use of mobile phones in people's everyday lives in given protest issues. Last but not least, with the rapid diffusion of smartphones and the increasing ubiquity of the internet, future studies will need to consider how new mobile affordances—such as access to social media platforms and location-based information—enabled by smartphones may shape the dynamics of contentious politics (e.g., Liu, forthcoming).

Notes

1. For instance, Rafael (2003) credits the Catholic Church as "an authority outside the [mobilizing] text messages themselves" (p. 409) in "People's Power II" in the Philippines. Similarly, Castells et al. (2007) point out that "the new media of mobile phones and texting have to *work closely with other media . . . in order to deliver actual political consequences*" (p. 193, emphasis added).
2. See, for instance, the mobile phone–mediated middle-class protests in Xiamen and Shanghai (Liu, 2013a; Weber, 2011); for mobile phone use by migrant workers for collective resistance, see, for instance, Barboza and Bradsher (2010).
3. For instance, for *guanxi* and job allocation in China, see Bian (1994); for studies on mobile phone use for job information among migrant workers, see Law and Chu (2008).
4. Paraxylene is used in the production of plastics, polyester, and other synthetic materials.
5. It is necessary to point out here that mobile communication normally happens among existing *guanxi* networks, while internet-based communication (e.g., through social

media platforms) is more likely and better able to distribute beyond existing *guanxi* networks.

6. Among them, 14 from the Xiamen case (male, nine; female, five), and the average educational level as college and university; eight from the Weng'an case (male, seven; female, one), and the average educational level as middle school; and 11 from the Fuzhou strike (all male), and the average educational level as high school.
7. Residents in Xiamen, personal interviews, December 13–18, 2008.
8. Journalists and editors in Fuzhou, personal interviews, December 13–17, 2010.
9. Taxi drivers in Fuzhou, personal interviews, December 3–5, 2010.
10. It is necessary to mention that the way of framing the contentions could legitimate them to an extent and influence government response (e.g., to go against local government's decision on the PX plant in the Xiamen case instead of challenging the regime's rule). Nevertheless, as the discussion in the methods section already notes, there are many contingent factors that can affect government response to contentions. This issue is beyond the purpose of this study.
11. A 33-year-old merchant in Weng'an, telephone interview, October 15, 2010.
12. A 42-year-old primary school teacher in Weng'an, telephone interview, October 15, 2010.
13. A 27-year-old white-collar worker in Xiamen, personal interview, September 26, 2010.
14. A 35-year-old editor in Xiamen, personal interview, September 27, 2010.
15. A 32-year-old university lecturer in Xiamen, personal interview, September 26, 2010.
16. A 33-year-old taxi driver in Fuzhou, personal interview, October 5, 2010.
17. A 43-year-old taxi driver in Fuzhou, personal interview, October 5, 2010.
18. A 33-year-old taxi driver in Fuzhou, personal interview, October 5, 2010.
19. Residents in Xiamen, personal interviews, September 2010.
20. A 43-year-old taxi driver in Fuzhou, personal interview, April 22, 2010.
21. A 43-year-old peasant in Weng'an, telephone interview, October 17, 2010.
22. Weng'an residents, telephone interviews, October 15–17, 2010.

References

Allagui, I., & Kuebler, J. (2011). The Arab spring and the role of ICTs. *International Journal of Communication, 5*, 1435–1442.

Aminzade, R., & McAdam, D. (2002). Emotions and contentious politics. *Mobilization: An International Quarterly, 7*(2), 107–109.

Barboza, D., & Bradsher, K. (2010, June 16). In China, labor movement enabled by technology, *New York Times*, p. B1.

Bennett, W. L. (2003). Communicating global activism. *Information, Communication & Society, 6*(2), 143–168.

Bian, Y. (1994). *Guanxi* and the allocation of jobs in urban China. *China Quarterly, 140*, 971–999.

Bourdieu, P. (1986). The forms of capital. In J. Richardson (Ed.), *Handbook of theory and research for the sociology of education* (pp. 241–258). New York: Greenwood.

Buckley, C. (2008). Girl's death sparks rioting in China. Retrieved from http://uk.reuters.com/article/latestCrisis/idUKPEK27256220080628?sp=true

Castells, M., Fernandez-Ardevol, M., Qiu, J. L., & Sey, A. (2007). *Mobile communication and society: A global perspective*. Cambridge, MA: MIT Press.

Chen, R., Yang, Y., Xue, H., & Huang, K. (2010, April 24). Eighty percent of taxi drivers went on strike. *Strait Metropolis Daily*, p. A2.

China Daily. (2010, April 23). Around China: Taxi drivers go on strike, *China Daily*, p. 7.

Christensen, K., & Levinson, D. (2003). *Guanxi*. In K. Christensen & D. Levinson (Eds.), *Encyclopedia of community: From the village to the virtual world* (pp. 572–574). London: Sage.

Chu, R., Fortunati, L., Law, P., & Yang, S. (2012). *Mobile communication and greater China.* New York: Routledge.

Deng, Y., & O'Brien, K. J. (2013). Relational repression in China. *China Quarterly, 215,* 533–552.

Diani, M. (2000). Social movement networks virtual and real. *Information, Communication & Society, 3*(3), 386–401.

Diani, M., & McAdam, D. (Eds.). (2003). *Social movements and networks: Relational approaches to collective action.* New York: Oxford University Press.

Ding, B. (2008, July 10). Weng'an, an unpeaceful county city. *Southern Weekend,* p. A1.

Flam, H., & King, D. (2005). Introduction. In H. Flam & D. King (Eds.), *Emotions and social movements* (pp. 1–18). New York: Routledge.

Friedman, D., & McAdam, D. (1992). Collective identity and activism. In A. D. Morris & C. M. Mueller (Eds.), *Frontiers in social movement theory* (pp. 156–173). New Haven, CT: Yale University Press.

Global Times. (2013). Taxi drivers take work woes off-road in May Day demo. Retrieved from http://www.globaltimes.cn/content/778702.shtml#.Uapk6WTjZqo

Gold, T., Guthrie, D., & Wank, D. (2002). An introduction to the study of *guanxi.* In T. Gold, D. Guthrie, & D. Wank (Eds.), *Social connections in China: Institutions, culture, and the changing nature of guanxi* (pp. 3–20). Cambridge: Cambridge University Press.

He, Z. (2008). SMS in China. *Information Society, 24*(3), 182–190.

Hermanns, H. (2008). Mobile democracy: Mobile phones as democratic tools. *Politics, 28*(2), 74–82.

Howard, P. N., & Hussain, M. M. (2011). The role of digital media. *Journal of Democracy, 22*(3), 35–48.

Huang, S., & Wills, K. (2011). Taxi drivers in eastern China strike over rising fuel costs. Retrieved from http://www.reuters.com/article/2011/08/01/china-taxis-strike-idUSL3E7J10HX20110801

Ibahrine, M. (2008). Mobile communication and sociopolitical change in the Arab world. In J. E. Katz (Ed.), *Handbook of mobile communication studies* (pp. 257–272). Cambridge, MA: MIT Press.

Lai, H. (2011, August 19). High growth can't hide problems. *China Daily.* Retrieved from http://www.china.org.cn/opinion/2011–08/19/content_23246056.htm

Lan, Y., & Zhang, Y. (2007, May 29). Millions of Xiamen residents spread crazily the same SMS to against high-pollution project. *Southern Metropolis Daily.* Retrieved from http://news.sina.com.cn/c/2007–05–30/082011922201s.shtml

Latham, K. (2007). SMS, communication, and citizenship in China's information society. *Critical Asian Studies, 39*(2), 295–314.

Law, P., & Chu, W. (2008). ICTs and migrant workers in contemporary China. *Knowledge, Technology & Policy, 21*(2), 43–45.

Ling, R. (2004). *The mobile connection.* San Francisco, CA: Morgan Kaufmann.

Ling, R. (2008). *New tech, new ties.* Cambridge, MA: MIT Press.

Ling, R., & Yttri, B. (2002). Hyper-coordination via mobile phones in Norway. In J. Katz & M. Aakhus (Eds.), *Perpetual contact* (pp. 139–169). Cambridge: Cambridge University Press.

Liu, J. (2013a). Mobile communication, popular protests and citizenship in China. *Modern Asian Studies, 47*(3), 995–1018.

Liu, J. (2013b). *Mobilized by mobile media: How Chinese people use mobile phones to change politics and democracy* (Doctoral thesis, University of Copenhagen).

Liu, J. (forthcoming). The dynamics of real-time contentious politics. In A. Bechmann & S. Lomborg (Eds.), *The ubiquitous internet*. New York: Routledge.

McAdam, D. (1988). Micromobilization contexts and recruitment to activism. *International Social Movement Research, 1*, 125–154.

Passy, F. (2003). Social networks matter. But how? In M. Diani & D. McAdam (Eds.), *Social movements and networks* (pp. 21–48). New York: Oxford University Press.

Qiu, J. L. (2008a). Mobile civil society in Asia. *Javnost—The Public, 15*(3), 39–58.

Qiu, J. L. (2008b). Working-class ICTs, migrants, and empowerment in South China. *Asian Journal of Communication, 18*(4), 333–347.

Rafael, V. L. (2003). The cell phone and the crowd. *Popular Culture, 15*(3), 399–425.

Rainie, H., & Wellman, B. (2012). *Networked: The new social operating system*. Cambridge, MA: MIT Press.

Reida, F.J.M., & Reida, D. J. (2010). The expressive and conversational affordances of mobile messaging. *Behaviour & Information Technology, 29*(1), 3–22.

Rheingold, H. (2002). *Smart mobs*. Cambridge: Perseus.

Rheingold, H. (2008). Mobile media and political collective action. In J. E. Katz (Ed.), *Handbook of mobile communication studies* (pp. 225–240). Cambridge, MA: MIT Press.

Shan, G., & Jiang, Z. (2009). The characteristics and conflicts of mass incidents at township level. Retrieved from the Consensus Website (Gongshiwang, 21ccom.net), http://www.21ccom.net/articles/zgyj/ggzhc/article_201001202212.html

Shi, F., & Cai, Y. (2006). Disaggregating the state. *China Quarterly, 186*, 314–332.

Snow, D. A., Louis, A., Zurcher, J., & Ekland-Olson, S. (1980). Social networks and social movements. *American Sociological Review, 45*(5), 787–801.

Suárez, S. L. (2006). Mobile democracy. *Representation, 42*(2), 117–128.

Tilly, C. (1978). *From mobilization to revolution*. Reading, MA: Addison-Wesley.

Tilly, C. (2005). *Trust and rule*. Cambridge: Cambridge University Press.

Wallis, C. (2013). *Technomobility in China*. New York: New York University Press.

Weber, I. (2011). Mobile, online and angry. *Critical Arts, 25*(1), 25–45.

Xie, L., & Zhao, L. (2007). The power of mobile messaging. *China Newsweek, 326*(20), 16–17.

Xinhua. (2013, January 25). China's mobile phone users reach 1.11 billion. Retrieved from http://www.chinadaily.com.cn/china/2013–01/25/content_16172589.htm

Yang, G. (2000). Achieving emotions in collective action. *Sociological Quarterly, 41*(4), 593–614.

Yin, R. K. (2009). *Case study research* (4th ed.). London: Sage.

Yu, J. (2008). A review of anger-venting mass incident. *South Wind View, 15*, 20–22.

Zhao, P., Zhou, F., & Liu, W. (2008). Weng'an focused on economy but neglected public opinion, the people won't tell the truth to the government. Retrieved from http://cpc.people.com.cn/GB/64093/64099/7508621.html

6

CAMPAIGNING ON WEIBO

Independent Candidates' Use of Social Media in Local People's Congress Elections in China

Fei Shen

New media technologies (e.g., blogs, social media, SMS, etc.) are often hailed as important tools for their democratizing potential in authoritarian regimes. Undoubtedly, there is a grain of truth in such belief. The rapid spread of information technologies in China offers unprecedented structural conduciveness to accessing a novel space for public communication. According to the most recent report from China Internet Network Information Center (CNNIC, 2014), there were a total of 618 million users in the country by the end of January 2014. Among them, around 500 million users accessed the Internet via mobile devices.

Incidents showcasing impressive grassroots utilization of new communication tools—in particular, microblogging services—are not rare in China. Weibo has been used to fight against child trafficking, to initiate crowd-funding projects for rural school kids, to expose corrupted government officials, and to urge the government to be responsive and responsible to the public. Nevertheless, the power of social media has to be assessed within local social and political contexts. An overly optimistic view toward new technologies tends to overlook cases that are more complex and less encouraging. Focusing on a "not-so-successful" case, this study aims to analyze grassroots' use of social media for participating in national politics. The outpouring of independent candidates and their fresh presence on the most popular Chinese microblogging site, Sina Weibo, in local People's Congress (LPC) elections in 2011 and 2012 is an intriguing phenomenon that deserves special scholarly attention. The value of scrutinizing this case lies in at least three aspects.

First, in contrast to most grassroots collective actions in China which could be seen as being reactive toward government corruption and infringement of citizen rights, participation in local congressional elections represents a proactive case where people seek positive freedom. Second, unlike most "mass incidents" that are constrained to a single locality, be it a province, a city, or a small village, competing for deputy seats in local People's Congress constitutes a nationwide phenomenon. Third and most importantly, the use of new communication technologies in the elections provides researchers a novel corpus of data for analysis. Rather than relying on personal recounts and media discourse describing collective actions, this study uses data collected from social media to systematically examine individuals' involvement in local politics.

Local People's Congress Elections in China

Elections under authoritarianism (Gandhi & Lust-Okar, 2009) around the globe constitute a complicated phenomenon for political scientists. Notwithstanding, being considered an authoritarian country by many, China holds direct election at the lowest levels of the people's congress.[1] Article 97 of the Chinese Constitution stipulates that "deputies to the people's congresses of counties, cities not divided into districts, municipal districts, townships, nationality townships and towns are elected directly by their constituencies" (Chinese Constitution, 1982). Competing for seats in the lowest bodies in the tiered parliamentary system is a legitimate and legal venue for ordinary Chinese citizens to participate in politics.

The impetus for grassroots participation was partly derived from a new election law which came into force in 1979. Different than the 1953 election law, the new law adopted an election system of more candidates than positions (*cha e xuanju*), allowed initial candidates to be nominated by voters jointly, required direct election of delegates to the county people's congresses, and enforced the use of secret ballots (Nathan, 1985; Womack, 1982). Such changes offered an institutional space for citizens' participation in politics and increased election competitiveness (Huang & Chen, 2011).

Despite these electoral reforms, however, LPC elections are tightly controlled by the Party through exerting formal and informal, legal and extralegal influences on the election process (Yuan, 2011). For ease of exposition, Figure 6.1 presents a flowchart illustrating the process of LPC elections. To run for deputy seats, one has to register to be a voter first. Chinese voters could stand in for LPC elections if they are nominated by the CCP, eight democratic parties, and official mass groups (i.e., party-nominated candidates), or are seconded by 10 or more voters (i.e., voter-nominated candidates). The success rate of candidates nominated by parties and mass groups is next to 100%, whereas in contrast, the success rate of voter-nominated candidates is only about 10% (Lei, 2009, p. 82). The number of initial candidates is usually large when compared to the number of seats available. For example, a university with five deputy seats could attract 600 initial candidates (He, 2008). Local electoral committees, whose positions are typically held by the current government officials, will vet the list by holding a series of democratic consultations between the election committee and the masses in order to reduce the candidates to a manageable number, which allows the government to weed out unwanted candidates. When agreement cannot be formed by democratic consultation and deliberation, the election law stipulates that electoral committees must adopt a primary election to select the final candidates. Those whose names are not on the final slate will have to run as write-in candidates and their chances of winning the elections are mostly slim.

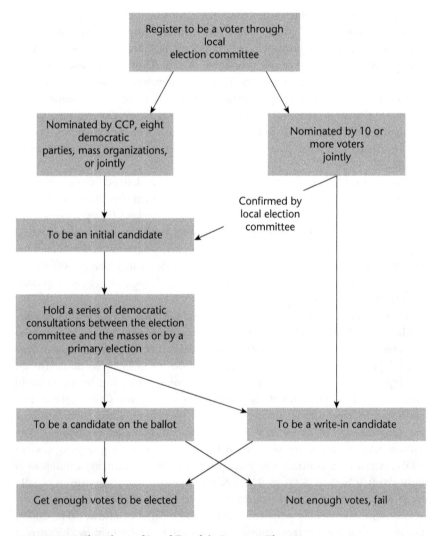

FIGURE 6.1 A Flowchart of Local People's Congress Elections

"Independent Candidates": A Misnomer

In elections that are considered to have a "limited choice" or be "semi-competitive" (e.g., Chen & Zhong, 2002; Shi, 1999), grassroots power should not be ignored. The emergence of independent candidates directly challenges the authoritative rule, fostering an undercurrent of tension between the government and the candidates. Simply put, independent candidates in Chinese LPC elections refer to those who run for deputy seats but are not handpicked by the Party.

Different titles have been given to these candidates by international news media including independent candidates (Richburg, 2011), citizen candidates (Branigan, 2011), and grassroots candidates (Wines, 2011). Even among scholars, no consensus has been reached. Some adopted the widely circulated term independent candidates (*duli houxuan ren*) (e.g., He & Liu, 2012; Luo, 2013), and others argued for terminologies such as autonomous campaigners (*zizhu canxuan ren*) (e.g., He, 2008) or self-initiated candidates (*zijian canxuan ren*) (e.g., Lei, 2013), and so on.

Independent candidates should not be understood as they are in elections of liberal democracies—candidates not affiliated with any existing parties. Contrarily, some "independent candidates" in China are Communist Party members, while many carefully vetted candidates nominated by the government are non-Party members, for the purpose of manufacturing demographic diversity of people's representatives. Furthermore, not all "voter-nominated candidates" are independent candidates. Many candidates nominated by 10 or more voters are actually Party-endorsed candidates (for a detailed description of the Party's control mechanism, see He, 2010). In extreme cases, candidates are not aware of their candidacy until they are successfully elected (He, 2008). To keep the proportion of "voter-nominated candidates" high, Party-endorsed candidates are arranged into different precincts according to their demographic features, and local governments then mobilize voters to nominate and to vote for the prearranged candidates.

Junzhi He (2008) noticed that being autonomous is the defining feature of independent candidates. Lei (2013) argued that self-initiation is a necessary condition for being an independent candidate, and thus "self-initiated candidates" is a more accurate term. Pu (2012) noted that self-motivation is not a sufficient condition for independent candidates because self-motivated or self-initiated candidates could possibly be those who bribed local authorities for deputy seats; instead, "publicized self-initiated candidates" is a better term. Taking these observations into account, it is appropriate to define independent candidates as voter-nominated LPC candidates who are self-motivated, running an active and publicized campaign, and relying on their own resources for garnering support.

New Media and Collective Actions

Independent candidacy is by no means a brand new phenomenon. University students started to run as independent candidates in 1980, after China amended its election law in 1979 (Nathan, 1985). Their presence abated throughout the

1990s, but independent candidates reemerged on a large scale in the 2003 elections (He, 2010; Lei, 2013) where people of different backgrounds (e.g., lawyers, property owners) started to join the fray. However, in 2004 the standing committee of the National People's Congress asked the media to tone down their coverage of independent candidates. Facing authoritative pressure, the media remained silent about independent candidates in the 2006–2007 elections.

Prior to the social media era, independent candidates have a very limited repertoire of campaign activities to carry out. The election law bans large-scale electoral competition and places many limitations on the duration and methods of campaigning (Shi & Lei, 1999). Independent candidates distribute leaflets and name cards to the public, visit voters, and make public speeches. Article 33 of the election law stipulates that local electoral committees must introduce the basic information of candidates to the voters at voters' meetings. But such ways of communication could attract little public attention, let alone garner support. Without mobilization organized by the Party, independent candidates are at a great disadvantage. They have to find ways to reach out to voters without transgressing the election law.

The Internet provides a low cost tool for large scale communication that transcends temporal and geographical constraints (Lupia & Sin, 2003). Resource mobilization theory (McCarthy & Zald, 1973; Zald & McCarthy, 1987) attributes the success of social movements to resources, organization, and political opportunities (Jenkins, 1983). New communication technology with low operating costs could be considered a type of indispensable resource in modern mobilization. Specific to Internet activism, the "swarming strategy" (Rheingold, 2002) is one of the emergent properties of ad hoc mobile computing networks. The ease of access to the Internet enables decentralized activity coordination for a common cause by activists from all over the world.

The rise of social media—Web applications created for facilitating interaction among users—further amplifies the political prowess of information technologies. Social media became an important resource for the organization of social movements in the Egyptian revolution (Eltantawy & Wiest, 2011). Social media help frame issues, disseminate unifying symbols, and translate online advocacy into offline protests (Lim, 2012). Velasquez and LaRose (2014) discovered a correspondence between efficacy perceptions and the level of political activities performed through social media.

Campaigning on Weibo: The 2011–2012 LPC Elections

Between September 1, 2011, and December 31, 2012, a total of around 2 million deputies to the People's Congresses at the counties and townships level in rural areas and at the district level in cities were reelected. The 2011–2012 LPC elections attracted an unprecedentedly large number of independent candidates (Lei, 2013). The Internet, social media in particular, is helping grow numbers of participants. On April 18, 2011, Ping Liu, a female worker who'd been laid off from her job, became the first person to express her intention to run in the LPC elections through Sina Weibo (Sina microblogging). Following Liu, a myriad of independent candidates started to use social media for the elections. About 217 candidates announced their candidacy on Weibo in 2011 (He & Liu, 2012).

Information dissemination, network formation, and mobilization seem to be the most important functions of social media advocacy. Nevertheless, free flow of information is rather limited in China. To control the domestic cyberspace, the government has a large variety of legal and administrative measures at their disposal, including promoting self-regulation, deploying human censors and Internet police force, and recruiting paid commentators (Shen, 2014). It is well known that social media applications such as Twitter and Facebook are blocked in China. Without access to international social media applications, independent candidates have to turn to the domestic platforms for their campaigns.

Among many others, Sina Weibo is the most popular Twitter-like microblogging service in China. In December 2012, there were a total of 309 million people, about 54.7% of all Chinese Internet users, using Weibo services. Sina's market share (57%) is higher than the combined share of its competitors (Tencent, Sohu, Netease, and Baidu).[2] Starting out as a Twitter clone, Sina Weibo has since added a variety of features to its products, which makes it a natural toolkit for creating visibility and momentum: (a) users can leave comments on a particular post formulating a discussion thread like those in online discussion forums; (b) users may exchange private messages when both users follow each other; and (c) users can post not only textual messages but also pictures and video clips.

Independent candidates are sensitive to changes in technology and political contexts. Once technological arrangements change, political actors adjust their behaviors accordingly. Independent candidates set up their Weibo accounts, announce their candidacy online, offer viewpoints on different social issues, and, to some extent, use mobilization strategies to gather public support. Different from the pre-Internet era, when campaigning required many offline efforts for reaching out to only a limited number of voters, nowadays candidates can rely on new media to get their messages out and to interact with voters and other candidates.

Weibo, along with its technical features, has made a considerable impact on Chinese politics since its inception in August 2009. Chinese users use Weibo for acquiring alternative news information, fulfilling emotional needs, and expressing their voices (Zhang & Pentina, 2012). Echoing Western scholars' research findings on new communication technologies and social movements, Chinese researchers find that convenience and low cost make Weibo a great tool for collective action (Huang & Sun, 2014). The speed with which information is transmitted on Weibo presents a new challenge to the Chinese government (Sullivan, 2014). But the government is adapting quickly and utilizing social media to its own advantage (Poell, de Kloet, & Zeng, 2014; Sullivan, 2014). Bamman, O'Connor, and Smith (2012) analyzed deletion practices in Chinese social media and demonstrated that politically sensitive terms have anomalously higher rates of deletion.

Given the restrained political and media environment, how do political actors make use of the new technologies? Previous studies of China's LPC elections have been primarily centered on the election law, the control mechanism of the government, and voting behavior (Chen & Zhong, 2002; Shi, 1999). Candidates' campaigning activities and advocacy strategies have received little scholarly attention. Although political science scholars (He & Liu, 2012; Lu, 2012; Wang, 2013) have noticed the new phenomenon of Weibo campaigning, few have systematically examined the features of independent candidates' online behavior. Against this background, this study will first ask two descriptive research questions.

RQ1: Who are the independent candidates that emerged on Weibo in the 2011–2012 LPC elections?

Roughly speaking, independent candidates include both well-educated groups (e.g., students, professors, lawyers) and the underprivileged groups (e.g., legal rights defenders, victims of government power abuse). Given the features of media technology outlined above, two observations are expected. First, because of the low cost of setting up a social media account and running an online campaign, the threshold of entering the races has been lowered and therefore the demographics of independent candidates in the 2011–2012 elections should be more diverse compared to the demographics of the independent candidates, who were mainly university students, in the early 1980s. Second, even if media technologies offer opportunities to everyone, inequality still exists, especially in a country where a serious rural-urban digital divide exists (Harwit, 2004; Xia & Lu, 2008). By the end of 2012, the average Internet penetration rate in urban areas (59.1%) was over 35 points higher than that in rural areas (23.7%),[3] but in 2007, the gap was approximately 20 percentage points, suggesting a widening divide.[4] Therefore, it is expected that most independent candidates who campaigned on Weibo were from cities rather than rural areas.

RQ2: How did independent candidates use social media to reach the electorate? In other words, what prominent features could be identified from their Weibo posts?

Guo and Saxton (2014) proposed a pyramid model of social media–based advocacy through examining nonprofit organizations' use of Twitter, including reaching out to people, keeping the flame alive, and stepping up to action. It would be an obvious logic fallacy to assume advocacy strategies in Western democracies will be replicated in China. Depending on the sensitivity of advocacy issues, flaming up Internet users and calling for action online could sometimes result in prison terms because of "inciting subversion of state power" and "gathering crowds to disrupt public order." King, Pan, and Roberts (2013) collected large-scale data to examine the censorship patterns on Chinese social media. They found that posts criticizing the state and its leaders and policies are not more likely to be censored. However, posts that call for collective action are most likely to be deleted from the cyberspace. Therefore, assuming that the independent candidates are "rational" actors, they would take a more conservative approach to the election: spending time and space discussing social issues on social media rather than mobilizing the public.

It is noteworthy to mention that not all candidates campaign with similar strategies. Lei (2013) argues that candidates of value-rationality aim at promotion of democratic practice and their bestowed rights written in the Constitution whereas candidates of goal-rationality attempt to boost their economic, political, and social status. Based on such conceptual differentiation, three types of candidates could be identified: idealists (i.e., value-rationalists), utilitarians (i.e., goal-rationalists), and legal rights defenders, who are neither value-rationalists nor goal-rationalists (Lei, 2013). He (2008, 2010), based on his observation of LPC elections in rural areas, distinguished four types of candidates: idealist intellectuals, legal rights defenders, heads of state-owned sectors, and grassroots elites. Idealists include professors, teachers, students, and lawyers; legal rights defenders include the unemployed, property owners, peasants, and professional human rights activists; heads of state-owned sectors include leaders of government departments, public-sectors, and companies; and grassroots elites include private entrepreneurs, village heads, and local party secretaries. Therefore, the following research question will be proposed:

RQ3: How do candidates of different backgrounds differ in terms of their social media behaviors?

Candidates of different backgrounds joined the races, and their strategies of campaigning might differ greatly. Independent candidates' motivations and campaign strategies are highly interrelated to their demographic features (He, 2010). Idealists avoid confrontation with the authorities, keep themselves away from foreign journalists, and campaign on their own; utilitarians try to maintain a good relationship with the government, and they are open to striking a deal with the government; and legal rights defenders seek collaboration with other candidates and confront the authorities with legal tools (Lei, 2013). However, uncertainty still remains regarding how independent candidates of different backgrounds campaign on Weibo. It is possible that intellectuals are more likely to focus on political systems as they are mostly idealists; utilitarians might make use of Weibo to discuss issues that concern them most; and legal rights defenders expose their mishaps online through emotional mobilization. In other words, these three groups of candidates treat social media as a platform for political debate, issue framing, and muckraking, respectively. Content feature differences could be identified accordingly.

Method

Data

The data for this study were collected from online. The data collection contains three major steps: candidate identification, candidates' Weibo content downloading, and content analysis. The whole process started from May 2011, after Ping Liu announced her candidacy on Weibo, and ended in December 2012, when the last province Yunnan finished its LPC elections.

First, a name list of independent candidates running for LPC election campaign was compiled according to information garnered from three sources: a crowd-sourced map, blogs and microblogging sites, and foreign news coverage. The major source is a customized Google map maintained by participants of the elections through crowdsourcing. Crowdsourcing is to take a job usually performed by a designated agent and to outsource it to an undefined large group of people. In early 2010, an independent candidate from Shanghai, Yaozhou Zhang, created a "China Open Constituency Map."[5] The map contains information about LPC election candidates from various parts of China and Internet users can update the map by adding new names onto it. There were also keen observers of the elections who created blog sites[6] and Weibo accounts[7] to document the participants, their progress, and important events of the elections. Although the domestic media strictly controlled the coverage of independent candidates, foreign media outlets such as VOA[8] and Boxun.com have been paying a great amount of attention to the elections. Different sources suggested that about 200 participants claimed their candidacy during the course of the elections, but among them around only 100 candidates took offline actions (He & Liu, 2012).

A total of 145 names were identified through aggregating information from all three sources mentioned above. Among them, nine candidates' Weibo accounts were closed or deleted for unknown reasons and six candidates announced their candidacy on Weibo but did not follow up with anything related to the elections since their announcements. These 15 names have been excluded from analysis, and the finalized list contains 130 independent candidates. It is not my intention to claim that the list contains every independent candidates, but it contains more cases than any other existing list and should thus be considered to possess high levels of validity. Nevertheless, it is necessary to point out that not all independent candidates used Weibo; in particular, those with low Internet literacy and from rural areas tended to use offline campaign strategies exclusively. Therefore, the cases to be analyzed in this study are acknowledgedly biased toward tech-empowered candidates.

Second, once a candidate was identified, content from his or her Weibo account was downloaded and updated on a daily basis until the end of the elections. But not all Weibo posts (or tweets) were used for analysis because (a) many candidates started using Weibo long before their announcement of candidacy and (b) quite a few candidates dropped out before the election days. To avoid analyzing irrelevant content, the starting point for analysis was set to the day when a candidate announced his or her candidacy online while the endpoint was defined to be one week after the local election voting day or one week after one's dropping out. Note that these two steps are concurrent as new candidates would appear during the course of the elections.

Third, Weibo posts within the defined time bracket were then coded into a series of items. The unit of analysis was a single piece of Weibo post. Categories of the coding items include post topics, themes, and emotional expressions, and so on. After all Weibo posts were coded, the content analysis data were aggregated at the level of each candidate; for instance, percentages of posts related to certain topics and themes, percentage of posts with explicit emotional expressions, and so on. Meanwhile, demographic and background information of all candidates was collected from account profiles and self-introductions, if available.

During their campaign period, independent candidates posted a total of 97,843 posts ($M = 752.64$; $SD = 1,030.21$). The most prolific candidate, the director of a grassroots think tank, posted 5,840 posts. For candidates who had posted more than 100 posts, one-tenth of all their posts were randomly selected using a systematic random sampling method. For those who had fewer than 100 posts, all posts were analyzed. A total of 10,509 posts were coded. Two trained research assistants participated in the coding. About 5% of all analyzed posts were coded by two independent research assistants. The Krippendorff's alpha for all coded items ranged from 0.728 to 1.

Measures

Demographic variables. Candidates' gender, age, occupation, geographical location, and voter registration affiliation were coded based on the information they disclosed through their Weibo posts and account profiles. Gender was a dichotomous variable (male = 1; female = 2). Age was an ordinal variable containing three categories: young (18–35), middle age (36–49), and old (50 or above). Occupation was a categorical variable. Location was coded at the province level according to where candidates ran their campaigns.

Election and campaign indicators. Prior experience of running an LPC election campaign was a dichotomous variable (1 = yes; 0 = no). Campaign longevity was calculated by number of days between one's candidacy announcement and voting day or dropping out day. Number of campaign issues took account of the number of social or community issues candidates discussed on Weibo and promised to make a change if elected; for instance, pollution in rural areas, noises in residential communities, free student dorms in university, public transportation, and so on. Public attention quantified the amount of name mentioning of a particular candidate in the first 10 pages of Google search results. Traditional media coverage counted the number of news articles related to a candidate from Chinese media by using Google news search. Finally, election outcome was a categorical variable containing four categories: lost, won, dropped out, and unknown.

Weibo usage indicators. Weibo usage indicators contained three items featuring Weibo use: number of followers, number of posts (daily average), and number of posts with original content (daily average). Number of followers characterized the popularity of the users; number of posts and number of original posts indicated the frequency of users' activity on Weibo.

Weibo content features. Weibo content featured include five dimensions. "Multimedia elements" referred to the percentages of candidates' posts that contained photos, hyperlinks, and video clips. "Topics" quantified the percentage of candidates' posts that included election related content (e.g., "According to the election law, voters could vote for write-in candidates."), discussions related to news and social issues (e.g., "The news revealed that the high-speed train in China is in huge deficit."), and personal life and work related content (e.g., "Hello everyone, greetings from Copenhagen. This is my fourth trip to Europe."). "Themes" quantified the percentages of candidates' posts posted for different purposes: (a) expose/muckraking (e.g., "Forced eviction ended up with one dead in Shanxi!"); (b) asking for help (e.g., "To better communicate with the electorate, I need ten campaign assistants."); (c) offering opinion (e.g., "I have nine suggestions regarding the university canteen."); (d) questioning authority (e.g., "Why did the Red Cross need to spend 5 million for auditing?"); (e) mobilizing (e.g., "Voters, reject government arranged candidates. You still have a choice, that is, to vote for me."); (f) emotional expressions (e.g., "I am so happy to know that Professor Li supports my campaign."); (g) satirical comments/parody (e.g., "Our government certainly did a good job protecting us from 'harmful information.'"); and (h) explanation (e.g., "I am running for the election because I wish to do something for my neighborhood."). "Emotional expressions types" quantified the percentages of candidates' posts that contained explicit emotional expressions. Five affective states related to the election and campaigning were selected according to prior work in psychology (Scherer, 2005): angry, happy, sad, surprised, and fearful. Finally, "Concepts mentioned" quantified the percentages of candidates' posts that contained different concepts and entities related to the elections: election committee/committee staff (*xuanju weiyuanhui*), law enforcement officers (*jingcha*), government officials (*zhengfu guanyuan*), voters/constituents (*xuanmin*), candidates (*canxuanren/houxuanren*), election law (*xuanju fa*), election procedure (*xuanju chengxu*), democracy (*minzhu*), CCP (*gongchandang*), state/government (*guojia/zhengfu*), and one-party rule or authoritarian system (*yidang zhuanzheng/jiquan*).

Candidate types. Based on Lei's (2013) and He's (2008, 2010) work on candidate typology, five types of candidates were identified in the current study. Intellectuals ($n = 57$), which included university/high school students, professors, lawyers, and journalists, and so on; legal rights defenders ($n = 21$), which included the laid-off workers, property owners, and farmers who mentioned on Weibo that their purpose was to reclaim their lost rights; grassroots elites (*n* = 14), which included business owners, village leaders, and large corporation top managers; heads of state-owned sectors (*n* = 2), which included leaders of government departments, public sectors, and companies; grassroots (*n* = 36), which included company clerks and other nonprofessional jobs dealing with front-line or low-level duties in an industry or company.

Findings

RQ1 concerns the demographic features of the independent candidates who campaigned on Weibo. Around 85% of the candidates were male and about 63.8% of the candidates were young people (between 18 to 35 years old). Females (14.6%) and the elderly (3.8%) are the minorities. Candidates came from a wide range of occupational backgrounds, but the top two categories were "university/high school student" (18.5%) and "retired, laid off, or unemployed" (16.2%). Besides, "company clerk/manager" (11.5%), "lawyer" (10%), "freelancer, artist, writer" (6.9%), "teacher/professor" (6.2%), and "journalist" (6.2%) also constituted major forces in the elections. Weibo-using independent candidates were more likely to appear in economically well-off and coastal areas such as Beijing (27.7%), Guangdong (26.9%), Zhejiang (8.5%), and Shanghai (6.2%) than in less developed and hinterland regions.

Among the 130 candidates, only a tiny portion (4.6%) had participated in previous elections. Most independent candidates were running the first political campaign in their lives. The average campaign longevity was around 3 months (M = 92.55 days; SD = 81.29). About 27.7% of the candidates' campaigns lasted less than a month; 24.6% lasted more than 1 month but less than 2 months; 35.4% lasted more than 2 months but less than half a year; and 12.3% lasted more than half a year but less than 1 year. Surprisingly, only 14.6% of the candidates mentioned or discussed election campaign issues on Weibo (M = 0.22; SD = .57). Most issues focused on people's livelihood such as education, food safety, environment protection, and community services. Domestic media coverage of the independent candidates was rather scant (M = 1.97; SD = 14.03): more than 70% of the candidates received zero news media attention. About 21.5% of the candidates were featured a few times (between one and five) in media coverage and 4.6% were covered more than five times. However, the Internet gave more attention to the independent candidates: more than 60% of the candidates were mentioned at least once by online sources, and 17.7% of them were mentioned more than 30 times in the first 10 pages of Google search results. Finally, the election results turned out to be not so encouraging: 20.8% dropped out and 50% lost, and only two candidates got elected. For the rest of the candidates, their election results were not announced on Weibo (27.7%), and it is reasonable to assume that people falling into this category lost.

RQ2 concerns independent candidates' social media use patterns (see Table 6.1). Over 31.5% of the candidates had more than 1,000 followers (or *fensi* in Chinese,

TABLE 6.1 Weibo Content Features

	0 *Never*	0–20% of *All Posts*	21–50%	51–100% of *All Posts*
Multimedia elements				
Containing pictures/photos/graphs	45 (34.6%)	66 (50.8%)	18 (13.8%)	1 (0.8%)
Containing hyperlinks	51 (39.2%)	63 (48.5%)	12 (9.2%)	4 (3.1%)
Containing video clips	105 (80.8%)	25 (19.2%)	0 (0%)	0 (0%)
Topics				
Local congress elections	0 (0%)	61 (46.9%)	36 (27.7%)	33 (25.4%)
News and social issues	20 (15.4%)	53 (40.8%)	49 (37.7%)	6 (6.1%)
Personal life	46 (35.4%)	65 (50%)	15 (11.5%)	4 (3.1%)
Work related	84 (64.6%)	42 (32.3%)	4 (3.1%)	0 (0%)
Themes (functional)				
Expose/muckraking	47 (36.2%)	77 (59.2%)	6 (4.6%)	0 (0%)
Asking for help	110 (84.6%)	20 (15.4%)	0 (0%)	0 (0%)
Offering opinion	8 (6.2%)	9 (6.9%)	71 (54.6%)	42 (32.3%)
Questioning	40 (30.8%)	85 (65.4%)	5 (3.8%)	0 (0%)
Mobilizing	59 (45.4%)	65 (50%)	5 (3.8%)	1 (0.8%)
Emotional expression	61 (46.9%)	66 (50.8%)	3 (2.3%)	0 (0%)
Satirical comments/parody	78 (60%)	50 (38.5%)	2 (2%)	0 (0%)
Explanation	62 (47.7%)	61 (46.9%)	7 (5.4%)	0 (0%)
Emotional expression type				
Angry	95 (73.1%)	33 (25.4%)	2 (1.5%)	0 (0%)
Happy	114 (87.7%)	15 (11.5%)	1 (0.8%)	0 (0%)
Sad	116 (89.2%)	14 (10.8%)	0 (0%)	0 (0%)
Surprised	128 (98.5%)	2 (1.5%)	0 (0%)	0 (0%)
Fearful	124 (95.4%)	6 (4.6%)	0 (0%)	0 (0%)
Entities/concepts mentioned				
Candidates	77 (59.2%)	43 (33.1%)	6 (4.6%)	4 (3%)
Voters/constituents	70 (53.8%)	43 (33.1%)	3 (6%)	0 (0%)
Election committee	78 (60%)	39 (30%)	12 (9.2%)	1 (0.8%)
Election law	86 (66.2%)	36 (27.7%)	8 (6.2%)	0 (0%)
Democracy	90 (69.2%)	32 (24.6%)	8 (6.2%)	0 (0%)
Election procedure	94 (72.3%)	33 (25.4%)	3 (2.3%)	0 (0%)
Law enforcement officers	115 (88.5%)	12 (9.2%)	2 (1.5%)	1 (0.8%)
State/government	105 (80.8%)	13 (10%)	2 (1.5%)	0 (0%)
CCP	116 (89.2%)	11 (8.5%)	3 (2.3%)	0 (0%)
Government officials	118 (90.8%)	12 (9.2%)	0 (0%)	0 (0%)
Authoritarian system	119 (91.5%)	11 (8.5%)	0 (0%)	0 (0%)

which means "fans"), and about 22.3% had more than 10,000 followers. The rest had fewer than 1,000 followers. The median was 1,166.5. Compared with celebrities, who usually have millions of followers, the numbers seems rather small. But considering the fact that a few thousand votes could help win representative seats, these candidates possessed a fair amount of supporters online. To a certain extent, the abundance of followers could be seen as the result of active campaign efforts. Most candidates were very active on Weibo. On average, they posted about seven tweets a day ($M = 7.37$; $SD = 17.37$). But, not all of these posted messages were original. Some were merely "re-tweets." Counting only posts with original content, they posted as many as five posts a day ($M = 5.26$; $SD = 13.13$). The correlation between online activity and one's number of followers is .523 (Spearman's rho,[9] $p < .001$). In other words, being active online is associated with popularity. However, it is not possible to ascertain the direction of causality due to the lack of temporal data.

In addition to Weibo-use frequency, five dimensions of content features were analyzed. More than 60% of the candidates included picture/photo/graphs or hyperlinks in their Weibo posts. The use of video clips was not prevalent; only 19.2% of the candidates embedded video clips in their posts. With regard to topics, all candidates discussed local congress elections, but the majority (74.6%) of them contributed less than half of the posts to this topic. About 86.4% of the candidates discussed news and social issues, 64.6% discussed personal life topics, and 35.4% discussed work-related topics.

Speaking of the themes of these posted messages, a large majority of the posts were aimed at offering personal opinions: 86.9% of the candidates devoted more than half of their posts to offering opinions on various topics. The next three top-ranked functions were questioning authority, muckraking, and mobilization: about 70% of the candidates had questioned authorities on different issues; more than 60% of the candidates posted muckraking information; and more than 50% of them used Weibo to mobilize potential voters. The themes that appeared relatively less frequently were cynical comments and asking for help.

Although explicit emotional expressions were few and far between, anger seemed to be the most frequently expressed emotion. About 26.9% of the candidates expressed anger on Weibo. A small portion of the candidates also expressed sadness and happiness but surprise and worry were rarely seen.

In terms of the election-related keywords, concepts akin to the elections were seen far more frequently than concepts related to the government and political system. For instance, the concepts mentioned most frequently were voters/constituents, candidates, election committee/committee staff, and election law. In contrast, discussions of the authoritarian system, government officials, CCP, and state/government were less popular. One exception was democracy; more than 30% of the candidates mentioned this in their Weibo posts. Interestingly, law enforcement officers (i.e., policemen) were mentioned by about 10% of the candidates.

RQ3 concerns the differences in candidates' campaigning behavior on Weibo across candidate types (see Table 6.2). Since the "heads of state-owned sectors" category only contained two cases, they were excluded from the analysis. Overall, only a few items demonstrated meaningful differences among four types of candidates. First, legal rights defenders seemed to run shorter campaigns than other types of candidates. On average, their campaigns lasted about 52 days while others' were longer than 3 months. Second, intellectuals and legal rights defenders tweeted more about the elections than grassroots elites. About 40% of the posts posted by intellectuals and legal rights defenders were about the elections, but for grassroots elites, the number was lower than 20%.

Third, legal rights defenders did not mention work-related content on their Weibo, while other candidates on average devoted 3% to 6% of their tweets to work-related topics (see Table 6.3). In terms of themes, the data showed that legal rights defenders were more likely than other candidates to use Weibo to muckrake, to expose social injustice, and to make cynical comments, but they were less likely to question the authority. Speaking of the keywords mentioned in tweets, legal rights defenders were more likely to mention law enforcement officers and candidates, and were less likely to mention voters. Finally, both intellectuals and legal rights defenders tended to mention election law more frequently than grassroots candidates.

TABLE 6.2 Election and Weibo Use Indicators by Candidate Type

	Intellectuals	Legal Rights Defenders	Grassroots Elites	Grassroots
	n = 57	n = 21	n = 14	n = 36
Previous experience	5.00%	0.00%	0.00%	8.00%
Campaign longevity	90.81	52.33	130.93	104.36
Number of campaign issues raised	0.26	0.14	0.29	0.17
Internet attention	20.35	19.48	19.21	8.44
Traditional media coverage	1.04	8.05	1.00	0.39
Election outcome				
Lost	26	14	8	16
Won	2	0	0	0
Dropped out	15	0	3	9
Results unknown	14	7	3	11
Number of followers	12,915.70	2,685.43	55,847.14	4,899.50
Number of posts (daily average)	8.66	5.69	10.27	5.58
Number of posts with original content (daily average)	6.54	2.87	8.43	3.62

TABLE 6.3 Weibo Content Features by Candidate Type

	Intellectuals	Legal Rights Defenders	Grassroots Elites	Grassroots
	n = 57	n = 21	n = 14	n = 36
Multimedia elements				
Containing pictures/photos/graphs	9.87%	7.44%	9.68%	11.16%
Containing hyperlinks	9.16%	8.62%	12.61%	7.53%
Containing video clips	1.05%	0.57%	0.17%	0.59%
Topics				
Local congress elections	37.35%	41.49%	18.81%	28.06%
News and social issues	23.28%	15.17%	24.17%	21.58%
Personal life	9.97%	6.18%	9.69%	9.50%
Work related	2.89%	0.20%	5.58%	3.15%
Themes (functional)				
Expose/muckraking	0.47%	5.57%	0.12%	1.13%
Asking for help	0.96%	0.59%	0.39%	0.53%
Offering opinion	42.74%	31.79%	40.69%	44.09%
Questioning	6.21%	2.40%	8.72%	6.91%
Mobilizing	4.99%	6.28%	2.18%	4.17%
Emotional expression	3.77.%	3.23%	4.59%	3.81%
Satirical comments/parody	1.78%	5.54%	2.78%	2.83%
Explanation	5.83%	2.41%	3.62%	5.39%
Emotional expression type				
Angry	0.92%	3.17%	0.99%	1.58%
Happy	0.55%	0.00%	1.06%	0.91%
Sad	0.34%	0.00%	0.08%	0.77%
Surprised	0.00%	0.00%	0.02%	0.10%
Fearful	0.05%	0.00%	0.02%	0.02%
Entities/concepts mentioned				
Election committee/residential committee staff	4.73%	9.17%	4.75%	8.80%
Law enforcement officers	1.26%	8.08%	0.09%	0.48%
Government officials	0.77%	0.24%	0.18%	0.58%
Voters/constituents	11.52%	1.64%	9.80%	7.15%
Candidates	5.21%	15.05%	7.31%	6.14%
Election law	4.89%	6.65%	2.48%	1.15%
Election procedure	2.77%	2.43%	1.07%	2.28%
Election results	0.55%	0.25%	0.55%	0.00%
Democracy	5.40%	3.82%	1.03%	2.36%
CCP	1.80%	1.50%	0.89%	1.81%
State/government	1.57%	0.88%	1.02%	2.78%
Authoritarian system	0.39%	0.00%	0.02%	0.27%

Discussion and Conclusion

The rapid spread of Internet technologies in China opens up a novel space for public and political communication. Although the Chinese government has made great efforts to curb the power of grassroots activism through legal and administrative measures, grey areas still exist in which netizens can utilize the new technologies for political empowerment. This study provides a first look at Chinese social media users' participation in political elections. The results, though preliminary and mostly descriptive, led us to a couple of observations and insights.

Foremost, Weibo campaigners in Chinese LPC elections showed distinctive demographic features. Young males from relatively well-off geographical regions constituted the major force. Beijing, Guangdong, Zhejiang, and Shanghai were the four provinces or direct-controlled municipalities with the largest numbers of Weibo campaigners. As a matter of fact, only two cases in the data set are candidates who were running for seats in rural areas. Most of the independent candidates in 2011–2012 LPC elections were intellectuals, grassroots elites, and victimized citizens who were trying to reclaim their rights. This is consistent with findings from previous studies (He, 2010; Yuan, 2011).

But why did Weibo campaigners mostly come from urban areas? There are two plausible explanations. First, while the adoption of the Internet has grown fast in China in the past decade, the digital gap between rural and urban areas is still large. If only a small portion of the electorate is online, it makes little sense to publicize oneself on the Internet. In addition to technological difference, societal difference seems to be a more robust explanation. Social ties in rural China are characterized by strong personal relationships, close-knit communities, strong families, and weak social institutions (i.e., *Gemeinschaft*). Therefore, campaigning in rural areas requires much face-to-face communication through which *guanxi* could be nurtured. In urban areas, secondary relationships are more important than familial and community ties (i.e., *Gesellschaft*). It is next to impossible for the candidates to know all the voters in their precincts. Social media such as Weibo provides a platform for candidates to introduce themselves to the voters and to interact with them.

The power of the new media technologies is at least twofold: reaching out to voters and creating new media buzz. The data showed more than half of the candidates had at least 1,000 followers, which is quite impressive. Without new media technologies, the candidates might need to spend a few weeks spreading their messages to such a large group of people by distributing pamphlets. To the extent that the government clamped down on news coverage of independent candidates, about 75% of the candidates got zero attention from domestic media. Nevertheless, candidates' names along with their stories could be seen in blogs, discussion forums, and elsewhere in cyberspace, where centralized gatekeeping is relatively weak. More than 60% of the candidates were mentioned by some Internet sources.

Seeing from the frequency of posted messages, obviously the candidates were highly active on Weibo. Discussions of local congress elections and social issues were the mainstay of the tweets. Offering opinion, questioning authority, muckraking, and mobilization were the most important themes of the tweets. Interestingly, the most frequently expressed emotion in posts was anger, which reflected the general dissatisfactory mood among the candidates. In terms of the election-related keywords, terms akin to the elections were far more frequently brought up than those related to government and the political system. From a brief summary of the content analysis indicators, two inferences could be made regarding independent candidates' campaigning strategies.

First, independent candidates tried to pose as opinion leaders who could provide insights regarding various types of social issues of the day and question government authority. They expected the voters to perceive them as knowledgeable, daring, and competent. Second, most independent candidates tried to avoid political risks by focusing on the election rather than challenge the status quo. Issues related the political system were considered as "sensitive" and downplayed. Yet, in sharp contrast to elections in Western democracies, where campaign issues are the key to winning voters' hearts and minds, campaign issues were rarely brought up by independent candidates in Chinese LPC elections. Less than 15% of them mentioned campaign issues on Weibo.

Notwithstanding the generic features of independent candidates mentioned above, they did exhibit differences—in particular, if we adopt a more liberal statistical criterion considering the small amount of cases available to us. Intellectuals and grassroots elites provided more campaign issues than legal rights defenders and grassroots participants. Legal rights defenders and grassroots candidates tweeted less frequently, but based on percentage, both intellectuals and legal rights defenders discussed more election-related topics, especially about the election law and democracy. Legal rights defender stood out as cynical, angry muckrakers. Despite that, they attracted plenty of domestic traditional media attention due to the news value they carried. Overall, compared to grassroots elites and grassroots candidates, intellectuals and legal rights defenders conveyed more vivid and sharp images through Weibo use.

On the surface, if we take a look at the election results, it seems that independent candidates had a limited impact on the political status quo of China (Yuan, 2011). But from a functionalism perspective, the use of social media has empowered the public. Weibo provides a platform for participating in politics by lowering the cost of running a campaign. Offline activities incur a large amount of time and money. The toolkits offered by Weibo work better than those offered by bulletin boards, instant message applications, and text-based Web pages. Nevertheless, technologies do not favor one side or another in social and political processes. Since Weibo messages are publicly available to everyone, candidates' use of social media for campaigning reveals much information that could be monitored by the government. Currently, new media technologies do not give independent candidates enough leverage over other Party-endorsed candidates in winning the elections. Both Cho (2008) and Xia (2007) doubt that the People's Congresses will be the driving force behind democratization. But the emergence of Internet campaigning might call for reassessment of such argument. It is true that institutional barriers to grassroots democracy in China still exist. Nevertheless, in the long run, a civic and democratic culture could be fostered through campaigning with social media tools. However, the future of grassroots political campaigns in the Chinese cyberspace remains largely uncertain because the authoritarian government has quickly adapted to manage the microblogosphere and control the flow of "undesirable" information.

Social media and politics demonstrate complex relationships in different social and political contexts. This study draws preliminary conclusions with regard to Chinese social media users' participation in political elections. Future research could follow up with a wide array of questions that might further our understanding of the phenomenon. First, candidates do not campaign in isolation, especially when they are not liked by the authorities. The key feature of social media for collective action is forming coalitions and groups in order to be less vulnerable. This raises two meaningful questions: How did candidates interact with each other? And what are the consequences of such interaction? Second, independent candidates and Weibo is just one case among many other online collective actions in China. How is this case different from others? What are the differences between these independent candidates on Weibo and those political candidates on Twitter in Western democracies? Comparative studies across contexts and societies could help reveal the cross-context variation of technology adoption and usage. Third, the future success of independent candidates in Chinese LPC elections very much depends on the way local governments in China respond to the campaigns. How did the government adapt to the new media environment, and how effective is it? A thorough and systematic analysis of the Chinese government's information control measures in the era of social media could help better forecast the efficacy of various types of digital activism tools available to Chinese social activists.

Notes

1. There are five levels of People's Congresses in China: the National People's Congress and four levels of local People's Congresses. Delegates at higher levels are indirectly elected by the congresses of the level immediately below.
2. See http://news.sina.com.cn/m/2011–06–29/121922726985.shtml
3. See http://www.cnnic.net.cn/hlwfzyj/hlwxzbg/ncbg/201311/P020131127389304711108.pdf
4. CNNIC, *2009 Report on the Development of the Internet in Rural Areas* (Beijing: CNNIC, 2010), retrieved from http://www.cnnic.cn/html/Dir/2010/04/15/5810.htm
5. See China Election Map: http://maps.google.com/maps/ms?ie=UTF8&hl=en&msa=0&msid=207218016920381578262.000484cad2a623d3ded44&ll=37.649034,107.050781&spn=37.746166,112.5&z=4

6. For instance, see http://blog.sohu.com/people/!cmRkYmVsZWN0aW9uQGdtYWls LmNvbQ==/
7. See http://weibo.com/u/2149652973 and http://weibo.com/xuanjuyuzhili
8. See http://www.voanews.com/chinese/news/20111115-Grassroots-people-china-133879338.html
9. Number of followers contains lots of extreme values and, therefore, Spearman's rho, instead of Pearson's correlation, is used.

References

Bamman, D., O'Connor, B., & Smith, N. (2012). Censorship and deletion practices in Chinese social media. *First Monday, 17*(3). doi:10.5210/fm.v17i3.3943

Branigan, T. (2011, September 19). China's boom in "citizen candidates" sparks backlash. *Guardian.* Retrieved from http://www.theguardian.com/world/2011/sep/19/china-citizen-candidates-clampdown

Chen, J., & Zhong, Y. (2002). Why do people vote in semicompetitive elections in China? *Journal of Politics, 64*(1), 178–197.

Chinese Constitution. (1982). Constitution of the People's Republic of China. Retrieved from http://english.people.com.cn/constitution/constitution.html

Cho, Y.-N. (2008). *Local People's Congresses in China: Development and transition.* New York: Cambridge University Press.

CNNIC. (2014). The 33rd statistical report on internet development. Retrieved from http://www.cnnic.net.cn/hlwfzyj/hlwxzbg/hlwtjbg/201403/t20140305_46240.htm

Eltantawy, N., & Wiest, J. B. (2011). The Arab Spring social media in the Egyptian revolution: Reconsidering resource mobilization theory. *International Journal of Communication, 5,* 18.

Gandhi, J., & Lust-Okar, E. (2009). Elections under authoritarianism. *Annual Review of Political Science, 12,* 403–422.

Guo, C., & Saxton, G. D. (2014). Tweeting social change: How social media are changing nonprofit advocacy. *Nonprofit and Voluntary Sector Quarterly, 43*(1), 57–79.

Harwit, E. (2004). Spreading telecommunications to developing areas in China: Telephones, the internet and the digital divide. *China Quarterly, 180,* 1010–1030.

He, J. (2008). The emergence of autonomous campaigner and new changes in the Chinese elections [Zizhu canxuan ren de xingqi yu zhongguo xuanju shengtai de xin bianhua]. *Fudan Political Science Review, 6,* 95–111.

He, J. (2010). Independent candidates in China's local People's Congresses: A typology. *Journal of Contemporary China, 19*(64), 311–333.

He, J., & Liu, L. (2012). The new features of independent candidates in China's local People's Congress elections [Gongmin zuzhu canxuan renda daibiao guocheng zhong de xin tezheng]. *Journal of Shanghai Administration Institute, 13*(4), 43–50.

Huang, R., & Sun, X. (2014). Weibo network, information diffusion and implications for collective action in China. *Information, Communication & Society, 17*(1), 86–104.

Huang, W., & Chen, J. (2011). China's grassroots democracy: Development and assessment. *International Journal of China Studies, 2*(2), 177–211.

Jenkins, J. C. (1983). Resource mobilization theory and the study of social movements. *Annual Review of Sociology, 9,* 527–553.

King, G., Pan, J., & Roberts, M. E. (2013). How censorship in China allows government criticism but silences collective expression. *American Political Science Review, 107*(2), 326–343.

Lei, T. (2009). *The logic of participation: A tracking study of Beijing voters' attitudes towards voting and participatory behavior [Canyu de luoji: Beijing xuanmin xuanju xintai yu canyu xingwei zhuizong yanjiu]*. Hong Kong: Morning Bell Press.

Lei, T. (2013). The reconfirmation of the "right to be elected": Examining self-initiated candidates in 2011–2012 local People's Congress elections ["Bei xuanju quan" hefaxing de shijian zai queren: 2011–2012 renda daibiao xuanju zijian canxuanren xianxiang jiexi]. *Journal of Gansu Institute of Public Administration, 1,* 56–127.

Lim, M. (2012). Clicks, cabs, and coffee houses: Social media and oppositional movements in Egypt, 2004–2011. *Journal of Communication, 62*(2), 231–248.

Lu, J. (2012). Social media and the political socialization of youth: The case of campaigning on Weibo [*Shejiao meiti yu qingshaonian de zhengzhi shehuihua: yi weibo zijian canxuan shijian weili*]. *China Youth Study, 8,* 35–41.

Luo, D. (2013). Independent candidates and the development of modern Chinese politics [Duli houxuanren yu dangdai zhongguo zhengzhi fazhan]. In W. Huang & Y. Wang (Eds.), *Reports on modern Chinese politics research [Dangdai zhongguo zhengzhi yanjiu baogao]* (Vol. 10, pp. 152–165). Beijing: Social Sciences Academic Press.

Lupia, A., & Sin, G. (2003). Which public goods are endangered? How evolving communication technologies affect the logic of collective action. *Public Choice, 117,* 315–331.

McCarthy, J. D., & Zald, M. (1973). *The trend of social movements in America: Professionalization and resource mobilization*. Morristown, NJ: General Learning Press.

Nathan, A. J. (1985). *Chinese Democracy*. New York: Alfred A. Knopf.

Poell, T., de Kloet, J., & Zeng, G. (2014). Will the real Weibo please stand up? Chinese online contention and actor-network theory. *Chinese Journal of Communication, 7*(1), 1–18.

Pu, X. (2012). An analysis of "independent candidates" ["Duli houxuanren" xianxiang bianxi], *Exploration and Free Views, 3,* 20–25.

Rheingold, H. (2002). *Smart mobs: The next social revolution*. Cambridge, MA: Basic Books.

Richburg, K. B. (2011, September 9). China sees surge of independent candidates. *Washington Post*. Retrieved from http://www.washingtonpost.com/world/asia-pacific/china-sees-surge-of-independent-candidates/2011/09/07/gIQAc7tNEK_story_1.html

Scherer, K. R. (2005). What are emotions? And how can they be measured? *Social Science Information, 44*(4), 695–729.

Shen, F. (2014). Great firewall of China. In K. Harvey (Ed.), *Encyclopedia of social media and politics* (Vol. 2, pp. 599–602). Thousand Oaks, CA: Sage.

Shi, T. (1999). Voting and nonvoting in China: Voting behavior in plebiscitary and limited choice elections. *Journal of Politics, 61*(4), 1115–1139.

Shi, W., & Lei, J. (1999). *Direct elections: The system and procedure [Zhijie xuanju: xitong he chengxu]*. Beijing: Chinese Academy of Social Sciences Press.

Sullivan, J. (2014). China's Weibo: Is faster different? *New Media & Society, 16*(1), 24–37.

Velasquez, A., & LaRose, R. (2014, January 7). Youth collective activism through social media: The role of collective efficacy. *New Media & Society*. doi:10.1177/1461444813518391

Wang, P. (2013). Electorate preference, new media use, and self-initiated political participation: Thoughts on young independent candidates in LPC elections [Xuanju pianhao, xinmeiti yunyong yu zizhu zhengzhi canyu: dui qingnian duli canxuan renda daibiao de guancha sikao]. *China Youth Study, 1,* 29–113.

Wines, J. (2011, June 9). China appears to be moving to halt grassroots candidates. *New York Times*. Retrieved from http://www.nytimes.com/2011/06/10/world/asia/10 china.html

Womack, B. (1982). The 1980 county-level elections in China: Experiment in democratic modernization. *Asian Survey, 22*(3), 261–277.

Xia, J., & Lu, T. J. (2008). Bridging the digital divide for rural communities: The case of China. *Telecommunications Policy, 32*(9), 686–696.

Xia, M. (2007). *The People's Congresses and governance in China: Toward a network mode of governance.* New York: Routledge.

Yuan, Z. (2011). Independent candidates in China's local people's congress elections. *Journal of Chinese Political Science, 16*, 389–405.

Zald, M., & McCarthy, J. D. (Eds.). (1987). *Social movements in an organizational society.* New Brunswick, NJ: Transaction Books.

Zhang, L., & Pentina, I. (2012). Motivations and usage patterns of Weibo. *Cyberpsychology, Behavior, and Social Networking, 15*(6), 312–317.

7

THE UNINTENDED CONSEQUENCES OF DELIBERATIVE DISCOURSE

A Democratic Attempt for HIV NGOs in China

Samuel Galler

In November 2010, long-brewing frustration over transparency regarding human immunodeficiency virus (HIV) prevention programs across China reached a breaking point. The Global Fund to Fight AIDS, Tuberculosis, and Malaria (the Global Fund), the main funding organization for nongovernmental organizations (NGOs) working on HIV-related projects, enacted a freeze on funding until an agreement could be reached on how to assure greater accountability for both the government and the NGOs with the management of the grants. The Chinese government had not disbursed a portion of the funding designated for NGOs, citing the NGOs' lack of accountability, and a finger-pointing contest ensued. No one could predict how long this freeze would last, and few would have guessed it would take almost 10 months for the Global Fund to resume funding again. In the meantime, while negotiations dragged on, the HIV NGO sector underwent a particularly difficult period. The majority of these groups in China relied on funding from the Global Fund, many were forced to delay or cancel projects, and a game of waiting and speculation began. The spread of the virus continued, however, and competition for grants intensified as funding shortages persisted (LaFraniere, 2011).

The dynamics of this scenario illustrate the fragility and complexity of the civil sector, while foregrounding questions about the role that NGOs should take in the fight against HIV in China. NGOs are embedded in a crisscrossing system of international partnerships, domestic relationships, political sensitivities, organizational ideologies, and economic competition. In addition to these factors, NGOs working on HIV also have to mediate cultural taboos, government oversight, and the difficulty of accessing marginalized communities. Although the organizations and missions of HIV NGOs vary greatly, these groups face a number of common obstacles and experiences. For instance, every NGO working on HIV must establish tacit or explicit agreements with Chinese state officials in order to operate sustainably, while also learning to overcome popular stigmas associated with this field. Under pressures from government restrictions, limited financial resources, and relatively weak support from domestic businesses and individuals, NGOs have had difficulty coordinating projects that address various problems related to HIV. Although there were only around one million estimated cases of HIV in China (approximately 0.1% of the population), the support network for people living with HIV in China leaves many without information or care, exacerbating suffering and making it easier for the virus to spread.

Because the HIV NGO sector includes diverse types of organizations, issues, and constituencies, it is a particularly difficult one to coordinate. The present lack of institutions that can successfully foster collaborative work represents an opportunity to improve the development of an effective Chinese civil sector that will complement the Chinese government's provision of care and social services to those affected by HIV. Information and communication technology (ICT) will bring with it many opportunities to improve coordination, but this cannot be taken for granted. Indeed, the institutional set of practices and guidelines for using ICT will shape the way that ICT affects civil coordination, especially in places characterized by a relatively thin civil society. This chapter examines a case in which an attempt to create a representative coordinating body failed within this sector and interprets what this might imply for the future of the Chinese civil sector.

Dissent Over Public Networks

This section focuses on an attempt to establish deliberative democracy among HIV NGOs that was carried out in ways that produced friction with distinct features of the Chinese NGO environment. By evaluating the extent to which Chinese HIV NGOs were able to achieve an instance of deliberative democracy in the context of the Global Fund's Country Coordinating Mechanism (CCM), it is possible to identify sources of disagreement that may have led to the failure to sustain these democratic processes. Drawing on interviews from a number of NGOs involved in this process as well as records from an independent organization that participated in these meetings,[1] I will argue the following points. First, distrust toward democratic procedures produced unwillingness to surrender individual interests to a group discussion. Second, the anonymous feature of online bulletin board forums may have contributed to greater polarization via breakdowns in traditional modes of interaction that typically would involve strong reliance on personal relationships to ensure accountability. We begin with an overview of the CCM and an account from the man who took on the task of democratizing the CCM's NGO representative election.

Established in 2002 by the Global Fund, the CCM is a representative body that provides input to the Global Fund on how to distribute small program implementation grants to address the problems of HIV, tuberculosis (TB), and malaria.[2] In each country the CCM brings together representatives from different sectors of society, including the government, NGOs, the private sector, and international organizations. It also reserves one seat for a representative who has one of these diseases. In China, the disease and NGO representatives typically all come from the HIV sector (personal interview, August 7, 2011).

Since 2002, the CCM has met at least twice per year to discuss how best to distribute grants from the Global Fund for the fight against HIV/AIDS, TB, and Malaria. Much of this funding has gone to the Chinese Ministry of Health, local health bureaus, and the China Center for Disease Control and Prevention (CDC) for broad programs to research and prevent the spread of these diseases (China CCM Secretariat, 2009, p. 17). In 2007, a grant was given to the CDC with the express indication that it be used for "Mobilizing Civil Society to Scale Up HIV/AIDS Control Efforts in China" (China CCM Secretariat, 2009, p. 19). This grant would provide over 14 million USD over the next five years and necessitated discussion between government officials and international stakeholders about how best to "utilize the unique strengths of NGOs and civil society to strengthen and fill gaps in existing AIDS control programs and . . . fill gaps in prevention efforts aimed at key vulnerable populations that are either not reached or under-served by existing interventions"(China CCM Secretariat, 2009, p. 19). Because of the current emphasis on the civil sector, the NGO representative has become an extremely influential seat on the CCM.

In China, NGOs and government officials have had mixed success in collaboration. In spite of some upward feedback and information flowing from NGOs to the government, when organizations have convened these two groups either in meetings or online correspondence, proximity has often led to the formation of negative impressions and loss of trust in the NGO sector. This has been particularly salient following an incident in the CCM, which involved abuse of democratic procedures and a failure to determine election procedures for the NGO sector (containing registered and unregistered groups).

This chapter argues that the use of Internet technology for deliberation among Chinese HIV NGOs actually contributed to the failure to establish democratic practices within a hierarchical and fragmented Chinese NGO environment. Second, it proposes an explanation for this failure that hinges on the role of relationship tension in the production of this conflict and considers the effects of these relationships and previous organizational tendencies alongside Habermas's theory on communicative action. This analysis has important implications for the future of deliberative democracy in China and suggests areas of improvement for governance and norms-setting in these types of forums.

Election Politics in the Country Coordinating Mechanism

One of my informants, a lawyer who graduated from a prestigious Chinese law school and a former visiting scholar at Columbia University, was a driving force behind efforts to democratize the CCM. He criticized the CCM for its nondemocratic procedures and was heavily involved in helping organize its first election in 2006. He saw his work as the realization of a long-held dream of transforming Chinese governance (personal interview, August 7, 2011). He took pride in his accomplishments in trying to democratize the NGO sector and currently publishes an independent monthly report on the activities of the CCM. However, he expressed frustration with the fact that reforms he had introduced to the CCM had been reversed.

Since the creation of the China CCM in 2002, this representative body suffered from problems of low efficiency and poor governance (Jia, 2009, p. 1), and the representatives were not being elected by their own sector, a stipulation from the Global Fund for all CCM organizations (personal interview, August 7, 2011). Rather, the government refused to allow NGO representatives who might challenge government opinions and would simply choose a representative from the NGO sector by appointment (Jia, 2009, p. 1). Thus, in 2005, a working group was established, which designed a new plan to adjust the structure of the CCM, with the primary change of allowing members from the NGO sector to elect their own representatives to the CCM. My informant successfully convened a series of meetings during which the procedures for electing representatives of the NGO sector to the CCM were established and approved.

Controversy arose over how to divide up constituencies of NGOs into representative categories. The first debate centered on whether NGOs should be divided by province or by sector (e.g., men who have sex with men [MSM], injection drug users [IDU], etc.). NGOs representatives from Henan argued that they deserved a greater number of representatives, due to the high prevalence of HIV in the province (Jia, 2009, p. 15). My informant was the convener of the meeting and successfully argued for sectoral representation, emphasizing the point that "[s]ex workers, IDU or TB related NGOs are far fewer in number, even though the number of people affected by HIV/AIDS, TB and malaria in these communities is disproportionately large" (Jia, 2009, p. 1). Ultimately, in order to best represent the diversity of communities served by HIV NGOs, the small groups discussing the issue agreed to this sectoral model, with NGO representatives serving each type of high-risk population. Following the determination of electorate divisions, in April 2006 a meeting was convened in Beijing with representatives from registered NGOs who had signed up to vote, and my informant was elected as the NGO representative to the CCM.

After the election occurred, however, another NGO activist, named Wan Yanhai, contacted Reuters with a story claiming that the vote had been illegitimate because it had not allowed representatives from unregistered NGOs to run for election (personal interview, August 7, 2011). Moreover, he organized a group of sixty NGOs that protested the results of the election, claiming that my informant had been chosen because of ties to the government. This group of NGOs threatened to hold a separate election, which would undermine the legitimacy of the NGO sector to the international community. After negotiations between the NGOs that convened the April election and the dissenting group of unregistered NGOs, there was an agreement to accept the results of the official election, with the stipulation that the term of these representatives be shortened to one year (Jia 2008, p. 7).

For the following year, my informant characterized his role as a facilitator, hopeful that the CCM would be able to set reasonable and sustainable procedures for democratic election. He described his belief in the democratic process, its value to the Chinese system, and his early aspirations for Chinese democracy: "I thought about reform at a very young age . . . I dreamed about it—I'm a lawyer you know—all I think about every day is reform . . . and everything I do is related to this. It's a tradition . . . my grandparents were lawyers under the Guomindang" (personal interview, August 7, 2011). He located himself in a Chinese historical narrative; his grandparents were some of China's first lawyers in the republican period, and he was one of the only lawyers actively involved in the realm of HIV NGOs. He spoke highly of his own qualifications to work with the CCM, pointing out his superior understanding of HIV, law, English, economics, democratic theories, and the Chinese NGO sector.

This attempt to promote democratic elections within the CCM illuminates some of the conflicts between his interpretation of the CCM guidelines and the culture of the Chinese HIV NGO sector. Looking back, my informant stated doubts about the feasibility of democracy in this small microcosm, citing the absence of precedent cultural standards necessary for institutionalized democracy. He claimed that the reason that only a limited number of NGOs showed up to the first democratic election for the sector representative to the CCM was their unfamiliarity with elections: "The other NGOs didn't send people [to the 2006 election] for a few reasons. First, they didn't understand the democratic process. Second, they didn't have money, and didn't know what was going on" (personal interview, August 7, 2011). Indeed, other scholars have observed cultural obstacles to adopting Western-style democracy in China. One such cultural barrier is a common assumption that such deliberations are merely symbolic. Hé Baogang, a scholar of Chinese politics, cites the fact that deliberative meetings in China often do not actually influence decision making:

> In some circumstances, policy has been predetermined, questions have been pre-arranged, no materials have been distributed beforehand, insufficient time has been available to digest information and engage in authentic debate, and consultation has been only a formality to gain legitimacy and to manufacture consensus.
>
> (Leib & Hé, 2006, p. 193)[3]

Because democratic processes have been carried out superficially in many situations in China, many Chinese NGOs were not willing to participate seriously in the election. Moreover, the assumption that the democratic procedure was a scheme to manufacture consensus may have led NGO leaders to engage in protest of the conveners of the election, believing that the organizers were trying to monopolize decision-making authority under the name of deliberative democracy.

My informant strove to organize a truly democratic election, and indeed the implementation of elections to select national representatives from grassroots organizations represented a radical political experiment in China. The following year, in March 2007, the CCM held a vote that was widely recognized as successful and democratic. Because unregistered organizations were also included, there was a much higher turnout compared to the previous election in 2006: "Over 150 NGOs took part in the election process" (Jia, 2008, p. 14). In this election, my informant stepped down, acknowledging his role as a facilitator, with confidence in the future of democratic elections for NGO representatives to the CCM:

> As Mr. Bernard Rivers, . . . senior expert of the Global Fund noted, this election represents an important milestone in the development of the Global Fund. China's experience could become a model for CCM NGO representative elections in countries around the globe. The election, organized by the NGO community itself, was comprehensive, highly participatory and sustainable.
>
> *(Jia, 2008, p. 20)*

Though he was no longer the NGO representative to the CCM after the 2007 election, he remained highly involved, working for an organization that oversees and publishes reports on activities related to the CCM (personal interview, August 7, 2011). Another informant of mine indicated that this organization's goal is to increase transparency for the CCM, to ensure that it adheres to the proper representative procedures (personal interview, July 8, 2011). However, two years later, these nascent signs of Chinese democratic institutions began to falter.

In the following election, in 2009, the CCM election underwent a crisis that challenged the reputation of the entire NGO sector. First, the number of NGOs registered surged to over 400 (Jia, 2009, p. 5), and many people in the NGO community questioned the legitimacy of these organizations (personal interview, August 7, 2011). Second, the election procedures had been rewritten, greatly reducing the involvement of HIV NGOs targeting MSM populations. Third, the NGO representatives explicitly forbade future involvement of previous representatives to the CCM. Since my informant was the only person who fit this description, he asserted that this policy was designed specifically to exclude him and claimed that this policy violated the self-determination principle of the Global Fund (personal interview, August 7, 2011).

In the following election, in 2011, the NGO Working Committee, representing the seven sectors of HIV NGOs, "designated the China HIV/AIDS Information Network (CHAIN) [Web site] as the only discussion platform for notices and feedback regarding the next election" (Jia, 2011, p. 8), sparking a controversy about who would be controlling the flow of information and whether organizations would be accurately represented on this online forum. The election was post-poned, and the incumbent representative remained in his seat beyond the prec-edent term of two years. In the summer of 2011, the election had been postponed indefinitely, and the CCM's attempt at democratic procedures had been undone.

Democratic Habits and Structures

Many members of the NGO sector accused Meng Lin, the CCM representa-tive elected in 2007 and 2009, of corruption and autocracy, even comparing his actions to the violent abuse of power during the Cultural Revolution (Jia, 2011, p. 10). Meng Lin defended the need to take power as a necessary step to protect the democratic interest:

> Sometimes when dealing with hooligans you have to use methods that make you even more of a hooligan than the hooligans are themselves; only then can democracy be kept on the true path and can innocent citizens be protected.
>
> *(Jia, 2011, p. 10)*[4]

In a sector with strong competition for international funding, strong NGO leaders are often reluctant to submit to a democratic body, since this would mean surrendering their own organization's position and access to capital. As one of the only instances in which representative voting procedures have been implemented in Chinese governance (Jia, 2009, p. 5), the CCM story sheds light on challenges faced by democratic institutions within the Chinese cultural and political environment and the ways in which new networks of communication may not solve coordination difficulties.

While it is possible that the failure of democratic institutions occurred due to specific features of the HIV NGO community, this may also suggest broader structural problems. A report on the CCM's election failures attributed them in part to a lack of cultural understanding:

> In reality, these problems were merely a reflection of greater societal defects. The absence of a democratic consciousness and the absence of a democratic tradition, in addition to a lack of experience conducting and participating in independent elections were at the heart of the election's shortcomings.
>
> *(Jia, 2008, p. 7)*

Though China has not had a history of democratic governance systems, the concept of democracy has been debated for over a century in China. In particu-lar, there has been strong debate over the role of the public sphere in the reform period. Jürgen Habermas has played a prominent role in the thinking about democratization in China and has been frequently cited by Chinese intellectuals who advocate for "deliberative democracy"(Davies, 2007, p. 66),[5] a form of democracy in which public forums exert a strong influence on central decision making. One of the reports on the CCM directly pointed to Habermas as one of the guiding voices for the design of this particular voting body (Jia, 2009, p. 7).

Although the first election of the CCM went successfully, a conflict over these procedures in 2009 resulted in what my informant called the "Great Tragedy of China's NGOs," in which his democratic procedures were undone, and the path to democracy among NGOs seemed more distant than before (personal interview, August 7, 2011). What specifically caused this group of HIV NGOs to divide and dissolve, ultimately discrediting the entire sector in the eyes of international donor organizations and the Chinese government?

Relationship-Based Accountability and Online Participation

This democratic failure represents a confluence of forces, yet by examining the ways in which various actors characterized the story of the conflict, we can better understand the reasons for what happened. One of the most active and volatile public forums through which much of this conflict developed was online chat rooms (personal interview, August 7, 2011). While online tools allowed more frequent communication between NGOs from different regions, the type of information communicated on these forums varied greatly in content and purpose. Another one of my informants described the format of the group's communication:

> Some of the QQ lists, email lists, and chat rooms that we use to facilitate HIV NGO communication are used to share information, like conferences, inviting others to attend, etc. This is a relatively good use. Other times, people will argue over different points of view, often fighting and attacking each other on these chat rooms. There can also be name-calling; really there are all kinds of things.
>
> *(personal interview, June 20, 2011)*

These online forums, which allowed for frequent long-distance communication, represented channels along which serious public disagreements within the HIV sector were aired. They subsequently contributed to a power struggle within the CCM election process, which discredited the attempt at democratic institution building. This example suggests a need for further analysis of the effect that certain features (e.g., relative anonymity) exert on the social systems that typically govern deliberation. In this case, escalation of conflicts within the divided NGO sector represented an unintended consequence of networking the various stakeholders in this field.

Given the relatively brief history of Chinese NGOs in their current form, and the even shorter period characterized by their widespread use of the Internet, it is difficult to design best practices for online forums as a means for coordinating civil discourse. Because in this case the Internet was the space in which NGO disputes were most commonly carried out (personal interview, June 20, 2011), it might seem that online deliberation contributed to strife among NGOs by providing a space that facilitated deepened philosophical disagreements and increased polarization in public forums. Those organizing online discussions may not have been aware of this risk and thus did not take action to prevent online disagreements from producing serious consequences for the entire sector serving people living with HIV. Before democratic institutions are to be established, the tension between various forms of interpersonal accountability and the public nature of Internet dialogue may have to be reconciled.

The use of the online deliberative space to facilitate social interaction threatened the traditional role of relationship-based accountability (*guanxi*) across social networks in the Chinese CCM deliberation. Traditionally, relationships have been documented as powerful tools for facilitating cooperation (Zhuang et al., 2010, p. 142) and are part of China's strongly relations-based system of civil and governmental interaction. Indeed, relationship-based accountability often supersedes legal and rule-based constraints. Because the nature of relationships must be generally both private and personal (Li, Park, & Li, 2003, p. 147), when they are transported to a public space, and communication occurs largely through chat rooms, the power of *guanxi* to lubricate collaboration wanes. Cass Sunstein, a sociologist who has studied deliberative processes, argues that anonymous Internet forums are likely to contribute to polarization (2000, p. 71). As Sunstein points out, the relative anonymity that individual representatives from NGOs have on the Internet has allowed room for public attacks in public spaces that would likely not occur in a face-to-face setting. Thus, the concept of *mianzi* (literally meaning *face* or *reputation*) that generally regulates discourse in the Chinese public sphere (Leib & Hé, 2006, p. 193)[6] has been reduced given the anonymity of the chat room. While this is true of many cultures, others have observed that it seems to constrain in-person deliberation to a greater degree in China than in the West. In the case of the CCM election process, online forums were the primary mode of communication, and the relations-based system in existence began to fail. The weakness of Internet-based participation has been observed in industry in China and evidently holds true in civil society as well:

> Thus, given the higher compatibility of IT [information technology] . . . with rule-based governance than with relation-based governance, the former will gain more in management efficiency from IT adoption than the latter. Relation-based firms typically use IT or [Management Information Systems] merely to digitize manual work; they fail to integrate it as part of the decision-making process.
>
> (Li, Park, & Li, 2003, p. 147)

Given China's strong tradition of relation-based governance, the implementation of deliberative democracy in an online public sphere must take into consideration preexisting structures of relationship-based negotiation. Without a preexisting tradition of rules-based decision-making procedures, the dangers of transferring a relation-based system into a relatively anonymous public sphere are clear. For instance, protocols setting out expectations for orderly conduct to prevent public shaming may help regulate public discourse. Otherwise, as this chapter illustrates, disagreements may escalate and polarization can be exacerbated through these more open forms of communication.

Shaomin Li argues that because the Internet favors rule-based systems of corporate governance, the spread of the Internet will encourage societies to transition from relations-based to rule-based systems,[7] since they will gain competitive advantages from using the Internet in more comprehensive ways (Li, 2010, p. 105). Consequently, Li argues, the spread of Internet technology will "accelerat[e] the transition of [Less Developed Countries] from relation-based to rule-based governance" (p. 119). Li also argues that culture is shaped by the political and economic systems (p. 119), downplaying the role of culture in shaping the interaction between Internet use and political change. The outcome of the China CCM elections demonstrates a counterexample to this, indicating that social and cultural forces can shape the use of IT, and it is not always a force for transition to rule-based governance. Other scholars, such as Guobin Yang, have pushed back against this perspective, detailing the mutual relationship between technology and its social uses (Yang, 2003). As scholars begin to focus on the more specific relationship between technology and political change, it will be important not to jump to conclusions and overemphasize the positive effects that open communication can have.

The experience of the CCM demonstrates that Internet communication does not necessarily lead to the adoption or strengthening of rule-based systems. In this example, online conflict led to the unraveling of rule-based governance, an outcome that runs contrary to what Li's argument would predict. The influence of the Internet on Chinese governance merits further study, but this example demonstrates that the Internet may have divergent effects on thin civil sectors due to conflicts with preexisting social and organizational patterns.

Communicative Action in the CCM's NGO Representative Election

Disagreements in the NGO sector have revealed many of the challenges of importing deliberative democracy to China, highlighting the need to better organize and facilitate the process of deliberation to avoid polarization. This conflict reveals issues of publicity and transparency that must be addressed in future attempts to create representative democratic systems in China. Indeed, while this attempt to recreate democratic systems in China borrowed heavily from Habermas's theory on communicative rationality, it ultimately backfired and resulted in an abuse of democratic principles to concentrate representative power and discredit the HIV NGO sector in the eyes of the government and international donor organizations. By analyzing this democratic failure from the perspective of Habermas's writings on deliberative democracy, which strongly influenced the ways the election procedures were designed, we can better see the reasons behind the unintended abuses of democratic process that occurred.

Habermas's theory of communicative action proposes that because rationality is defined in societal and cultural spheres rather than by the individual subject, communities can make decisions that best reflect universal moral insights through discourse and deliberation (Habermas, 1992, pp. 107–109). Shared ideas best approximate rationality, Habermas argues, an idea that has motivated many Chinese scholars to argue for the development of a public sphere with open avenues for discussion. However, in the case of the China CCM election, this attempt to implement this theory did not suit existing institutions and decision-making practices, ultimately producing a reversion to undemocratic systems and discrediting the representative function of the NGO members. This illustrates a critical aspect of Habermas's theory—namely, the importance of procedures that govern communication. The new adaptation of online forums as the means for communication in this Chinese democratic experiment did not provide institutional regulation of discourse, causing polarization and disincentives to cooperation. Habermas notes that procedures to guarantee the relevance of communicative deliberation to establishing consensus are essential:

> Discourse theory has the success of deliberative politics depend not on a collectively acting citizenry but on the institutionalization of the corresponding procedures and conditions of communication.
>
> *(White, 1995, p. 2015)*

In China, the establishment of democratic institutions is complicated by the additional need for functional "procedures and conditions of communication." For NGO groups across China that are not able to convene regularly, the Internet provides a valuable resource in which ideas and perspectives may be shared across large distances. However, online forums lack regulatory systems of etiquette and orderly procedures (personal interview, July 24, 2011), and thus it may be necessary to establish procedures that will increase the Internet's ability to facilitate communicative action in budding deliberative democracies.[8] Because of the unregulated nature of information flow on the Internet, it may have exerted a destabilizing and polarizing effect on the HIV NGO discursive space.

The solidarity established by communicative action must exist alongside competing forces that serve to bring people together. In China, relationship-based accountability systems constitute one example of such an organizing force, insofar as they rely on a tacit system of gestures, favors, and gifts to maintain trust and cooperation.

The story of the China CCM reveals tension between these two types of social integration. On the one hand, one faction in the CCM attempted to create democratic procedures that would ideally enhance the traditional systems of governance that determined the NGO representative. On the other hand, others still upheld the old system ruled by social relationships and individual pursuit of self-interest. Meng Lin described democracy as a superficial sham built on the same systems of connections and corruption:

> Think of today's Chinese society, out there it's all corruption, profiteers, trouble makers . . . The field of AIDS is really very similar, and surprisingly so. Almost everyone is shouting for fairness and justice, and they're all dancing wildly, waving the flag of care for infected people, and prevention of HIV. But what is it really? . . . The government is fraudulent, corruption is clearly prevalent in grassroots organizations. . . . Behind the piercing screams of democracy, openness, and transparency is often hidden another lightly printed line: give us money. If you don't give it to us, we'll cut you down.
>
> *(Meng, 2011b)*

Thus, the CCM's failure to democratize might also be accounted for by the presence of a conflicting ideology of representation. In addition to deliberative democracy, there existed conflicting conceptions of how liberal democracy should function. This other view held that an individual representative should wield moral authority checked only at the time of the election process. Under this system, many of the organizational characteristics of Chinese NGOs can be replicated; there can still be a single actor with the authority to make decisions on behalf of the organization, thus preserving a top-down moral hierarchy. Given the way in which Chinese NGOs typically form, with an individual actor who becomes the leader of a group after an insight into a need for caregiving, liberal democracy more closely matches this organizational structure. Tong, a Chinese scholar on Habermas, comments on the moral shift implied by deliberative democracy: "Communicative rationality . . . no longer allows any subject— whether an individual or a group—to declare itself the embodiment of reason" (Davies, 2007, p. 66). Because Chinese organizations are often governed with a high degree of hierarchy, in which the leader possesses a sense of moral leadership (Li, Tsui, & Weldon, 2000, p. 86), many of these organizations have not adopted procedures that transfer moral authority from the leader to the group.

The CCM story complicates the idea that directly importing foreign democratic procedures will bring functioning democracy to China. First, the absence of democratic habits means that in most Chinese organizations there may be cultural barriers to overcome before a representative body like the CCM can implement fully democratic procedures. Second, the role of Internet technology in fostering participatory democracy is not clear—in the case of the CCM, it seems to have interfered with the usual manner in which collaborations are formed, and by bringing relationships into the public sphere, it exacerbated disagreements and contributed to the polarization of the HIV NGO community. This sector's relationship-based system of governance (*guanxi*) conflicted with the way that NGO leaders were adapting online forums for discourse, and this affected their perception of reputation (*mianzi*) as well. Third, an attempt to follow Habermas's model of deliberative discourse and communicative action under democratic institutions may have failed because of clashes with hierarchical structures and institutional habits that preserved the idea of leadership morality. Habermas explains that institutional and cultural factors form the basis for communicative action and that civil society undergirds the ability for communicative action to function:

> Strictly speaking, this communicative power springs from the interactions between legally institutionalized will-formation and culturally mobilized publics. The latter for their part find a basis in the associations of a civil society quite distinct from both state and economy alike.
>
> *(Habermas, 1994, p. 10)*

The Chinese NGO sector can claim none of these conditions; both institutional and cultural systems were not conducive to this process of deliberative consensus, and civil society remains wrapped up in state and economic constraints. The China CCM case illustrates the difficulty of direct application of foreign models for governance on Chinese civil society and sheds light on factors that democratization efforts in China must consider. Moreover, as a direct result of these failures to cooperate, the Global Fund froze funding for 10 months, affecting over 80% of HIV NGOs in China that depended on these grants.

The Aftermath of the CCM Crisis

In late August 2011, the Global Fund lifted the freeze on funding for Chinese NGOs, stating that it would continue to provide grants for work on TB, malaria, and HIV.[9] However, this good news turned out to be short-lived. The following year, the Global Fund announced that it would not renew funding for HIV in China beyond 2012, including grants that would go to nongovernmental organizations dedicated to providing services for HIV (Shan, 2011). Two reasons were given for this decision. First, the Global Fund faced serious shortages of donations due to financial crises affecting national budgets in Europe and the United States. Second, the Global Fund's decision to cut funding to China coincided with an approach aimed to maximize the impact of grants given out from 2012 to 2016, meaning a de-emphasis on middle-income countries in favor of low-income countries (Global Fund Strategy 2012–2016, 2011). Although certain areas of China have experienced severe HIV outbreaks, China's low overall prevalence makes it much less appealing from an approach that attempts to maximize impact per country. Furthermore, the 10-month funding hiatus and intense negotiations to try to achieve greater transparency probably raised doubts to the Global Fund about the value of continuing to invest in China.

Western Influence in the Chinese Civil Sector

The influx of Western influence and funding has certainly played a strong role in the development of Chinese NGOs and has allowed a small number of NGOs to follow the model of the permanent, sustainable NGO advocated by the United Nations Development Programme (UNDP) and to participate in international discussions. However, the vast majority of grassroots NGOs face multiple factors preventing them from achieving stable and sustainable operation, including difficulties gaining symbolic and bureaucratic recognition from the government (personal interview, July 6, 2011), challenges raising funds (personal interview, July 6, 2011), and challenges maintaining full-time staff (personal interview, August 3, 2011). These factors have created an environment in which governance over these organizations is weak and competition for the limited funding available for HIV has yielded conflict and disagreement rather than cooperation and compromise. As scholars studying experiments with local elections in China have observed, it is crucial to develop institutions in China based on preexisting social structures rather than trying to import them from the West: "The task of identifying and designing deliberative institutions that enhance collective solidarity without further harming the interests of the worst-off is perhaps the biggest challenge for defenders of local deliberative democracy in China" (Leib & Hé, 2006, pp. 150–157).

One of the great challenges for the Chinese civil sector will be developing institutions to provide governance over civil organizations despite strong government opposition to a strong civil society. Within this area of research there is a need to understand how new forms of communications will facilitate or hinder the development of robust civil institutions. Now that funding sources have shifted from international to domestic actors, China has an opportunity to develop its own institutions to manage the development of NGOs without dependence on foreign grant-making organizations. However, given the reluctance of the Chinese government to support civil organizations, this process will not be without obstacles. Moreover, the politically charged nature of communications in China further complicates the ability for researchers to predict how ICT will shape civil development.

Discussion

In China, a confluence of societal changes has contributed to rapid and disorganized expansion of civil society. However, due to the particular relationship between the Chinese state and nongovernmental entities, NGOs have developed differently than in other developing countries. Paradoxically, in spite of (and because of) the fact that the Chinese state regulates and pervades society to a deep extent, Chinese NGOs have developed in a space strongly influenced by funding from international organizations. Accordingly, this chapter challenges assumptions about the implications of an influx of technology and international organizations for the development of Chinese NGOs.

The story of the CCM brings to life the problems with adapting democratic procedures to Chinese NGOs due to their distinctive historical development and relationship with the state. The effects of Internet participation on deliberative discourse are mixed. On the one hand, people can communicate across great distances, more openly and quickly than ever before. On the other hand, online anonymity seems to undermine the regulatory function of relationship-based accountability systems, and in the CCM election it seems to have escalated disagreements between NGO leaders in unproductive ways. My informants' discussions highlight the fact that different interpretations of democratic systems exist and that certain features of Chinese organizational structures may conflict with true deliberative democracy. The Internet may have a destabilizing effect on both democratic and authoritarian systems, though further research will be needed to test these conditions and hypotheses. At the same time, NGO leaders may have to rethink how to better regulate Internet communication in a way that promotes consensus rather than polarization. By studying the CCM election controversy and the resultant Global Fund grant suspensions that reduced funding for tens of thousands of people living with HIV, we gain insight into the importance and subtlety of attending to the local contexts into which new forms of governance are deployed.

An understanding of the global interactions linking international organizations, government bureaucracies, and community groups will be impossible without probing the individuals caught in the middle of these networks. While macroscopic trends can lend useful predictive power, cultural specificity begins with the human experience, which constitutes the basis for this case study. The accounts involved in this controversy suggest that the online discussions through which the details of the CCM were debated deepened factions in the HIV NGO community. The sector likely would have benefited from a set of common guidelines for deliberation before allowing this disagreement to damage the entire HIV sector's relationship with the Global Fund.

Future research into the impact of communication on establishing deliberative institutions in areas with weak civil societies will give insight into ways to encourage coordination between NGOs and the development of effective governance systems. As technology begins to facilitate linkages between countries, sectors, and cultures, protocols for preventing polarization will become increasingly important, with concrete implications for both politics and international relations. Indeed, exploring mechanisms that encourage cooperation over competition within open, forum-based communication spaces presents promising opportunities for further research.

Acknowledgments

First I must thank the many brave NGO leaders who graciously took time to share their experiences with me, often allowing me to observe their offices and daily work. I am also grateful to professor Jing Jun, Mr. Zhang Jun, and

Mr. Zhang Xiaohu in the Medical Sociology Office at Tsinghua University in Beijing, for their fieldwork support and for sponsoring me to attend a number of HIV-related conferences. I am indebted to the David Roux Fund and Cordeiro Global Health Grants for covering my research costs. I am very grateful for all who helped design, carry out, and revise this study, including Professor Arthur Kleinman, Felicity Aulino, Lindsey Alexander, Bruce Galler, Grace Galler, Enid Galler, Chase Hu, Stephanie Sandhu, David Sawicki, Mikaël Schinazi, Alyssa Yamamoto, Gu Yuchen, Qu Zhi, Professor Stephen Reese, and Professor Wenhong Chen.

Notes

1. This organization publishes the "China Development Brief."
2. According to a report issued by the Global Fund, the CCM's purpose is to coordinate this distribution of capital: "[The CCM] exists to review, approve, and coordinate applications to the Global Fund; to monitor and guide the implementation of programs approved by the Global Fund for China with its members from government sectors, non-governmental organizations, private enterprises, international multilateral and bilateral organizations, and people living with HIV/AIDS and/or TB and/or malaria, etcetera . . . The CCM represents the broad participation of the whole society in tackling AIDS, TB and malaria" (Peter Dale, personal interview, July 25, 2011). The Joint UN Nations Programme on HIV/AIDS (UNAIDS) closely partners with the Global Fund as well as the CCM. Along with the Chinese Ministry of Health, UNAIDS helps organize the CCM in an attempt to improve intersectoral cooperation, to bridge the social and ideological barriers separating different sectors of society, and to improve trust between different types of organizations.
3. See also Fishkin and Laslett (2003).
4. See also Meng (2011a).
5. See also Leib and Hé (2006), p. 23.
6. This volume argues the following: "Due to the influence of traditional culture, sharp criticisms are not appreciated, and deliberation tends to be soft talk in a warm atmosphere. Participants can be superficially agreeable, refusing to deepen disagreements aggressively and productively. Participants occasionally talk past one another. There are many situations where deliberation results in false unanimity because participants do not want to emphasize how they disagree. In some cases, participants say only what leaders want to hear."
7. A rule-based system can be understood as a governance structure in which decision-making behavior is governed by written rules and codes rather than by negotiated, relationship-based agreements.
8. An important comparison must be drawn here between Chinese Internet democratization and the Arab Spring movement. While this is outside the scope of this chapter, it is important to note that in this instance of democratic governance, we evaluate the success of an attempt to achieve deliberative democracy, not the ability for the Internet to destabilize authoritarian governments. In fact, it may be relevant to examine the way that the Internet has led to destabilization in both cases, since arguing that the Internet leads to "democratization" simplifies this complex process.
9. See both "Global Fund to Resume Disbursements for Grants to China" (2011) and "China: Health Fund Will Again Finance Programs" (2011).

References

China CCM Secretariat. (2009). The Global Fund to Fight AIDS, Tuberculosis and Malaria. Retrieved from http://www.unaids.org.cn/download/China%20Global%20Fund%20CCM%20Brochure%20en.pdf

Davies, G. (2007, January). Habermas in China: Theory as catalyst. *China Journal, 57*, 61–85. doi:10.2307/20066241

Fishkin, J. S., & Laslett, P. (Eds.). (2003). *Debating deliberative democracy.* Malden, MA: Blackwell.

Global Fund Strategy 2012–2016: Investing For Impact. (2011, November). *The Global Fund.* Retrieved from www.theglobalfund.org/documents/core/strategies/Core_Global Fund_Strategy_en

Habermas, J. (1992). *Moral consciousness and communicative action.* Cambridge, MA: MIT Press.

Habermas, J. (1994, December). Three normative models of democracy. *Constellations, 1*(1), 1–10. doi:10.1111/j.1467-8675.1994.tb00001.x

Jia, P. (2008, February). Report on the election of community-based organizations and NGO sector representatives to the China CCM of the Global Fund 2006–2007. *China Global Fund Watch, 1*, 1–22. Retrieved from www.cgfwatch.org/files/pdf_e/ChinaGl obalFundWatchInitiativeNewsletter%5B1%5D_final.pdf

Jia, P. (2009, January). *China Global Fund watch newsletter, 5.* Retrieved from www. cgfwatch.org/c9990/w10045835.asp

Jia, P. (2011, March). *China Global Fund watch newsletter, 14* (C. J. Miller, Trans.). Retrieved from www.cgfwatch.org/c9990/w10047995.asp

LaFraniere, S. (2011, May 20). AIDS funds frozen for China in grant dispute. *New York Times.* Retrieved from www.nytimes.com/2011/05/21/world/asia/21china.html

Leib, E. J., & Hé, B. (Eds.). (2006). *The search for deliberative democracy in China.* New York: Palgrave Macmillan. doi:10.1057/9780312376154

Li, J. T., Tsui, A., & Weldon, E. (2000). *Management and organizations in the Chinese context.* New York: St. Martin's Press.

Li, S. (2010). The impact of information and communication technology on relation-based governance systems. *Information Technology for Development, 11*(2). doi:10.1002/ itdj.20010

Li, S., Park, S. H., & Li, S. (2003). The great leap forward: The transition from relation-based governance to rule-based governance. *Organizational Dynamics, 33*(1), 63–78. Retrieved from ssrn.com/abstract=904336

Meng, L. (2011a, February 28). Manma yu weigong 谩骂与围攻. *Huxi Jiu You Xiwang.* 呼吸就有希. Retrieved from blog.sina.com.cn/s/blog_4ba22e420101715m.html

Meng, L. (2011b, January 5). Rang Zidan Fei 让子弹飞. Retrieved from blog.sina.com. cn/s/blog_4ba22e4201017hvu.html

Shan, J. (2011, November 1). Fight will go on despite grant cut. *China Daily.* Retrieved from usa.chinadaily.com.cn/china/2011–11/01/content_14012172.htm

White, S. K. (Ed.). (1995). *The Cambridge companion to Habermas.* Cambridge: Cambridge University Press.

Yang, G. (2003, May/June). The co-evolution of the Internet and civil society in China. *Asian Survey, 43*(3), 405–422. doi:10.1525/as.2003.43.3.405

Zhuang, G., Xi, Y., & Tsang, A.S.L. (2010, January). Power, conflict, and cooperation: The impact of guanxi in Chinese marketing channels. *Industrial Marketing Management, 39*(1), 137–149.

PART II

Glocalized Media Space

Emergence, Composition, and Function

8

THE IMPORTANCE OF "BRIDGES" IN THE GLOBAL NEWS ARENA

A Network Study of Bridge Blogs About China

Nan Zheng

China is one of the world regions that attracts a high demand of news and information from the English-speaking world. In the United States, for example, a survey conducted in 2011 by Pew Research Center found that 34% of Americans say they are very interested in news from China, which far exceeds those who say the same about Great Britain (17%), Germany (11%), Italy (11%), and France (6%). On the supply side, China is one of the most challenging nations to cover by foreign correspondents because of its large geographic size and censored domestic media environment. The gap between the demand and supply of English language news about China has given rise to bridge blogs about China: a type of current event blog with authors writing about Chinese news and public opinion for overseas audiences.

The concept of a "bridge blog" was first coined by Zuckerman (2008) to describe blogs that serve as bridges between bloggers' local communities and the rest of the world. The metaphor of a bridge implies that bridge blogs function to translate and explain local media coverage and public opinion to the overseas audiences. These practices enable bridge blogs to serve as "weak ties" (Granovetter, 1982) that close the communication gaps between distant locations with religious, cultural, and political differences, and eventually help to facilitate a more informed public discourse across the world.

The emergence of bridge blogs in China is a phenomenon recognized and discussed by news media and media scholars, but the functions of bridge blogs as bridges in communication networks still lacks theoretical grounding and empirical examination. This chapter is making the first attempt to point out the theoretical importance of bridge blogs and to investigate how, if at all, they help to span the gap between the Chinese domestic media landscape and the English language news coverage and commentary on China. To answer this question, this chapter will track the hyperlinks that go in and out of bridge blogs in order to assess their betweenness level—a network measurement assessing to what extent one network actor serves as the intermediate point between otherwise isolated parts in a network. Further, this chapter will study how the betweenness level, as a defining characteristic of their bridging role in the global news arena, leads bridge blogs to adopt communication practices as reflected in the choices of sources and content structures.

Tangible Forms of Global Journalism

Over the years, researchers have been searching for global journalism in tangible forms. A review of global media studies from three main theoretical traditions will offer a critical understanding of the key assumptions regarding the global characteristics of a media platform.

One of the early studies of global media equates transnational media channels such as CNN International as a platform of global journalism, broadcasting the news to and from all over the world, thus representing a global political communication not catering to interests from any particular nation (Volkmer, 1999, 2002). The spatial reach of a media platform helps to make the global transmission of information possible. However, when the spatial reach is treated as the defining characteristic of global media, it overlooks the global features in news content. For example, these features can be found in the appearance of international news sources and the references to international issues (Ruigrok & Atteveldt, 2007), the reporting styles that manage the visibilities of human suffering stories in the world (Chaoliaraki, 2008), and the news coverage of global crises that have origins and outcomes exceeding the boundary of one nation (Cottle, 2011).

From a political economic view, media globalization is characterized by the concentration of media ownership under fewer and fewer transnational media corporations (e.g., McChesney, 2000; Schiller, 2001), therefore leading to the adoption of similar commercial production patterns and news values in news outlets across the world (e.g., Thussu, 2003, 2007). Despite the dominance in ownership of a few multinational media brands, the rise of regional geo-linguistic channels under global media brands that serve regional audiences has made it inaccurate to assume the homogenous outlook of news content under the same media ownership (Rai & Cottle, 2007).

Others have found enduring national differences in journalistic ethical standards and professional attitudes in survey studies of journalists from a variety of countries (Weaver & Wu, 1998; Weaver & Willnat, 2012), as well as the persistence of journalistic principles formed within specific national political and economic environments (Benson & Hallin, 2007). These studies of journalism practices and institutions have conducted their analyses within the national boundaries. Thus, using a national model of journalism as a comparative basis, these studies do not aim to identify the emerging global journalism values shared worldwide.

Since the above theoretical traditions focus their analyses of global media at either the global level or national level, the understanding of the increasing interconnectedness in the global media landscape is underdeveloped in these theoretical assumptions. To fill this void, I want to apply the network way of thinking and consider the discursive communication space across different world regions as a fruitful site for the emergence of citizen media platforms with global nature. In network society theory, the globalization process is defined as the intensified connections formed worldwide in the realms of politics, economy, and culture (Castells, 2008). Accordingly, what characterizes the globalization-era media system is a global network of communication formed across local, national, and regional spaces. Applying such a network perspective to define global journalism, Reese (2008) proposes the concept of the global news arena, a space that mediates the increasing mutual awareness and interactions among regional, national, and local news outlets as well as user-generated news content on the Internet (e.g., blogs, social media, online forums). Such mutual awareness and interactions are accomplished when news events and public opinions in local settings are repackaged to reach audiences in distant places; this is also accomplished when international media coverage and perspectives on local issues are informed by local views. As a result of engagements taking place all over the world, one can expect to see a global news environment in which "people know how they are portrayed, and others know that they know (or soon will)" (Reese & Dai, 2009, p. 223).

Bridge blogs have the potential to increase interconnectedness in the global news arena with a self-claimed goal to bridge the communication gap between the geographical areas they cover in the blog content and the audiences they try to reach. Based on a general observation of their daily practices, the geographical proximity and language skills of bridge blogs enable them to have access to exclusive information rising locally from a particular region in the world, while their intentions to reach audiences across the world may lead them to survey a broad-based conversation about a specific region (Zuckerman, 2008). Thus, bridge blogs enable local focus and global connections that lead this chapter to consider them as a form of global journalism.

Understanding Bridge Blogs From a Network Perspective

In network terms, bridge blogs resemble what Granovetter (1982) described as the strength of the weak tie. According to Granovetter, weak ties are social relations people form with others who do not belong to their intimate social circles, which consist of close friends and family members. However, weak ties are not merely the trivial acquaintance ties in one's social network. The value of weak ties resides in their ability to grant individuals access to resources from other social groups that are separate from their own close social circles due to barriers such as different ethnic identities, social class, divisions of labor, or geographical distance. Therefore, it is through weak ties that information and ideas can travel across different social groups that are otherwise not in touch with one another.

Bridge blogs have the potential to become important weak ties that may close the gaps in the global news arena. In network theory, the gaps between the disconnected parts of a network are defined as structural holes (Burt, 1992). In the global news arena, the structural holes are caused by the predominance of insulated national views in international news coverage. Over the years, studies have repeatedly shown that national news organizations are oriented toward domestic interests in their international news reporting, which results in international news coverage that only caters to the national interests (Chang, 1999; Choi, 2009; Kim, 2003; Nossek, 2004). The national media become a site for nations to express, and thus reinforce, their enduring values and ideologies without recognizing and engaging in conversation with other nations (Lee, Chan, Pan, & So, 2002).

This tendency to present unilateral views on international events has resulted in the lack of hyperlink references across national media outlets. A study of 28 online news media sources in 15 countries found that 91% of stories covering foreign countries did not contain links to news resources other than those based in the home country of the news site (Chang, Himelboim, & Dong, 2009). When reporting a major international conflict such as the start of the Iraq War, a total of 75% of the links in 246 Web sites from all over the world simply connected to the sites' own archives, as opposed to referring readers to news coverage of the Iraq War from other nations (Dimitrova, Connolly-Ahern, Williams, Kaid, & Reid, 2003). This national-centric linking pattern is also apparent in the top U.S. political blogs, which linked mainly to U.S. media and content created by U.S. authors (Reese, Rutigliano, Hyun, & Jeong, 2007).

In sum, the international news environment still consists of closed national news circles with rare connections in between, leaving structural holes in the global news arena. Bridge blogs play the same bridging role in the global news arena as weak ties play in an individual's social network. Bridging actors in the network can not only transmit information but also create alternative perspectives and fresh ideas by contrasting or synthesizing dissimilar ways of thinking across structural holes (Burt, 2004). Thus, according to this network way of thinking, if bridge blogs indeed are bridges that close the structural holes in the global news arena, we can expect that they will help bring information and present alternative perspectives between regions of the world that lack communication with one another.

Bridge Blogs in China

Since bridge blogs are geographically based within the nation they are blogging about, their popularity mainly depends on whether or not the location they blog about attracts overseas attention. For instance, there is increasing international attention paid to English-language blogs from countries in the Middle

East because of U.S. military presence, terrorist activities, and the uprising social movements in the area (Heller, 2005). In addition, when blogging about a region of the world with a censored media system and limited access by the international media, the information from bridge blogs is all the more valuable for the international community (Zuckerman, 2008).

China is one of the nations that provides fertile soil for the growth of bridge blogs. While China attracts media attention from all over the world, it is also one of the most challenging regions for foreign correspondents to cover. The array of rules imposed by the Chinese government has limited foreign media access to Chinese society, including the necessity to obtain government permission in order to travel around China and conduct interviews (McLaughlin, 2008). One of the first bridge bloggers in China, Roland Soong (2006), sees bridge blogs in China as a value-added service to English language media coverage of China because they provide a wider range of news stories and extended coverage on issues otherwise mentioned only briefly by foreign media. Conducting a survey of foreign correspondents in China, former CNN Beijing and Tokyo Bureau Chief Rebecca MacKinnon (2008) found that bridge blogs are commonly used as information sources by foreign correspondents in China to identify story ideas.

The Internet is an indispensable component of the Chinese media environment. In particular, the BBS forums (Yang, 2003; Zhou & Moy, 2007) and the blogosphere (Esarey & Qiang, 2008; Zhou, 2009) are two important platforms for online deliberation that provide opportunities for citizens' voices to be heard in the authoritarian regime. However, online citizen media, which cover a broad range of issues in China, are not available to outside audiences primarily due to the language barrier. Therefore, bridge blogs play an important role in cross-nation communication by providing English translations of the dynamic public opinions emerging on the Chinese Internet, which are viewed as a weather vane of public opinion in Chinese society ("China's 'Bridge Blogs,'" 2010).

Research Questions

In this chapter, I propose an analytical framework to examine how bridge blogs' betweenness is related to their communicative practices. This rationale follows the logic of network analysis, which focuses on a communicator's relationships with others rather than its own attributes as the defining characteristics for the nature of communication (Monge & Contractor, 2003). Just as one person's age and income level can be used as attributes to predict his or her consumption behavior in a survey study, the betweenness level of a bridge blog may inform the bloggers' practices in choosing (1) the type of sources to link and (2) content structures of the blog posts.

The betweenness is a direct test of the ability of bridge blogs to fill the gap between information resources that provide news and opinions about China. In network analysis, betweenness is the extent to which an actor mediates between other actors who are not directly tied to one another in a network (Monge & Contractor, 2003). Actors with high betweenness scores are those who act as brokers and interpreters of information between disconnected social groups. Therefore, the betweenness measure can be used to examine the extent to which bridge blogs fill the projected role as bridges to bring isolated coverage and commentaries about China into a well-rounded conversation.

As the defining characteristic of its role in the global news arena, the betweenness level of a bridge blog is expected to affect how they behave in their actual blogging practices. What sets bridge blogs about China apart from other current events blogs and traditional media outlets is that they aim to bring information and perspectives originating within China to English-language audiences with distinct cultural backgrounds. To fulfill this communication goal, bridge blogs may have different preferences for Chinese or Western sources: choosing to present the local perspective to the outside world or to discuss outside coverage of local issues. Thus, this chapter intends to answer the following question:

> RQ1: What is the relationship between a bridge blog's betweenness and the extent to which it depends on Chinese and Western news sources?

In their daily practices, bridge blogs attend to both citizen-based media and professional media as their information sources. One reason to examine the professional and citizen sources of blogs is that the blogosphere is a space for citizen and professional voices to engage with each other. Compared with professional news media, blogs treat news production as "knowledge-as-process," rather than "knowledge-as-product," in which blogs provide hyperlinks for readers to explore the facts and perspectives surrounding a news issue instead of presenting a fixed narrative of a news story (Matheson, 2004, p. 458). In the process of producing political knowledge and adding to the deliberation of public affairs, blogs depend heavily on professional news media for information (Cornfield, Carson, Kalis, & Simon, 2005). Studying the content of political blogs during the 2004 U.S. presidential election, Scott (2007) described their performance as "mediated reporting," since the surveillance and correlation functions carried out in political blogs are based on media sources rather than firsthand reporting. Since bridge blogs are a special type of current events blog, monitoring and translating coverage of China produced by professional media are important practices to inform global audiences about news from China. Another reason to include the distinction between professional and citizen media is that citizen media in China is largely inaccessible to the outside world due to the language barrier, as discussed above. Thus, bridge blogs have the provide opportunities to bring underrepresented citizens' voices to the global stage. Bridge blogs' links to citizen-based and professional media will reveal to what extent the communication about China is carried out within the professional news arena or expanded to include citizens' voices. Therefore, the following research question is proposed:

> RQ2: What is the relationship between the betweenness of a bridge blog and the extent to which it depends on citizen-based media and professional news media?

Beyond linking preferences, communication practices of bridge blogs are also examined through the communicative frames bridge blogs use to structure a blog post. I adopt the communicative frames that Cottle and Rai (2008) developed as the measuring framework for posts in bridge blogs in order to assess the democratic potential of global news content. On a theoretical level, communicative frames are designed to evaluate the capacity of news media to facilitate open, equal, and deliberative communication in the world, which is in accordance with the self-claimed goal of bridge blogs, to increase mutual awareness and understanding in cross-cultural communication. On an analytical level, communicative frames are the generic frames that can be used to study different content topics rather than the issue frames that are identified through the content patterns of one particular issue.

Since bridge bloggers construct their content by referring to, adding onto, and accumulating from other information sources on the Web, this dynamic nature of a blog is different from traditional media, which tend to set the boundaries of their content within a fixed structure of a news story without reference to other information sources. Therefore, I extended the scope of analysis to include the nature of the content they link to. If the blog post simply refers to other sources or publishes translated content, it is then categorized based on the communicative frames used in the content being linked or translated. Finally, this chapter will examine bridge blogs for the research question below:

> RQ3: What is the relationship between the betweenness of a bridge blog and how often different types of communicative frames appear in its content?

Method

In order to conduct an empirical study using the aforementioned framework, I selected a sample of bridge blogs about China using the following criteria derived from the definition and developed from practical considerations to separate bridge blogs from other similar genres. First, I examined blogs that write about issues surrounding China in English. Second, I chose bridge blogs that cover general public affairs categories such as social, political, and cultural issues about China and exclude those writing about special topics such as technology, business law, and fashion. Finally, I did not include blogs affiliated with professional media outlets that follow the editorial guidelines of a news organization.

Eventually, I identified the 11 most popular and constantly updated bridge blogs out of approximately 30 blogs that fit the above criteria. Although this sample is far from a true representative sample of the overall bridge blogging community in China, the 11 selected blogs may be seen as a gateway to find the larger bridge blogging community and the cross-national information resources surrounding them.

To obtain a sample that can represent one year of content from bridge blogs, this study searched within each of the 11 selected blogs and obtained blog posts published in two constructed-weeks, which were obtained by randomly selecting each of the seven days in a week (Sunday, Monday, etc.) twice between November 2009 and November 2010.

The betweenness of bridge blogs was measured through both the outgoing and incoming hyperlink connections one blog can form with other online information resources. In order to systematically document the network location of a blog on the Internet, this study adopted a publicly available online crawling tool, IssueCrawler, which was used in a previous study to trace the hyperlinks in selected blog posts (Bruns, 2007). Blog posts published in the two constructed-weeks are put into IssueCrawler as the starting points of a crawl to map an online territory that are two steps away from the 11 selected bridge blogs[1] (see the illustration of the crawl process in Figure 8.1). The network data generated based on the link-tracing process in IssueCrawler helps to measure the betweenness levels of bridge blogs.

In addition to the blog post samples that were used to measure the betweenness level of bridge blogs, this chapter obtained another three constructed-weeks sample of blog posts from the 11 bridge blogs during the same time period to assess bridge bloggers' choices of sources and communicative frames. This sample contains a total of 426 blog posts and 1,026 linked sources.

Link Type

In the coding process of link types, coders classified all the content units (a total of 1,026 linked sources) into one of the following categories: (1) Chinese citizen media; (2) Chinese professional media; (3) Western citizen media; (4) Western professional media; (5) Asian professional media (including Hong Kong and Taiwan); (6) Asian citizen media; (7) bridge blogs; (8) self-linking; (9) others. The intercoder reliability is calculated using Cohen's kappa, a conservative measurement controlling for the agreement achieved by chance between two coders (Neuendorf, 2002). The observed reliability coefficient of link types (.88) reached the acceptable level.

Communicative Frames

The intercoder reliability of the communicative frames (.73) was calculated using Cohen's kappa; this also reached the acceptance level. The following

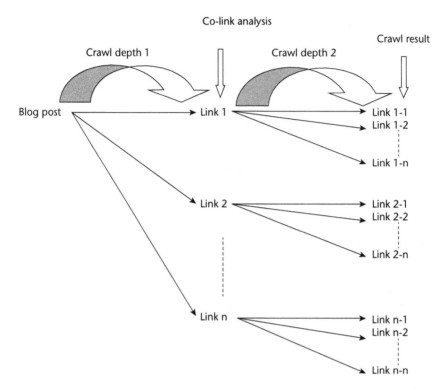

FIGURE 8.1 Blog Network Diagram and the Procedures in IssueCrawler

section provides explanations to each of the communicative frames used in this chapter.

The *contrast and contention* frame is used to contrast opposite ideas against each other or present a variety of different perspectives surrounding an issue.

Culture recognition is mainly used to help outsiders to understand issues in China with an insiders' perspective. Blog posts using the cultural recognition frame often highlight the perspectives or opinions emerging from China's society, thus providing contextualized interpretations of an issue or news event.

The *investigative* frame is found when a bridge blog publishes its self-initiated investigation on an issue or provides fact-checking on a news story produced by professional media. The investigative frame is also used when bridge blogs directly link to or translate pieces of investigative reporting from professional media outlets.

The *reportage* frame involves bloggers' firsthand reporting or experience. This is different from the cultural recognition frame, which is often written with information from third-party resources.

In addition to the frames developed by Cottle and Rai (2008), I used the following two frames to describe the basic blogging practices adopted by bridge blogs to monitor the information environment inside and outside of China.

Translation is used to capture the practice of translating the basic factual reporting of news events or information found from other media outlets. If the translated content exhibits the features in one of the communicative frames shown above, the blog post is coded accordingly instead of coded as a translation frame.

Referral describes the cases when a blog post simply refers to the content at another online source but does not offer any arguments or analysis on the content it refers to (e.g., "This is a big story in China, but this is all you are going to get in English."). Again, the blog posts are not coded as using a referral frame if the content referred to in the post fits the description of any communicative frames.

Data Analysis

The variables measuring the characteristics of bridge blogs are on different levels of analysis. The betweenness is measured on the blog level. On the level of the blog post, each post is examined for its format of communication (communicative frames). On the level of linking units, the content linked to by blog posts is analyzed for geographical location (e.g., Western, Chinese) and institutional affiliation (i.e., professional, citizen-based).

In this study, the probit regression[2] (Garson, 2006) was adopted in order to conduct this cross-level analysis. Specifically, probit regression helps to reveal how a bridge blog's betweenness level affects the probability of using a certain link type or communicative frame in the content. The variable link type is dummy-coded into four separate variables representing the four link types that are at the primary interest of this study: Western media, Chinese media, professional media, and citizen-based media. Then the number of times a particular link type is present in each blog is divided by the total number of links in that blog, to obtain the percentage for a certain type of link to be used in each blog. A similar dummy-coding procedure was used to convert the number of a certain communicative frame into the percentage of a frame to appear in a blog. Finally, a blog's level of betweenness is regressed on the percentage for each type of link and communicative frame to appear in its content.

Results

Betweenness

The betweenness of bridge blogs tests the extent to which blogs play the role of bridges between information resources that have no direct links to one another. The Freeman betweenness[3] of each bridge blog is calculated in UCINET 6. As shown in Table 8.1, CNReviews, Danwei, and ESWN have the highest

TABLE 8.1 Betweenness of Bridge Blogs

Ranking	Bridge Blogs	Betweenness
1	CNReviews	695.846
2	Danwei	651.027
3	ESWN	581.838
4	China Geeks	319.592
5	China Smack	279.425
6	Peking Duck	259.253
7	China Beat	198.049
8	Shanghaiist	182.828
9	Shanghaiscrap	130.560
10	China Digital Times	94.778
11	China Hush	74.391

$M = 60.701$; $SD = 145.818$

betweenness scores in the current sample. These three blogs are devoted to surveying and translating Chinese language news content and opinions, which are often used as the resources to provide insights on China-related news by overseas current events blogs and occasionally professional English-language media. Different from the focus of these top three bridge blogs, China Smack's betweenness level is built upon its role of providing translations of popular issues emerging from Chinese citizen media, such as online forums and social media.

Shanghaiist and China Digital Times, which serve primarily as aggregators of English language content about China, have lower betweenness scores. China Hush, which has a similar focus as China Smack to translate the hot topics on the Chinese Internet, scores lowest on the betweenness measure. Since it started a year later than China Smack, it is still building on its level of recognition on the Internet.

> RQ1: What is the relationship between a bridge blog's betweenness and the extent to which it depends on Chinese and Western news sources?

Table 8.2 shows the breakdowns of sources on the geographic origins of bridge blogs. The categories of main interest, Western (33.1%) and Chinese (24.8%) media outlets, have relatively equal proportions among the overall blog posts analyzed. Besides these two main regions that the bridge blogs tend to communicate across, they also link to their peer group (bridge blogs about China) (8.6%) and Asian media outlets (6.7%) for coverage and discussion of China.

The betweenness of the bridge blogs was found to be positively related to the proportion of Chinese sources in their content ($b = .004$; $t(10) = 11.055$; $p < .001$). By contrast, betweenness yields a significant negative relationship with the

TABLE 8.2 Geographic Origins of Links in Bridge Blogs

	CDT	Shanghaiist	China Beat	Peking Duck	Shanghai scrap	China Hush	China Smack	Danwei	ESWN	China Geeks	CN Reviews	Total (%)
Chinese media	8.6	15.6	7.1	7.1	4	68.9	78.6	61.5	48.6	28	11.1	24.8
Western media	62.3	32.5	10.7	39.3	48	4.4	0	16.7	14.9	32	33.3	33.1
Bridge blogs	6.4	11.4	1.8	28.6	6	6.7	0	12.8	2.7	4	22.2	8.6
Self-linking	7.3	30.9	8.9	10.7	20	8.9	12.5	7.7	1.4	28	22.2	17.5
Asian media	3.6	8.1	16.1	0	0	0	0	1.3	27	0	0	6.7
Others	11.8	1.6	55.4	4.3	22	11.1	8.9	0	5.4	8	11.1	9.3
Total (%)	100	100	100	100	100	100	100	100	100	100	100	100
N	220	385	56	28	50	45	56	78	74	25	9	1,026

proportion of Western sources ($b = -.001$; $t(10) = -4.159$; $p < .001$). It indicates that bridge blogs playing a more important intermediary role in the network are more likely to go to Chinese sources for information and opinion, whereas bridge blogs that are less likely to mediate between other sites in the network depend more on Western sources.

> RQ2: What is the relationship between a bridge blog's betweenness and the extent to which it depends on citizen-based media and professional news media?

Table 8.3 shows the distribution of professional and citizen-based media links in bridge blogs' content. Overall, about half of the links (47.9%) are going to professional media sites, while only about one-fourth (25.3%) point to citizen-based media.

Using probit regression, the betweenness of bridge blogs is found to be negatively related to the proportion of links to professional media outlets ($b = -.004$; $t(10) = -5.805$, $p < .001$). There is a significant positive relationship found between the betweenness and the proportion of links to the citizen-based media outlets ($b = .002$; $t = 7.378$; $p < .001$). It shows that bridge blogs that are important liaisons in the network have higher proportions of links going to citizen media outlets, but have a lower proportion of links to professional media sites.

> RQ3: What is the relationship between a bridge blog's betweenness and how often different types of communicative frames appear in its content?

Overall, the most commonly used communicative frame among bridge blogs is the referral (54.7%), which means more than half of the posts just make reference to factual information or quote an opinion from other sources on the Web (see Table 8.4). The next most common practice of bridge blogs is to translate Chinese content into English (16.8%). In the overall blog post sample, bridge blogs rarely present or link to the content in reportage (6.1%), cultural recognition (4.5%), contrast/contest (4%), and investigative reporting (2.7%) frames.

The level of betweenness of bridge blogs yields a significant positive relationship with the proportion of translation frames ($b = .004$; $t = 10.065$; $p < .001$). In contrast, the betweenness is found to be negatively related to the proportion of referral frames ($b = -.003$; $t = -7.714$; $p < .001$). The level of betweenness of bridge blogs is not a significant predictor of contrast/contest frames ($p = .513$), cultural recognition frames ($p = .768$), reportage frames ($p = .185$), and investigative frames ($p = .333$). These findings show that bridge blogs that are important bridges among isolated information sources about China tend to translate more Chinese content into English but are less likely to simply refer readers to other information sources.

TABLE 8.3 Institutional Affiliation of Links in Bridge Blogs

	CDT	Shanghaiist	China Beat	Peking Duck	Shanghai scrap	China Hush	China Smack	Danwei	ESWN	China Geeks	CN Reviews	Total (%)
Professional media	70	39	30.4	39.3	42	48.9	12.5	62.8	64.9	40	22.2	47.9
Citizen media	10.9	28.6	5.4	35.7	16	31.1	66.1	29.5	28.4	24	44.4	25.3
Self-linking	7.3	30.9	8.9	10.7	20	8.9	12.5	7.7	1.4	28	22.2	17.5
Others	11.8	1.6	55.4	14.3	22	11.1	8.9	0	5.4	8	11.1	9.3
Total (%)	100	100	100	100	100	100	100	100	100	100	100	100
N	220	385	56	28	50	45	56	78	74	25	9	1,026

TABLE 8.4 Communicative Frames in Bridge Blogs

	CDT	Shanghaiist	China Beat	Peking Duck	Shanghai scrap	China Hush	China Smack	Danwei	ESWN	China Geeks	CN Reviews	Total (%)
Contest/contrast	1.3	1.6	0	16.7	20	11.1	23.8	6.5	2.2	0	0	4
Cultural recognition	2	3.1	7.1	8.3	0	22.2	14.3	3.2	0	9.1	40	4.5
Reportage	2.6	10.2	21.4	0	40	0	4.8	0	0	9.1	20	6.1
Investigative	2	3.1	0	0	0	0	0	3.2	4.4	18.2	0	2.7
Referral	88.2	52.8	57.1	58.3	20	11.1	19	38.7	11.1	18.2	20	54.7
Translation	2	.8	0	0	0	50	38.1	41.9	80	36.4	20	16.8
Others	2	28.3	14.3	16.7	20	5.6	0	6.5	2.2	9.1	0	11.2
Total (%)	100	100	100	100	100	100	100	100	100	100	100	100
N	152	127	14	12	10	18	21	31	45	11	5	446

Conclusion and Discussion

This chapter emphasizes interconnectedness emerging at or across the local, national, and regional media landscapes as the essential characteristic that defines global journalism. The main contribution of this chapter provides theoretical grounding and empirical examination of a tangible form of global journalism: bridge blogs. Broadly speaking, the impact of bridge blogs lies in their location within a larger communication network: the global news arena, a news gathering and distributing network marked by the quality of facilitating mutual awareness and understanding that transcends national boundaries (Reese, 2010). As one component of the global news arena, bridge blogs help to intensify the quality of interconnectivity within this arena by breaking away from the national insularity and boundary between professional and citizen media to create a broader market of news and commentary to inform global audiences about a region of the world.

The empirical findings in this chapter suggest that bridge blogs that play a more important bridging role refer more to Chinese media as opposed to Western media. It shows that bridge blogs have the potential to raise awareness about Chinese public affairs and citizens' voices to a larger global audience. This increased transparency can contribute to the global visibility and understanding of public affairs in China and make it more difficult for the Chinese government to hide its wrongdoing or social unrest from the outside world. As professional news organizations cut resources for foreign bureaus, bridge blogs about China have become one of the emerging online citizen-based media formats that have begun to complement and compete with the professional news coverage of foreign affairs, thus enriching the information and broadening the perspectives that world audiences can receive about news happening in distant places (Hamilton & Jenner, 2004; Trammel & Perlmutter, 2007).

When testing the relationship between the betweenness level of bridge blogs and the choices of content structures, the findings show that bridge blogs with higher betweenness scores have a higher proportion of posts providing English translations of Chinese media content and a lower proportion of posts using referral practices. Apparently, the translation of Chinese content—which contributes more to the flow of information and views from China to the outside world—is valued more by bridge blogs that are important for interconnecting actors in the network. These findings help to confirm the self-claimed bridging role of bridge blogs in the global news arena; they help overseas audiences gain access to information about China that is otherwise not available to them due to cultural and language barriers.

This study has opened promising directions for future studies. First, the varying preferences of link types and communication structures found in different bridge blogs call for a further understanding of the implications of different bridging functions. Second, this study is based on the online network of bridge blogs. In the future, inquiries into bridge blogs need to look into the offline network of bridge blogs. The offline network that shows how bridge blogs cooperate with other media organizations, activist groups, NGOs, and so on across national borders can further illustrate the potential of the social network behind bridge blogs to facilitate a global public sphere, as well as the contribution of bridge blogs to the democratic process in China.

Notes

1. IssueCrawler first traced the 310 blog posts in the current sample and retrieved the Web pages that these blog posts linked to. Then, only those pages linked by at least two blog posts were retained. The retained Web pages represent a group of information resources that are common points of references for at least two blog posts in the sample. This process is performed in order to eliminate sites that appear in the network only by chance. In the next step, IssueCrawler traced the links in these retained Web pages and the original sample of blog posts to fetch another layer of Web pages. The second crawling cycle further broadened the network and surrounded the sample bridge blogs. This network includes not only the sample bridge blogs and the community of information resources they refer to but also the Web pages linked to by the community of information resources surrounding bridge blogs. Finally, this network was constructed based on the results from the second round of crawling.
2. The probit regression is often conducted to see the effect of independent variables on the likelihood of a binary outcome to occur. The dependent variable in probit regression models is the probability for a desired binary outcome to occur under a particular level of an independent variable. The number of a binary response is counted under each condition of independent variable. Then, this count is divided by the total number of cases that are under each independent variable condition in order to calculate the percentage for that response to take place among these cases.
3. Freeman betweenness is the sum of probabilities for an actor to go between any pair of actors in a network (Scott, 2000). For example, the Freeman betweenness of actor A is calculated as follows in the network analysis software UCINET: first, UCINET counts the paths between any two actors in a network. Second, among all these paths, it identifies the number of paths that go through actor A. Third, the possibility for actor A to go between any two actors can be calculated by dividing the number of paths going through A by the total number of paths. Finally, the Freeman betweenness of actor A is the sum of possibilities for A to go between any pair of actors in a network.

References

Benson, R., & Hallin, D. C. (2007). How states, markets and globalization shape the news. *European Journal of Communication, 22*(1), 27–48. doi:10.1177/0267323107073746

Bruns, A. (2007). Methodologies for mapping the political blogosphere: An exploration using the IssueCrawler research tool. *First Monday, 12*(5). Retrieved from http://eprints.qut.edu.au/7832/

Burt, R. S. (1992). *Structural holes: The social structure of competition.* Cambridge, MA: Harvard University Press.

Burt, R. S. (2004). Structural holes and good ideas. *American Journal of Sociology, 110*(2), 349–399. doi:10.1086/421787

Castells, M. (2008). The new public sphere: Global civil society, communication networks, and global governance. *ANNALS of the American Academy of Political and Social Science, 616*(1), 78–93. doi:10.1177/0002716207311877

Chang, K. (1999). Auto trade policy and the press: Auto elite as a source of the media agenda. *Journalism and Mass Communication Quarterly, 76*(2), 312–324. doi:10.1177/107769909907600209

Chang, T., Himelboim, I., & Dong, D. (2009). Open global networks, closed international flows: World system and political economy of hyperlinks in cyberspace. *International Communication Gazette, 71*(3), 137–159. doi:10.1177/1748048508100910

China's "bridge blogs" show great firewall's other side. (2010, February 21). *Independent*. Retrieved from http://www.independent.co.uk/news/media/chinas-bridge-blogs-show-great-firewalls-other-side-1906068.html

Choi, J. (2009). Diversity in foreign news in US newspapers before and after the invasion of Iraq. *International Communication Gazette, 71*(6), 525–542. doi:10.1177/1748048509339788

Chouliaraki, L. (2008). The symbolic power of transnational media. *Global Media and Communication, 4*(3), 329–351. doi:10.1177/1742766508096084

Cornfield, M., Carson, J., Kalis, A., & Simon, S. (2005). Buzz, blogs, and beyond. Retrieved from http://www.pewtrusts.org/uploadedFiles/wwwpewtrustsorg/News/Press_Releases/Society_and_the_Internet/PIP_Blogs_051605.pdf

Cottle, S. (2011). Taking global crises in the news seriously: Notes from the dark side of globalization. *Global Media & Communication, 7*(2), 77–95. doi:10.1177/1742766511410217

Cottle, S., & Rai, M. (2008). Global 24/7 news providers: Emissaries of global dominance or global public sphere? *Global Media and Communication, 4*(2), 157–181. doi:10.1177/1742766508091518

Dimitrova, D. V., Connolly-Ahern, C., Williams, A. P., Kaid, L. L., & Reid, A. (2003). Hyperlinking as gatekeeping: Online newspaper coverage of the execution of an American terrorist. *Journalism Studies, 4*(3), 401–414. doi:10.1080/14616700306488

Esarey, A., & Qiang, X. (2008). Political expression in the Chinese blogosphere: Below the radar. *Asian Survey, 48*(5), 752–772. doi:10.1525/AS.2008.48.5.752

Garson, D. (2006). Probit and logit response models. *Statnotes: Topics in Multivariate Analysis*. Retrieved from http://faculty.chass.ncsu.edu/garson/PA765/probit.htm

Granovetter, M. (1982). The strength of weak ties: A network theory revisited. *Sociology Theory, 1*, 105–130. doi:10.2307/202051

Hamilton, J. M., & Jenner, E. (2004). Redefining foreign correspondence. *Journalism, 5*(3), 301–321. doi:10.1177/1464884904044938

Heller, Z. (2005). Building blogs. *AlterNet*. Retrieved from http://www.alternet.org/media/21316?page = 1

Kim, K. K. (2003). It's all about trade: United States press coverage of cigarette export talks and policy. *Mass Communication and Society, 6*(1), 75. doi:10.1207/S15327825MCS0601_6

Lee, C.-C., Chan, J. M., Pan, Z., & So, C.Y.K. (2002). *Global media spectacle: News war over Hong Kong*. Hong Kong: Hong Kong University Press.

MacKinnon, R. (2008). Blogs and China correspondence: Lessons about global information flows. *Chinese Journal of Communication, 1*(2), 242–257. doi:10.1080/17544750802288081

Matheson, D. (2004). Weblogs and the epistemology of news: Some trends in online journalism. *New Media & Society, 6*(4), 443–467. doi:10.1177/146144804044329

McChesney, R. W. (2000). *Rich media, poor democracy*. Urbana: University of Illinois Press.

McLaughlin, K. E. (2008, June/July). A bad omen. *American Journalism Review*. Retrieved from http://www.ajr.org/Article.asp?id=4534

Monge, P. R., & Contractor, N. S. (2003). *Theories of communication networks*. Oxford: Oxford University Press.

Neuendorf, K. A. (2002). *The content analysis guidebook*. Thousand Oaks, CA: SAGE.

Nossek, H. (2004). Our news and their news: The role of national identity in the coverage of foreign news. *Journalism, 5*(3), 343–368. doi:10.1177/1464884904044941

Pew Research Center. (2011). Friend or foe? How Americans see China. Retrieved from http://www.pewresearch.org/2011/01/13/friend-or-foe-how-americans-see-china/

Rai, M., & Cottle, S. (2007). Global mediations: On the changing ecology of satellite television news. *Global Media and Communication, 3*(1), 51–78. doi:10.1177/1742766507074359

Reese, S. (2008). Theorizing a globalized journalism. In M. Löffelholz, D. Weaver, & A. Schwarz (Eds.), *Global journalism research: Theories, methods, findings, future* (pp. 240–252). London: Blackwell.

Reese, S. (2010). Journalism and globalization. *Sociology Compass, 4*(2), 1–10. doi:10.1111/j.1751-9020.2010.00282.x

Reese, S., & Dai, J. (2009). Citizen journalism in the global news arena: China's new media critics. In S. Allan & E. Thorsen (Eds.), *Citizen journalism: Global perspectives* (pp. 221–231). New York: Peter Lang.

Reese, S., Rutigliano, L., Hyun, K., & Jeong, J. (2007). Mapping the blogosphere: Professional and citizen-based media in the global news arena. *Journalism, 8*(3), 235–261. doi:10.1177/1464884907076459

Ruigrok, N., & van Atteveldt, W. (2007). Global angling with a local angle: How U.S., British, and Dutch newspapers frame global and local terrorist attacks. *Harvard International Journal of Press/Politics, 12*(1), 68–90. doi:10.1177/1081180X06297436.

Schiller, H. (2001). Not yet the post-imperialist era. In M. G. Durham & D. M. Kellner (Eds.), *Media and cultural studies: Keyword* (pp. 295–310). Malden, MA: Blackwell.

Scott, J. (2000). *Social network analysis: A handbook*. Thousand Oaks, CA: SAGE.

Scott, T. (2007). Pundits in muckrakers' clothing: Political blogs and the 2004 U.S. president election. In M. Tremayne (Ed.), *Blogging, citizenship, and the future of media* (pp. 39–58). New York: Routledge.

Soong, R. (2006, September 15). Influencing foreign correspondents. *EastSouthWestNorth*. Retrieved from http://www.zonaeuropa.com/20060915_1.htm

Thussu, D. K. (2003). Live TV and bloodless death: Warm infotainment and 24/7 news. In D. K. Thussu & D. Freedman (Eds.), *War and the media: Reporting conflict 24/7* (pp. 117–132). London: Sage.

Thussu, D. (2007). The "Murdochization" of news? The case of Star TV in India. *Media, Culture & Society, 29*(4), 593–611. doi:10.1177/0163443707076191

Trammel, K. S. & Perlmutter, D. D. (2007). Bloggers as the new foreign correspondents personal publishing as public affairs. In D. D. Perlmutter & J. M. Hamilton (Eds.), *From pigeons to news portals: Foreign reporting and the challenge of new technology* (pp. 70–88). Baton Rouge: Louisiana State University Press.

Volkmer, I. (1999). *News in the global sphere: A study of CNN and its impact on global communication*. Luton, UK: University of Luton Press.

Volkmer, I. (2002). Journalism and political crises. In B. Zelizer & S. Allan (Eds.), *Journalism after September 11* (pp. 235–246). New York: Routledge.

Weaver, D. H., & Willnat, L. (Eds.). (2012). *The global journalist in the 21st century*. New York: Routledge.

Weaver, D. H., & Wu, W. (1998). *The global journalist: News people around the world*. Cresskill, NJ: Hampton Press.

Yang, G. (2003). The Internet and civil society in China: A preliminary assessment. *Journal of Contemporary China, 12*(36), 453–475. doi:10.1080/10670560305471

Zhou, X. (2009). The political blogosphere in China: A content analysis of the blogs regarding the dismissal of Shanghai leader Chen Liangyu. *New Media & Society, 11*(6), 1003–1022. doi:10.1177/1461444809336552

Zhou, Y. Q., & Moy, P. (2007). Parsing framing processes: The interplay between online public opinion and media coverage. *Journal of Communication, 57*(1), 79–98. doi:10.1111/j.0021-9916.2007.00330.x

Zuckerman, E. (2008). Meet the bridgebloggers. *Public Choice, 134*(1), 47–65. doi:10.1007/s11127-007-9200-y

9

ONLINE POLITICAL DISCUSSION IN ENGLISH AND CHINESE

The Case of Bo Xilai

Ericka Menchen-Trevino and Yuping Mao

Twitter users discuss global political issues in a worldwide public forum. Despite being a U.S.-based company, 70% of Twitter accounts came from outside the United States in 2013, when the company claimed that it had become a "global town square" (Rao, 2013). A comparative approach is needed to better understand the different social dynamics that shape such discussions around the world. Despite their technological proximity on the same social network, the conversations of different linguistic groups are rarely compared regarding what they actually say. We examined a sample of over 10,000 tweets from early 2013 in order to compare the Chinese and English language conversation around the disgraced Chinese politician Bo Xilai. We used human coders to classify tweets in both languages by topic, and we followed the links within the tweets to outside sources to examine which organizations were most prominent. A research agenda is proposed for further examining political discussion across languages in a transnational digital context.

The Chinese government has blocked access to Twitter since 2009 (Woollaston, 2013) and actively censors China-based social media platforms such as Sina Weibo (Zhu, Phipps, Pridgen, Crandall, & Wallach, 2013). A Chinese military official described Twitter as one of the "powerful subversion tools for hostile Western forces" (Tze-wel, 2012). Despite this blockade there is an active conversation in the Chinese language on Twitter, some portion of which comes from users within China who circumvent the country's restrictions, while the rest comes from Chinese speakers outside of mainland China.[1] These users may be particularly interested in the free speech opportunities that Twitter offers.

What we are concerned with is not the identity of the users but the transnational and networked public sphere as enacted on Twitter and its interconnections with the fourth estate of journalism. Does the forum provided by Twitter open up a fifth estate (Dutton, 2009) capable of holding politicians and others in power accountable? What would this mean in an international context? Dutton (2009) argues that information technologies are enabling users to "reconfigure access to alternative sources of information, people, and other resources" (p. 2). We address the nature of this reconfiguration by examining a case of political corruption in China that reverberated around the world.

On February 6, 2012, the former police chief of Chongqing, Wang Lijun, sought refuge at the United States Consulate in the city of Chengdu (Wong, 2014). There he implicated Gu KaiLai, wife of Bo Xilai—then mayor of Chongqing—in the murder of British businessman Neil Heywood and made corruption allegations against Bo Xilai, Wang's boss at the time (2012). He apparently did not wish to bring these allegations directly to Chinese authorities. Bo Xilai comes from a powerful family; he's the son of Bo Yibo, a high-ranking official who was once Chairman Mao's regular swimming partner (Gittings, 2007). Bo Xilai's story soon garnered international attention, and discussion of the case was removed and blocked from mainland Chinese social media (Boxun.com, 2012b; Branigan, 2012). In August 2012 Bo's wife, Gu, was tried and convicted of the Heywood murder (Jacobs, 2012). Bo was jailed, pending corruption charges. He was convicted in September 2013 (Jiang, 2013), and his appeal was denied in October 2013 (Sudworth, 2013). Our data for this study comes from early 2013 after Gu's conviction when Bo was awaiting trial, and there was a rumor that his trial would begin in late January.

The United States and the West, in general, sometimes view China as an ideological or economic threat (Xia, 2006). A major corruption trial in China would receive coverage in Western media, but the connection to the murder of a British businessman gave the story additional relevance in the West. The English language discussion of the Bo Xilai case on Twitter was substantial, offering an opportunity to compare the discussion in Chinese with that in English in order to provide an exploratory analysis of this global town square.

Twitter, Spheres, and the Transnational Media Coverage of Bo Xilai

Twitter Enters the Networked Public Sphere

Each online platform has technical features and a history of use, adoption, and development that shapes its social norms. Twitter was founded in 2006 in San Francisco. A cofounder of the site describes the name's origin, "[W]e came across the word 'twitter,' and it was just perfect. The definition was 'a short burst of inconsequential information,' and 'chirps from birds.' And that's exactly what the product was" (Sarno, 2009). Until 2011 the mainstream public perception of the service was that it was filled with inconsequential information, based on the descriptions of the service by its founders and the press.

Then in 2009, Twitter was partially credited with facilitating the Green movement in Iran and subsequently the uprisings of the Arab Spring (Wolman, 2013). Whatever the role Twitter actually played, perceptions of social media changed to include the potential for political disruption. While Western democracies largely welcomed this as a way to promote the development of democratic social change (Shirky, 2011), it was seen as dangerous interventionism by non-democratic states (Tze-wel, 2012). Access to Twitter has been blocked temporarily in countries experiencing political unrest, such as Turkey (Sezer, 2014) and Venezuela (Laya, Frier, & Kurmanaev, 2014), and it has been blocked frequently in Iran since 2009. China has blocked the site except for in a small free-trade zone since 2009 (Liebelson, 2014).

Clearly, Twitter has entered the political realm, now calling itself a "global town square" (Rao, 2013) rather than "inconsequential information" (Sarno, 2009). The town squares, cafes, and early pamphlets and newsletters of old are all associated with the idea of the "public sphere." This is an idealized construct based on European historical developments in the early modern period where "access is guaranteed to all citizens" (Habermas, 1974, p. 49) and a rational-critical public opinion can be formed (Habermas, 1962/1989).

The idealized nature of the public sphere concept allows researchers studying very different contexts to use it as a source of inspiration, such as non-Western societies (for the case of China, see Huang, 1993) and online communication platforms (discussed further below). However, the idealized quality of the concept also invited many criticisms of the public sphere ideal as proposed by Habermas. Some have pointed out that the ideal public sphere has never existed: in early modern Europe, the vast majority of the population was excluded from the public sphere (e.g., women, non-land-owning men and minority groups) (Frasier, 1992; Schudson, 1997). However, Habermas (1962/1989) placed communication and media at the center of normative democratic theory, and the idea of the public sphere continues to spark many investigations into political communication.

Since the beginning of the wide adoption of the Internet there has been considerable interest in whether various new digital technologies might be able to provide a virtual public sphere. Like most attempts to measure empirical reality against this idealized vision, these technologies have largely fallen short of enabling a virtual sphere (for a review, see Papacharissi, 2009). Digital technologies do, however, open a public space for discourse, which is sometimes used for deliberation (reasoned and otherwise) (Papacharissi, 2002, 2009).

Rather than compare public discourse on the Internet to a potentially unrealizable ideal such as Habermas's public sphere, Benkler (2006) compared it to the mass mediated sphere, and he found that what he called the networked public sphere "has a capacity to take in, filter, and synthesize observations and opinions from a population that is orders of magnitude larger than the population that was capable of being captured by the mass media" (p. 261). Research on Twitter has borne out this idea, finding that although incumbent voices—mainstream media, politicians, celebrities—influence the discourse, outsiders regularly enter and gain prominence (Ausserhofer & Maireder, 2013; Papacharissi & de Fatima Oliveira, 2012).

Transnational Spheres and the Fifth Estate

The Internet and satellite television have enabled media to cross national borders with ease. International organizations such as the European Union and civil society groups have tried to use the Internet to create a transnational public sphere, unbounded by the nation-state (Cammaerts & Audenhove, 2005; Wodak & Wright, 2006). However, as Cammaerts and Audenhove observed, the idea of transnational or unbounded citizenship may be "a rather empty concept, as there is an absence of accountability, of rights, but also of duties" (2005, p. 194). On the other hand, online movements can spur action from governments feeling the pressure of international media attention as in the case of the Nigerian schoolgirl kidnapping (Litoff, 2014).

Twitter is highly relevant to journalism, as one study found that over 85% of trending topics were news-related (including political news and soft news) (Kwak, Lee, Park, & Moon, 2010). The independent press is considered to be an important part of democratic societies, and as such it is often called the fourth estate, which makes implicit reference to the social order of medieval Europe, which was divided into three estates (see Fitzsimmons, 2003). Calling the press the fourth estate means that it has significant but unofficial power in governance. Dutton (2009) theorized that online media may be forming a fifth estate, which offers an "alternative source of authority to professional expertise by offering citizens, patients, students and others alternative sources of information, analysis and opinion" (2009, p. 11). In this study we examined the resources (primarily news articles) referenced by Twitter users in addition to the content of tweets.

Media Coverage of Bo Xilai

Many English-speaking Twitter users come from the United States and other democracies and have access to the English language media, which tend to be independent from direct government control. Chinese users have access to independent and Chinese government sources. Bo Xilai was rarely covered in English language media before the allegations of corruption that surfaced in 2012, with just 35 articles in the *New York Times* mentioning his name from 1992 to 2011, and 261 between 2012 and 2013 (LexisNexis Academic, 2014). As a high-level politician and son of a famous revolutionary leader, Bo Xilai was much more familiar to Chinese-speaking media audiences.

The implications of Bo's case were often portrayed quite differently in official Chinese media than in other sources. When the Xinhua News Agency, an official Chinese news outlet, mentioned Bo Xilai it often used Bo's downfall as an indication that the Chinese government was fighting corruption, noting "China investigates 30 ministerial-level officials within five years" (Xuequan, 2013a) and "Xinhua Insight: China's anti-graft efforts to get institutional impetus" (Xuequan, 2013b). In other cases Xinhua portrayed Bo as out of step with the Communist Party, and in particular the Party's new leadership (Shasha, 2013). Nonstate Chinese language media, including citizen media, tended to report a variety of events and people that were directly or indirectly related to Bo, such as politicians who were his associates (Boxun.com, 2012a) and celebrities that may have been his mistresses, presented in a tabloid-like style in some cases (Baidutata, 2013). Western media tended to portray Bo as a symbol of widespread and often shocking levels of corruption among the Chinese Communist Party leadership by emphasizing his insider status as the son of a top official (MacKinnon, 2012) or his strong bid to become a part of the 2013 new leadership of the Communist Party ("No longer immune," 2012).

Beyond this black-and-white representation of Bo as outcast, tabloid wrongdoer, or consummate insider, some English and many Chinese language sources covered Bo's case with more nuance. Bo was quite popular in the city where he served as mayor, Chongqing, where he pioneered a leftist style of governance called the "Chongqing model" (Chun, 2012; Keck, 2013). He was known for his personal style of leadership as mayor, as well as his cleanup of organized crime in Chongqing. These policies aligned him with the leftist faction within the Chinese Communist Party, and some speculated whether Bo's downfall was based on political tensions within the Communist Party, rather than his alleged crimes (Chun, 2012).

Will these different fourth estate contexts impact the topics discussed and the types of sources used within the Twitter discussions in each language?

Methods

Our sample of 13,035 tweets was gathered from the Twitter application programming interface (API) from January 11 through March 18, 2013. We used the search terms "薄熙来" (Bo Xilai in simplified Chinese characters), "boxilai" (case insensitive), and "bo xilai." We gathered the tweets available via the API that matched these terms.[2] The amount of tweets downloaded during each session varied based on how many users were employing our search terms at that moment. If discussion of the case was very active, more tweets would be available at that time. Thus our sample more heavily reflects the discourse that was present during peak discussion periods within this timeframe. The largest peak of activity occurred in late January when the rumor of Bo's impending trial emerged; thus 39% of our content was gathered between January 25 and January 29. The volume of tweets was far higher in Chinese compared to other languages, as our sample contained 76% in Chinese, 22% in English, and 3% in other languages. The remainder of the analysis will focus only on the tweets that were in English or Chinese, with $N = 12{,}665$.

This strategy of using search terms gathered a wide range of tweets about this topic. Unlike Twitter data based on a hashtag, which is a conscious social construction, these users were not necessarily contributing to a particular shared conversation on this topic but communicating with a wide variety of intended audiences. The data thus covers a broad range of conversations in each language.

Although the Twitter platform has the same technical features worldwide, it has different implications in a global context. The basic unit of Chinese writing is the character, which is ideographic in origin (Schmitt, Pan, & Tavassoli, 1994). Chinese words vary from one to six characters, and over 60% of Chinese words are two characters (Huang & Wang, 1992). In comparison, most English words contain more than two letters. Therefore, Twitter's limit of 140 characters has different implications based on whether they are Chinese characters or English letters. The same number of Chinese characters can carry much more meaning than English letters, making Twitter a more expressive medium in Chinese. We address this issue further in the discussion and conclusion.

Content Analysis of Tweets

We created a unified coding scheme for the English and Chinese content using an inductive approach to category development (Mayring, 2000). Our goal was to reflect the prominent topics specific to this case across languages, so we had to create our own codes. We developed this scheme based on an initial analysis of 100 random Tweets in English (performed by the first author) and 100 in Chinese (performed by the second author). We compared our analyses and considered the cases provided by content in the other language and came up with an initial (lengthy) typology, which we pretested and simplified into the final scheme. The coding scheme contained three facets: (1) whether the tweet appeared to be a news headline or a comment from the Twitter user, (2) if the tweet mentioned the timing of Bo Xilai's trial, and (3) which of eight mutually exclusive topic categories was the best fit for the overall meaning of the tweet (see Table 9.2 for a list of the topic categories, and see below for descriptions with examples).

Distinguishing between news headlines alone and commentary by the Twitter users allowed us to assess the contributions of the fourth and fifth estates within the content. News headlines without any commentary by the user may or may not reflect the views of the user, and the degree to which retweeted news content is perceived as reflecting the views of the user may differ in the English and Chinese language contexts. It is common for English language Twitter users to indicate in their profile that "RT ≠ endorsement" (Sreenivasan, 2013), pointing out the assumption that retweets—repeating content from others, including news headlines—are generally perceived as endorsements. This may be less true in the Chinese language content where providing the link and title of a state-run media outlet's content may not imply endorsement but simply sharing important information. The timing of the trial was the major news story during the time of our data collection. It was measured separately from other topics so that it did not overwhelm more specific themes in the content. The exclusive topic categories were somewhat broad so that they could capture the information provided in both languages given the low context of a single tweet.

Two native English speakers and three native Chinese speakers (including both authors) coded the tweets according to this scheme. Overall, the coding system has a high intercoder reliability, but the English data had higher reliability than the Chinese. This was likely due to the higher complexity of the Chinese data. Chinese tweets have a greater expressive potential because the characters express more than individual English characters, as discussed above, and because the Chinese discussion involved a wider cast of characters and events. See Table 9.1 for a summary of intercoder reliability for each language.

Examining the dataset, we saw that some tweets were repeated many times by the same user at different times, sometimes posted just seconds apart. For example, the user mynte5 repeated the exact same 34 tweets 656 times in our dataset. To prevent such repetition from dominating our analysis we deduplicated exact replicate tweets coming from the same user at different times, such that mynte5's tweets counted as 34 rather than 642 in the following analysis. Overall this reduced our dataset by 19% from 12,665 tweets to 10,236. This impacted only the Chinese dataset, as this was not a strategy used in the English data (less than 1% of the removed tweets were in English). This moderate approach to deduplication does not completely neuter the impact of political activists who intensively advocate specific views. Such users are an important part of an open

TABLE 9.1 Intercoder Reliability

Coding Categories	Percent Agreement (English Tweets)	Percent Agreement (Chinese Tweets)	Average Percent Agreement
News or comments	0.91	0.93	0.92
Trial date	0.92	0.95	0.94
Legal system	0.93	0.86	0.90
Politics	0.96	0.78	0.87
Corruption	0.98	0.98	0.98
Non-corruption allegations or scandals	0.98	0.93	0.96
Defense or advocacy for Bo and his family	1.00	0.94	0.97
Comments about media	0.93	0.97	0.95

platform like Twitter. However, this moderate data cleaning does allow us to see a broader spectrum of topics beyond those issues that were advocated by activists. Retweets are included in our analysis, as those are the same text coming from different users.

Analysis of Links Referred to in Tweets

We also analyzed the links provided in Tweets to determine which sources of information were popular among users. In the dataset of 10,236 tweets, 88% of all tweets in English ($N = 2,804$) and 80% of all tweets in Chinese ($N = 7,432$) contained at least one link. The vast majority (80%) of all tweets with links had only one link, so only the first link per tweet was analyzed. Since most links shared in tweets are shortened due to Twitter's character limit, the final destination of the link was determined by visiting the link using a programmable Web browser that logged the final URL and this was added to the dataset. All analysis refers to the final destination of the link. This destination link revealed the domain of the Web site referred to (e.g., cnn.com) and the specific Web page (e.g., http://www.cnn.com/boarticle123.htm), each of which were analyzed for frequency. Before presenting the results we provide a brief overview of how the Bo Xilai case was reported in our sample.

Results

Overview of Content Across Languages

The majority ($N = 7,895$, 77.1%) of the tweets appear to be a news headline or text from a news story without any further comment by the Twitter user; for example, "NY Times: Report of Trial for Bo Xilai Proves to Be False Alarm: Dozens of journalists gathered in Guiyang after . . . http://t.co/9Pw2WCLT." The remainder ($N = 2,341$, 22.9%) have the Twitter users' comments. In most cases these were comments added to news stories; for example, "@theaccidentalec Did you see this turnaround in the case? Chinese blogger who mocked Bo Xilai wins court case http://t.co/O6k6ZyJH," and some were comments without links to specific news stories; for example, "It's obvious president Xi Jinping will be lenient with Bo Xilai since Bo belonged to the Jiang faction which also put Xi on the throne." According to a chi-squared test of a cross tabulation, there are significantly more tweets that are only reporting news headlines than expected by chance, with an adjusted residual greater than 2.00 ($\chi^2 = 573.31$, $df = 1$, $p < .01$, $R = 25.9$).

Among all tweets three main topics were dominant. The legal system category ($N = 3,284$, 32.1%) included tweets simply announcing the trial date (or lack thereof); for example, "Trial of China's Bo Xilai opens next week, says Beijing-backed paper—Asahi Shimbun: http://t.co/3ATE9rov," as well as discussion of

Bo's lawyers, "DeHeng Partners Tapped for Bo Xilai Defense—The American Lawyer http://t.co/xq2aGlVt"; possible punishments, "More signs that Bo Xilai may face the death penalty http://t.co/S3aEVYmf"; and issues of credibility or fairness of the Chinese legal system, "Judgment Day for princeling Bo Xilai Hard time or 'Chinese-style rule by law' http://t.co/MkV8dc6a #china #poli tics #cn."

The politics theme (N = 2,905, 28.4%) incorporated tweets addressing the consequences of the case for China's new leadership, "Bo Xilai Trial Facilitates Infighting Within High Level. http://t.co/s8kIOrh4," and Bo's relationships with other politicians, "China's Chongqing mayor says has banished Bo Xilai's influence http://t.co/SWLDKLKo," as well as his political achievements, mistakes, or leadership style.

Third, defense or advocacy for Bo and his family was another important topic: "RT @BloombergNews: Bo Xilai's supporters demonstrate outside south China courthouse | http://t.co/FSiIYLEB" (N = 1,681, 16.4%). This theme included tweets that described the actions of advocates for Bo, either among the public or prominent figures, including members of Bo's family or Bo himself. Together these three themes constituted 76.9% of the total tweets.

The remaining four themes (excluding "other") altogether constituted about 10% of the tweets. The category noncorruption allegations or scandals (N = 501, 4.9%) involved allegations of Bo's or Bo's family members' sexual improprieties, ties to gangsters, and other nonfinancial misdeeds: "Ten Chinese officials fired over sex scandal in former Bo Xilai fiefdom: Developers secretly filmed men sleeping with women then used." Second, comments about media outlets and the coverage of Bo's case were a minor topic overall (N = 372, 3.6%), and they included issues of censorship, lack of information accuracy, comparison of Chinese and overseas media, and attacks on journalists who reported Bo's case: "The South China Morning Post has poured lukewarm water on earlier reports, originating in state media, that the . . . http://t.co/U9ThY9Sn." Corruption, surprisingly, was quite a minor theme (N = 220, 2.1%), encompassing allegations that Bo, his family, associates, or the Communist Party were taking advantage of their power to gain wealth for themselves in some way, or that such allegations were inflated or false: "A senior land official in Chongqing, under Bo Xilai's administration, is being investigated on suspicion of serious violations!" One category in the coding scheme was very infrequent, accounting for less than 1% of the content: Bo's story as it related to international politics or political figures; for example, "Chavez and Bo Xilai Gone: Death of a Political Model?—http://t.co/yAm8CdMgqV." The remainder of the content was coded as "Other" and covered a wide range of largely tangential topics or comparisons; for example, "Huckleberry Hound looks a bit like Bo Xilai it's not just me right?"

As mentioned above, the biggest news story during our data collection time period was the rumor of Bo's imminent trial. The content of about one-fourth

(N = 2,524, 24.7%) of the tweets we analyzed were about the date or timing of Bo Xilai's trial. However, these were overwhelmingly news headlines, as only 4% (N = 102, R = 25.9) of comment tweets were about timing. Among the tweets about timing, the majority fell into the legal system (N = 1,756, 69.6%) or politics (N = 591, 23.4%) category.

Comparing English and Chinese Content

We compared the Chinese and English tweets and found important differences in the content. The results for each language are visualized in Figure 9.1. Overall, significantly more (χ^2 = 498.90, df = 1, p < .01) Chinese tweets contained the Twitter users' comments (N = 2,123, 28.6%, R = 22.3) as compared to the English tweets, which tended to contain more news headlines without commentary (N = 2,586, 92.2%, R = 22.3). The change of the trial date of Bo's case received proportionally

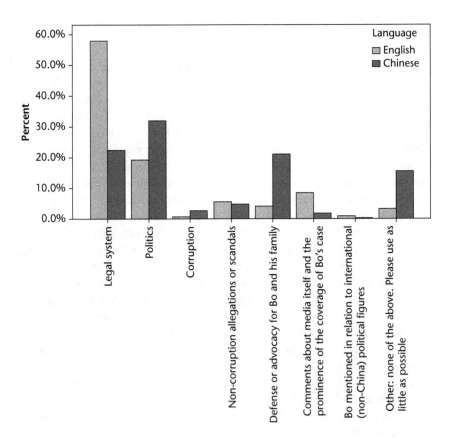

FIGURE 9.1 Percent of Content in Each Topic Category by Language

Source: http://www.baidutata.com/2992.html

more attention among users who tweeted in English, nearly 49% of the content, compared to those in Chinese, just 15.5% (χ^2 = 1,224.67, df = 1, p < .01). News-only tweets that were also about the timing of the trial were largely breaking news headlines; for example "BEIJING (Reuters)—China's disgraced former senior politician, Bo Xilai, will go on trial next week, a Beijing- . . . http://t.co/cunexv8X." In the English data, 47% of the tweets were news headlines about the timing of the trial, versus just 15% of the Chinese tweets.

Turning to the eight exclusive topic categories, many differences were found here, as well (χ^2 = 1,851.86, df = 7, p < .01; see Figure 9.1). Significantly more Chinese tweets were about corruption and politics, defense or advocacy for Bo and his family, while more English tweets were about the legal system, noncorruption allegations or scandals, media and media coverage, as well as Bo's story in relation to non-China political figures. Figure 9.1 provides a clear contrast between Chinese tweets and English tweets as apparent in their respective distribution of different topics. Table 9.2 provides the statistically significant results of the comparison.

Clearly, Chinese and English tweets show different patterns in the focus of Twitter discussion about Bo's case. Among Chinese tweets, politics dominates. English tweets focused more on breaking news about the timing of the trial, which fit into the legal system topic category of the coding scheme.

When Twitter users made their own comments in their tweets on Bo's case, the most dominant categories, in descending order, among Chinese tweets are as follows: politics (N = 817, 38.5%); for example, "Part of power reshuffle in Chongqing after the fall of Bo Xilai. On the evening of January 24, the Media

TABLE 9.2 Comparison of English and Chinese Tweet Content

	Chinese Tweets			English Tweets		
	N	Percentage	Adjusted Residual (R^1)	N	Percentage	Adjusted Residual (R)
Legal system	1,663	22.4%	−34.3	1,621	57.8%	34.3
Politics	2,363	31.8%	12.5	542	19.3	−12.5
Defense	1,565	21.1%	20.6	116	4.1	−20.6
Non-corruption allegation	343	4.6%	−2.1	158	5.6	2.1
Corruption	203	2.7%	6.6	17	0.6	−6.6
Media	131	1.8%	−16.5	241	8.6	16.5
International figure	5	0.1%	−5.3	17	0.6	5.3
Other	1,159	15.6%	17.0	92	3.3	−17.0

[1]Adjusted residuals greater than 2 in absolute value indicate that the categorical differences are statistically significant.

Office of Chongqing Government announced a few position changes of government officials"; defense or advocacy for Bo and his family (N = 413, 19.5%), "Call for impartial trial for Bo Xilai's case, Beijing teacher wrote a public letter to Xi Jinping and other party leaders"; and legal system (N = 193, 9.1%), "Bo Xilai case transferred to judicial departments." Differently, the most dominant categories with descending order among English comment tweets were as follows: legal system (N = 83, 38.1%), "Bo Xilai trial-flavoured punishment ceremony to finally start next week, says Dagongbao: http://t.co/nPZ2qZAv"; politics (N = 45, 20.6%), "RT @johncbussey: The problem for China isn't Bo, it's the pervasiveness of Bo's: 'Official: Bo Xilai Could Face Severe Punishment' @WSJ http://t.co/Wytn9tde"; and comments about media outlets or media coverage (N = 28, 12.8%), "RT @JoshGartner: Journalists eagerly await next destination in Bo Xilai trial scavenger hunt." The retweets of this particular tweet (and slight variations thereof) seem to have pushed this topic category ahead of others, accounting for 43% (12 of 28) of the media category tweets in English.

The following compares Twitter's perspectives on media coverage between languages, which were significantly different (χ^2 = 1,303.96, df = 7, p < .01). The majority (N = 7,895, 77.1%) of tweets across languages appear to be a news headline or text from a news story without any further comment by the Twitter user, of which 2,586 tweets were in English and 5,309 tweets were in Chinese. Both Chinese and English news-only tweets were strongly related to the legal system and politics, but significantly more English news-only tweets were about the legal system (N = 1,538, 59.5%, R = 27.3), compared to 27.7% of Chinese tweets. Significantly fewer English news-only tweets (N = 497, 19.2%) were about politics, compared to those of Chinese tweets, which comprised 29.1% of the content. Chinese news-only tweets (N = 1,152, 21.7%, R = 20.3) had heavy coverage of defense or advocacy for Bo and his family, while English news-only tweets (N = 102, 3.9%, R = –20.3) did not. Significantly more English news-only tweets (N = 213, 8.2%, R = 12.4) were about media outlets and media coverage compared to Chinese tweets (N = 120, 2.3%).

Analysis of Links in the Tweets

Domains

The most cited Chinese Web sites among the Chinese tweets in this study are chinafree.greatzhonghua.org and zyzc.greatzhonghua.org, which are referenced in 37.5% of the tweets (see Table 9.3). The chinafree Web site is a home page with news stories, while zyzc is a discussion board. Both Web sites belong to the domain greatzhonghua.org, which is the Web site for the United States of Great Zhonghua, a fictitious state with false information for the postal address and phone number of the Web site operator. There is no information regarding the actual owner or administrator of the Web site. This is clearly an anti–Chinese government

TABLE 9.3 Top 10 Domains in the Chinese Dataset (N = 5,943)

Domain	Affiliation	% Links
chinafree.greatzhonghua.org	Anti-Chinese government group	28.6
zyzc.greatzhonghua.org	Anti-Chinese government group	8.9
chinadigitaltimes.net	U.S.-based Web site	7.1
news.sina.com.cn	Mainland China news site	5.9
epochtimes.com	Falun Gong	5.0
bbc.co.uk	U.K.-based news organization	3.3
secretchina.com	Falun Gong	3.3
peacehall.com	U.S.-based Web site	2.7
news.ifeng.com	Hong Kong-based news portal	2.4
news.qq.com	Mainland China news portal	2.2

Web site, with the mission statement provided in Chinese and English: "To elimi-nate commie is our duty in the twenty-first century. Give us back our freedom, human rights, democracy, justice, and the vote." The popularity on Twitter of cit-ing information from these Web sites seems to be the result of just 25 Twitter users out of the total 1,337 Chinese language Twitter users in our dataset, five of whom linked to these two Web sites more than 100 times in our sample.

Other Web sites among the top 10 sites most cited in Chinese tweets were each cited in 2% to 7% of the tweets. Three of these Web sites are independent Chinese language news Web sites in the United States or United Kingdom (chi-nadigitaltimes.net, bbc.co.uk, and peacehall.com) and are free of media censor-ship from the Chinese government. Two of these Web sites (epochtimes.com and secretchina.com) are associated with Falun Gong, a religious group sup-pressed by the Chinese government that advocates for anti–Communist Party positions. The Falun Gong–affiliated Web sites support different positions than the Chinese Communist Party on issues such as human rights and democracy. The remaining two domains are well-known Chinese news Web sites, one based in Mainland China (news.sina.com.cn) and the other in Hong Kong (news.ifeng. com). The press freedom of these two Web sites is somewhat constrained by the Chinese government.

In the English dataset, eight of the 10 most prominent domains were wire services, news organizations, or blogs free of Chinese government censorship (see Table 9.4). None of these sites have explicit political statements or affiliations with political organizations, although they tend to criticize authoritarian policies and media restrictions in China. Based in Hong Kong, scmp.com has somewhat more freedom than the Mainland China site globaltimes.cn, although the free-dom of the press in Hong Kong has been declining in recent years (Freedom House, 2013).

TABLE 9.4 Top 10 Domains in the English Dataset ($N = 2,477$)

Domain	Location or Affiliation	% Links
reuters.com	U.S.-based wire service	26.2
news.yahoo.com	U.S.-based news portal	7.7
nytimes.com	U.S.-based news organization	6.0
wsj.com	U.S.-based news organization	4.5
guardian.co.uk	U.K.-based news organization	4.4
scmp.com	Hong Kong-based news organization	4.1
bbc.co.uk	U.K.-based news organization	4.0
telegraph.co.uk	U.K.-based news organization	3.3
globaltimes.cn	Mainland China-based news organization	1.9
shanghaiist.com	U.S.-based blog	1.5

Web Pages

Of the top 10 links in the Chinese dataset of tweets, six are all from one well-known news Web site in Mainland China, news.sina.com (see Table 9.5). However, a large proportion of the tweets—13.6%, compared to just 6.5% for all other links combined—linked to an article on the anti–Chinese government Web site chinafree.greatzhonghua.org. Only two Twitter users linked to this article in the dataset, one of whom did so 803 times, the other tweeted it 7 times. These users changed the text of the tweet slightly each time so the tweets were not removed from the dataset as duplicates according to the data cleaning procedure described above. The second most popular link, a news story titled "Bo's Trial Will Be In Guiyang Tomorrow, and Might Conclude Before the Two Political Meetings" (translated from Chinese by the authors), was linked to by 55 different users: 17 of them shared it twice using different tweet text, and one shared it five times. The remaining three links came from Web sites based in the United Kingdom and United States that provide news in Chinese. Most of the top 10 links are about legal issues such as Bo's trial date, assessments of Bo's wife's trial, and Bo's lawyers, while the top link is a call for political change.

The top 10 links in the English data represent a greater overall proportion of the links in the dataset (39.8%) compared to the Chinese top 10 (20.1%), indicating that the English Twitter users focused more on the most popular links (see Table 9.6). Unlike the Chinese top link, the English top link was widely shared by different users more than the other links: 258 out of 1,604 English language users shared this link. Nine out of the 10 top links in English came from mainstream U.S. or U.K. news sites or wire services, with one from a Mainland China–based English language site.

TABLE 9.5 Top 10 Links in the Chinese Dataset (N = 5,943)

Title, Translated from Chinese	Domain	% Links
Let's all make a political change! Attached Bo Xilai's letter to the public.	chinafree. greatzhonghua.org	13.6
Bo's trial will be in Guiyang tomorrow, and might conclude before the two political meetings	news.sina.com.cn	1.0
Bo Xilai hired two lawyers in Beijing to defend his case	news.sina.com.cn	1.0
Qifan Huang claims Chongqing was stable last year	news.sina.com.cn	0.8
Bo-Gu Kailai's murder was selected to be one of the top 10 most influential law suits last year	news.sina.com.cn	0.8
Bo's trial will be in Guiyang before the two political meetings, Bo's family have hired two lawyers	news.sina.com.cn	0.7
The Anhui provincial court received an award for judging Bo-Gu Kailai's law suit	news.sina.com.cn	0.7
Bo Xilai will be on trial after the two political meetings	bbc.co.uk	0.6
Freedom Asia | AFP: Bo Xilai and his family hired two defense lawyers	chinadigitaltimes.net	0.5
Hong Kong news: Bo Xilai will be on trial in Guiyang next Monday	chinadigitaltimes.net	0.4

TABLE 9.6 Top 10 Links in the English Dataset (N = 2,477)

Title	Domain	% Links
Trial of China's Bo Xilai opens next week, says Beijing-backed paper	reuters.com	11.5
Dead end trail to Bo trial in China's south	reuters.com	6.7
Rumours swirl around Bo Xilai trial	bbc.co.uk	3.9
China's Chongqing mayor says has banished Bo Xilai's influence	reuters.com	3.8
China to Hit Bo Hard, Official Signals	wsj.com	2.7
Bo Xilai trial not in Guiyang today—court official	news.yahoo.com	2.5
Former student at University of Leeds to defend Bo Xilai in court	telegraph.co.uk	2.5
Trial of China's Bo Xilai opens next week, says Beijing-backed paper	news.yahoo.com	2.4
Report of Trial for Bo Xilai Proves to Be False Alarm	nytimes.com	1.9
Officials deny rumor of Bo Xilai's imminent trial	globaltimes.cn	1.9

Differences Within Categories and Among User Strategies

In addition to differences at the category level, there are also important differences in the content within the same category of each language. The top two categories of both datasets were legal system and politics. While the Chinese content in the legal system category discusses issues of credibility or fairness of the Chinese legal system with some regularity, this is rare in the English data, where the vast majority of tweets simply announce breaking news about Bo's judicial process or lawyers.

Even greater differences appear in the politics category, where most of the English data in this category simply makes reference to the political meetings in March, referred to as the Langhui or "two meetings" in Chinese; for example, "RT @taniabranigan: Bo Xilai trial unlikely until after March political meetings the National People's Congress (NPC) and Chinese People's Political Consultative Conference (CPPCC).- my quick round-up http://t.co/wLZ2z4Yu." Of the English language tweets, 38% (205 of 542) refer to one story originally reported by Reuters (and republished on several Web sites) titled "China's Chongqing Mayor Says Has Banished Bo Xilai's Influence." The Chinese data on politics, however, covers a wider range of issues, with 41% of the posts having links in this category citing unique Web pages, versus 30% in the English language data. For instance, some Chinese tweets range from news related to Bo's case to the power dynamic within the Chinese Communist Party: "Fanhua Internet retorted: The Communist Party criticized Bo, Xi Jinping purposefully set this media agenda." With a more in-depth understanding of Chinese politics, some news quoted by Twitter users analyzed the potential impact of Bo's case on his political alliances: "Bo's alliances are dismantled, Tang Jianhua, the previous vice chief police officer of Chongqing, was given an reprieve."

The other important difference in the content of the two datasets was the presence of political activists who promoted specific ideas in the Chinese data, which were lacking in English. Initially this may seem like a greater concentration of power among users in the Chinese dataset, with one user contributing more than 15% of the initial dataset while the top English user contributed less than 4%. Overall in English tweets, the links appearing most frequently in the tweets were also shared by the most different users, but in the Chinese tweets only a few users determined some of the top links. These political activists were not particularly influential, however, as their content was only referenced by a few users. Rather than having different levels of power concentration, it may be more accurate to say that a few Chinese users choose a strategy of high volume repetition, whereas the majority of Chinese and English users did not.[3]

Discussion and Conclusion

This study explored a case where two different language groups discussed the same political event on the same platform at the same time. The concept of the fifth estate (Dutton, 2009) and the networked public sphere (Benkler, 2006) were used as theoretical starting points. Here we begin by returning to these concepts to discuss them in light of what this case offers, and we end with a research agenda for further investigating networked public spheres in international contexts.

At the center of the fifth estate concept is the notion of holding those in power accountable, which is complicated in transnational contexts. The mechanism for this accountability—particularly in the case of the English language discussion—is the perception of the Chinese government that the world is watching. In this case, the English language Twitter conversation largely served to amplify mainstream journalism, as little additional commentary was offered. The topics, and thus the critiques, in English were limited compared to the Chinese language content. But given that this story was told with an international audience not familiar with the details of the case, this simplicity was required.

The Chinese language Twitter content amplified a wider range of journalism and offered more original commentary. Users from Mainland China who scaled the "great firewall" to access Twitter may use it as an escape outlet for political speech that is otherwise suppressed. Certainly the Chinese content was quite critical of the Communist Party, and the topic of Bo Xilai provided an opportunity to express dissatisfaction with the government. At the same time, the "filtering" process Benkler (2006) describes as promoting only widely valued content seems to have dampened the attempts of these particular political activists to spread their message widely.

During Bo's trial, the court posted regular updates to China's microblogging service Sina Weibo; unprecedented, this was seen as a response to calls for greater transparency in the Chinese legal system (Tang, 2013). We do not know what prompted the government to make this move, but Chinese language Twitter users did call for greater transparency in the Chinese system of justice in this case, perhaps reflecting some segment of public opinion. Whether or not the microblogging of Bo's trial by the court actually increased transparency in a meaningful way is debatable, but it did set the media agenda. A Chinese television anchorwoman went so far as to check her phone for updates during a live broadcast (Tang, 2013, p. 1). This choice of the government to "go public" (Kernell, 2007)—that is, to cut out the journalistic middleman—is difficult to understand in a country where the government holds sway over the broadcast media, but it does seem like a response strategy that takes into account the fifth estate.

Research Agenda

Comparing social media content about the same news story in different languages allows researchers to explore the relationship between the fourth and fifth estates in a transnational perspective. The role of government and commercial interests are quite different in the fourth estate of China as compared to the United States, the most populous nations speaking each language we studied, respectively. Social media, and particularly Twitter, may perform a distinct function based on their context in a different media system. Future research considering additional news topics would help to distinguish among a number of possible explanations for the greater role of commentary in the Chinese data, and the presence of political activists only in the Chinese language. These possible explanations are described below, followed by further suggestions for future research directions.

The more prominent role of commentary in the Chinese data could be related to a lack of trust in the media. Expressing skepticism of news reports (directly or indirectly) seemed to be more common in the Chinese data. For instance, a tweet from a Chinese user stated, "Chinese politics is complicated. Information on Bo's trial kept being reported firstly by overseas media, and the Chinese government did not deny it." However, there are alternative explanations for the greater commentary in the Chinese content. Due to different writing systems, there is simply more semantic space available within a tweet from Chinese language Twitter users. In addition, the high context Chinese culture may influence Chinese Twitter users' indirectness and use of nuance in their tweets. Assessing additional cases with different characteristics would help distinguish among these possibilities.

Similarly, there are several possible reasons why political activists may have appeared in the Chinese content but not in the English content. The political relevance of the case to Chinese speakers may be much higher. Another factor may have been the censorship practices of China, which produce marginalized political actors who have very few ways of disseminating information. Also, social media information campaigns, such as those run by the Chinese government (Bristow, 2008), may inform the social norms of some Chinese language Twitter users, thus making it more acceptable to promote information in this way. Analyses of different news stories could help disentangle these possibilities.

Ausserhofer and Maireder's (2013) study of the Austrian Twittersphere found that the relationship between mainstream media content and conversations on Twitter both converged and diverged over time. Although we did not analyze the mainstream media outside of what was cited in the tweets, we did find mainstream sources at the center of the conversation on Twitter in both languages, with the exception of content pushed by political activists in the Chinese language. In the Austrian case, Twitter was used to organize political activity around a planned event, and short-term stories were emphasized more so on Twitter than in mainstream media. Political organizing is not generally carried out through mainstream media, so this type of case would necessarily diverge from a focus on mainstream media content.

Regarding methods, comparing the content itself through human coding was important to begin to understand the complexities of making cross-linguistic comparisons. However, larger-scale analysis could be facilitated by machine learning techniques that begin with human coded examples (e.g., Hopkins &

King, 2010). The authors feel that their collaboration as native speakers of the languages in question is quite valuable in developing the cross-linguistic code-book, and such collaboration is recommended for future such projects. Following the links within the tweets to their sources proved particularly valuable in investigating the highly intertwined nature of the fourth and fifth estates. Future research can take this technique even further by analyzing the content of the linked articles in addition to the source. Another avenue for qualitative inquiry may be to take an in-depth look at the small but potentially important set of users who bridged this boundary by tweeting in both English and Chinese.

Notes

1. Circumventing the blockade masks the true country of origin of the user. We are not aware of any reliable way to determine the country of origin based on publicly available information, which is important for user privacy. All Twitter users' geographic information is subject to this same lack of verifiability. However, in the case of Chinese language Twitter content, location data problems are highly likely to be present to the extent that such information is not useful as a guide to which country the tweets originate from. This study is focused on discourse about a political issue in China in the English and Chinese languages, not the identity or geography of users.
2. We also searched for Bo's wife's name in both languages, as well as Bo's name in traditional Chinese characters, but found very few results that were not already included in our dataset. We downloaded the data from the API every hour in January and early February and slowed to every two hours from mid-February through March. This slowdown did not impact the amount of data gathered, as all available matches from the API were retrieved during this period of lower activity. Only a subset of Twitter data is available via the API (see Morstatter, Pfeffer, Liu, & Carley, 2013). For the purpose of analyzing the discourse, we believe a large sample—rather than a complete census—is sufficient.
3. Because the data used for analysis lacked these tweets, the extent of political activism was *less* prominent in the content than it would have been without this data cleaning.

References

Ausserhofer, J., & Maireder, A. (2013). National politics on Twitter. *Information, Communication & Society, 16*(3), 291–314. doi:10.1080/1369118X.2012.756050

Baidutata. (2013, July 23). 和薄熙来有染的女人是谁？ 张姓女星被确认 [Who is the women having an affair with Bo Xilai? Actress Zhang is identified]. Retrieved from http://www.baidutata.com/rytata/2992.html

Benkler, Y. (2006). *The wealth of networks: How social production transforms markets and freedom.* New Haven, CT: Yale University Press.

Boxun.com. (2012a, February 8). 疑王立军成都美国领馆避难被拒 [U.S. Consulate in Chengdu suspect Wang Lijun asylum rejected]. Retrieved from http://boxun.com/news/gb/china/2012/02/201202080447.shtml#.Ua9N4mSA1F8

Boxun.com. (2012b, June 2). 令公子高速车震死亡牵出令计划、周永康、薄熙来三角政治同盟 [Shocking high-speed car death of Ling Jihua's son reveals Ling Jihua, Zhou Yongkang, and Bo Xilai triangle political allies]. Retrieved from http://www.boxun.com/news/gb/china/2012/06/201206022347.shtml#.U2DOd62SxqF

Branigan, T. (2012, April 16). China's censors tested by microbloggers who keep one step ahead of state media. Retrieved from http://www.theguardian.com/technology/2012/apr/16/internet-china-censorship-weibo-microblogs

Bristow, M. (2008). China's Internet "spin doctors." *BBC*. Retrieved from http://news.bbc.co.uk/2/hi/7783640.stm

Cammaerts, B., & Audenhove, L. V. (2005). Online political debate, unbounded citizenship, and the problematic nature of a transnational public sphere. *Political Communication, 22*(2), 179–196. doi:10.1080/10584600590933188

Chun, L. (2012). China's leaders are cracking down on Bo Xilai and his Chongqing model. *Guardian*. Retrieved from http://www.theguardian.com/commentisfree/2012/apr/22/china-leaders-cracking-down-chongqing-xilai

Dutton, W. H. (2009). The fifth estate emerging through the network of networks. *Prometheus, 27*(1), 1–15. doi:10.1080/08109020802657453

Fitzsimmons, M. P. (2003). *The night the old regime ended: August 4, 1789 and the French revolution*. University Park: Pennsylvania State University Press.

Frasier, N. (1992). Rethinking the public sphere: A contribution to the critique of actually existing democracy. In C. Calhoun (Ed.), *Habermas and the public sphere* (pp. 109–142). Cambridge, MA: MIT Press.

Freedom House. (2013). *Freedom of the press data*. Retrieved from http://www.freedomhouse.org/sites/default/files/FOTP%20Category%20Breakdown%201989–2013.xls

Gittings, J. (2007, January 1). Bo Yibo: Veteran Chinese leader and "immortal" whose loyalty to the party survived its purges, obituary. *Guardian*. Retrieved from http://www.theguardian.com/news/2007/jan/24/guardianobituaries.obituaries1

Habermas, J. (1974). The public sphere: An encyclopedia article (1964) (S. Lennox & F. Lennox, Eds.). *New German Critique, 3*, 49–55.

Habermas, J. (1989). *The structural transformation of the public sphere: An inquiry into a category of Bourgeois society* (T. Burger & F. Lawrence, Trans.). Cambridge: Polity. (Original work published 1962)

Hopkins, D. J., & King, G. (2010). A method of automated nonparametric content analysis for social science. *American Journal of Political Science, 54*(1), 229–247.

Huang, J.-T., & Wang, M.-Y. (1992). From unit to gestalt: Perceptual dynamics in recognizing Chinese characters. In H. C. Chen & O.J.L. Tzeng (Eds.), *Language process in Chinese* (pp. 3–36). Amsterdam: Elsevier Science.

Huang, P.C.C. (1993). "Public sphere"/"civil society" in China?: The third realm between state and society. *Modern China, 19*(2), 216–240. doi:10.2307/189381

Jacobs, A. (2012, August 20). China defers death penalty for disgraced official's wife. *New York Times*. Retrieved from http://www.nytimes.com/2012/08/21/world/asia/china-defers-death-penalty-for-gu-kailai.html

Jiang, S. (2013, September 23). Bo Xilai found guilty on all charges, sentenced to life in prison. *CNN*. Retrieved from http://edition.cnn.com/2013/09/21/world/asia/china-bo-xilai-verdict/

Keck, Z. (2013, August 21). With Bo Xilai on trial, China adopts Chongqing model. *Diplomat*. Retrieved from http://thediplomat.com/2013/08/with-bo-xilai-on-trial-china-adopts-chongqing-model/

Kernell, S. (2007). *Going public: New strategies of presidential leadership*. Washington, DC: CQ Press.

Kwak, H., Lee, C., Park, H., & Moon, S. (2010, April 26–30). *What is Twitter, a social network or a news media?* Paper presented at WWW2010: The Nineteenth International WWW Conference, Raleigh, NC.

Laya, P., Frier, S., & Kurmanaev, A. (2014, February 15). Venezuelans blocked on Twitter as opposition protests mount. *Bloomberg.* Retrieved from http://www.bloomberg.com/news/2014–02–14/twitter-says-venezuela-blocks-its-images-amid-protest-crackdown.html

LexisNexis Academic. (2014). Retrieved from http://academic.lexisnexis.nl/

Liebelson, D. (2014, March 28). MAP: Here are the countries that block Facebook, Twitter, and YouTube. *Mother Jones.* Retrieved from http://www.motherjones.com/politics/2014/03/turkey-facebook-youtube-twitter-blocked

Litoff, A. (2014, May 6). "Bring back our girls" becomes rallying cry for kidnapped Nigerian schoolgirls. *ABC News.* Retrieved from http://abcnews.go.com/International/bring-back-girls-rallying-cry-kidnapped-nigerian-schoolgirls/story?id=23611012

MacKinnon, M. (2012, August 21). The Bo family saga grips China. *Globe and Mail,* p. A10.

Mayring, P. (2000). Qualitative content analysis. *Forum Qualitative Sozialforschung/Forum: Qualitative Social Research, 1*(2). Retrieved from http://www.qualitative-research.net/index.php/fqs/article/view/1089/2385%3E%3B

Morstatter, F., Pfeffer, J., Liu, H., & Carley, K. M. (2013). *Is the sample good enough? Comparing data from Twitter's streaming API with Twitter's firehose.* Proceedings of the Seventh International Conference on Weblogs and Social Media. Palo Alto, CA: AAAI Press.

No longer immune, former top Chinese politician faces inquiry. (2012, October 27). *New York Times,* p. 7.

Papacharissi, Z. (2002). The virtual sphere. *New Media & Society, 4*(1), 9–27.

Papacharissi, Z. (2009). The virtual sphere 2.0: The Internet, the public sphere and beyond. In A. Chadwick & P. N. Howard (Eds.), *The Routledge handbook of Internet politics* (pp. 230–245). New York: Routledge.

Papacharissi, Z., & de Fatima Oliveira, M. (2012). Affective news and networked publics: The rhythms of news storytelling on #Egypt. *Journal of Communication, 62*(2), 266–282.

Rao, S. (2013, January 22). Connecting advertisers to Twitter users around the world. *Twitter.* Retrieved from https://blog.twitter.com/2013/connecting-advertisers-twitter-users-around-world

Sarno, D. (2009, February 18). Twitter creator Jack Dorsey illuminates the site's founding document, part I. *Los Angeles Times.* Retrieved from http://latimesblogs.latimes.com/technology/2009/02/twitter-creator.html

Schmitt, B. H., Pan, Y., & Tavassoli, N. T. (1994). Language and consumer memory: The impact of linguistic differences between Chinese and English. *Journal of Consumer Research, 21*(3), 419–431.

Schudson, M. (1997). Why conversation is not the soul of democracy. *Critical Studies in Mass Communication, 14*(4), 297–309. doi:10.1080/15295039709367020

Sezer, S. (2014, April 20). Turkey Twitter accounts appear blocked after Erdogan court action. *Reuters.* Retrieved from http://www.reuters.com/article/2014/04/20/us-turkey-twitter-idUSBREA3J0ET20140420

Shasha, D. (2013, March 17). Profile: Chinese top legislature has younger leaders. *Xinhua News Agency.* Retrieved from http://news.xinhuanet.com/english/china/2013–03/17/c_132240957.htm

Shirky, C. (2011). The political power of social media: Technology, the public sphere, and political change. *Foreign Affairs, 90*(January/February), 28–40.

Sreenivasan, S. (2013, May 3). RT ≠ endorsement. *Washington Post.* Retrieved from http://wapo.st/YjvCRd

Sudworth, J. (2013). Chinese court rejects Bo Xilai appeal and upholds life sentence. *BBC*. Retrieved from http://www.bbc.com/news/world-asia-china-24652525

Tang, D. (2013, August 22). In rare openness, China microblogs Bo Xilai trial. *Associated Press*. Retrieved from http://bigstory.ap.org/article/rare-show-openness-china-tweets-bos-trial

Tze-wel, N. (2012, April 3). Warning over Twitter, YouTube "subversion." *South China Morning Post*. Retrieved from http://www.scmp.com/article/689105/warning-over-twitter-youtube-subversion

Wodak, R., & Wright, S. (2006). The European Union in cyberspace: Multilingual democratic participation in a virtual public sphere? *Journal of Language and Politics, 5*(2), 251–275. doi:10.1075/jlp.5.2.07wod

Wolman, D. (2013, April 16). Facebook, Twitter help the Arab Spring blossom. *Wired*. Retrieved from http://www.wired.com/magazine/2013/04/arabspring/

Wong, E. (2014, January 10). New detail emerges about Bo Xilai's downfall. *Sinosphere: Dispatches from China*. Retrieved from http://sinosphere.blogs.nytimes.com/2014/01/10/new-detail-emerges-about-bo-xilais-downfall/?_php=true&_type=blogs&_r=0

Woollaston, V. (2013, September 25). China lifts ban on Facebook—but only for people living in a 17 square mile area of Shanghai. *Daily Mail*. Retrieved from http://www.dailymail.co.uk/sciencetech/article-2431861/China-lifts-ban-Facebook—people-living-working-small-area-Shanghai.html

Xia, M. (2006). "China threat" or a "peaceful rise of China"? *New York Times*. Retrieved from http://www.nytimes.com/ref/college/coll-china-politics-007.html

Xuequan, M. (2013a, March 10). China investigates 30 ministerial-level officials within five years. *Xinhua News Agency*. Retrieved from http://news.xinhuanet.com/english/china/2013–03/10/c_124439560.htm

Xuequan, M. (2013b, March 15). China's anti-graft efforts to get institutional impetus. *Xinhua News Agency*. Retrieved from http://news.xinhuanet.com/english/indepth/2013–03/15/c_124465397.htm

Zhu, T., Phipps, D., Pridgen, A., Crandall, J. R., & Wallach, D. S. (2013). *The velocity of censorship: High-fidelity detection of microblog post deletions*. Retrieved from http://arxiv.org/abs/1303.0597

10

FANDOM OF FOREIGN REALITY TV SHOWS IN THE CHINESE CYBER SPHERE

Weiyu Zhang and Lize Zhang

Susan Boyle, the Scottish singer who claimed her fame in the reality show *Britain's Got Talent*, finally made her debut in China in 2011. Media coverage repeatedly cited multiple cancelations of her planned visits to China as a disappointment to Chinese audiences and the debut visit as a fulfillment of many longings. The previously failed attempts included inviting Boyle to sing three songs in the 2010 New Year's Eve Gala organized by a major TV network Jiangsu TV, which was said to cost the station 500,000 USD. The visit that was finally successful was made to support the Chinese version of *Britain's Got Talent*, produced by another major TV network, Dragon TV from Shanghai. This case of Auntie Susan, a nickname used by Chinese media and audiences, is an illustration of the popularity of transcultural media products in contemporary China. However, the reality show, itself, has never been broadcast on any Chinese mainstream TV channels.

The majority of Chinese audiences access and consume foreign reality shows on the Internet due to the unavailability of such shows on TV. Audiences often put a considerable amount of effort into searching online sources for the shows and translating the episodes into Chinese subtitles. Their intense commitment has granted them the title of fans and their activities, fandom. This recent wave of fandom of foreign reality shows is a continuation of the fandom of transcultural media products such as TV shows (e.g., *Friends*) and movies (e.g., Hollywood blockbusters). The fans, old and new, share similar motivation of taking the flow of entertainment content under their own control, against commercial control by the local TV networks and political control by the Chinese government. Whereas this rhetoric has been heard many times in fan communities, scholarly thinking regarding the globalization of cultural market points out that these fans serve as immaterial labor, or people who conduct activities that are not normally recognized as "work" yet produce the "cultural content" of the commodity, for transnational media corporations. The competing interpretation mirrors the theoretical debate in the research field of cultural industries: How much autonomy does the local have compared to the global?

This chapter attempts to follow the recommendations made by prior studies (e.g., Wang, 2009) to complicate the dichotomy between the local and the global by integrating the political, economic, cross-cultural, and aesthetic analyses of the fandom over foreign reality TV shows in China. Drawing evidence from our months of participant observation and 23 in-depth interviews with active fans, we first describe in detail how the viewing experience is fully mediated by the Internet, a space in which various forces such as the state, global capital, and local capital mutually influence each other in interacting with users. A cross-cultural comparison between foreign and local shows elicited from the interviewees is presented with an emphasis on the fans' evaluation of aesthetic standards (i.e., their critique of local shows as being *Jia*) and their own perception regarding the impact of foreign shows. We conclude with a discussion on how the state must be included in analyses of transcultural media products, as well as a discussion considering how the views of immaterial labor versus fan activists can be reconciled without denying each other.

Beyond the Dichotomy

The globalization of the market economy, aided by the new wave of information and communication technologies (ICTs) such as the Internet, has certainly changed the way of producing, circulating, and consuming cultural products. Transnational flow of information and entertainment goods has proliferated greatly around the world, as seen in the popularity of Hollywood movies in the global market. As Wang (2009) argues, the globalization of cultural markets is often viewed through two contrasting perspectives, one of which is the critical tradition that prognosticates cultural imperialism rising. Since it is impossible that "today a country or region could isolate or de-link itself from the global networks of power" (Hardt & Negri, 2000, p. 284), cultural imperialism is argued to be inevitable when those with more power force their cultural products to those with less power, resulting in homogenization of various cultures, deprivation of audience choices, and denial of local autonomy.

The critical school points out that even local consumers who actively participate in the consumption process (e.g., fan fiction) are not able to break free from the logic of capitalist exploitation. Scholars such as Terranova (2000) and Cote and Pybus (2007) called the active participation of engaged consumers "free labor" or "immaterial labor." Both concepts frame the active reading and creative reconstruction of global cultural products as "value-enhancing labor" that helps cultural industries to "offload some market research labor onto viewers" (Andrejevic, 2008, p. 24). ICTs such as the Internet are the basic infrastructure upon which such new forms of labor are built. Andrejevic (2008) argues that online spaces for active consumption are sites of production that blur the boundary between office and home, work and leisure, as well as paid and unpaid labor. Without dismissing the creativity and enjoyment embedded in active audience participation, the critical school disagrees that such activities necessarily destabilize the corporate control over popular culture.

On the other hand, a postmodern perspective (Wang, 2009) celebrates popular democratization that is enabled by the gradual "dedifferentiation" between the economic and the cultural. At this stage of global capitalism, Jameson (1998) argues, cultural forces are no longer separable from economic forces, both of which are major productive forces. As such, local cultures strive to survive and flourish through market means, such as producing one culture's own goods, made by local teams and targeted at local audiences. Instead of being homogenized by the culture in power, this perspective suggests that a decentered or de-Westernized cultural landscape is possible (Curran & Park, 2000). The emergence of cultural trading blocs and regional centers partially supports this perspective, showing that the complete dominance of Hollywood as predicted by cultural imperialism has not been the reality.

The collective efforts of local cultures to resist cultural imperialism are grounded in the dispersed consciousness of local communities and individuals. The active audience perspective (Fiske, 1989; Hall, 1980; Morley, 1993) suggests that audiences, as located in communities and histories, are actively negotiating, if not subverting, the meanings conveyed in cultural products. For instance, Radway (1984) finds that romance readers form "interpretative communities" to collectively make sense of texts. Ang (1985) observes the cultural differences in reading *Dallas* among audiences that come from different countries that vary in their histories, values, and traditions. The variance in cultural proximity and cultural capital has been used to explain the emerging phenomenon of cultural trading blocs, which demonstrates that globalization is by no means a one-way process (Hoskins & Mirus, 1988; Straubhaar, 1991).

Fans are the most active component of audiences and display an intense engagement with cultural products. Jenkins (2006) uses the term "fan activism" to refer to the efforts fans make to bring the flow of media under their own control. Noting that fan activism has changed the relationship between consumers and corporate media, Jenkins proposes further that the "participatory culture" accumulated through fan activism could be transferred to the political domain, as well. An example of fan activism cited by Jenkins points out how fans on YouTube appropriate their video-editing skills to make viral videos that support their favored candidates in political elections. Van Zoonen (2004) explicitly argues that there are significant similarities between fan communities and political constituencies: both come into being as a result of performance; both are involved in activities such as discussion, participation, and imagination of alternatives; and both rest on emotional investments that lead to affective intelligence. Although online spaces are dispersed, networked fan communities allow their members to "move amongst a complex ecosystem of sites" (Baym, 2007) without losing the shared identification with the fan objects (Soukup, 2006). In addition, virtual fan communities allow fans to effectively organize themselves to influence the fan objects they are attracted to, enabling them to reshape their relationship with artists or stars (Theberge, 2005) or rewrite commercial television narratives (Costello & Moore, 2007).

The dichotomy between cultural imperialism and popular democratization (i.e., immaterial labor and fan activism) sets the limits of our theoretical framework regarding the implications of the active consumption of transcultural media products. Many scholars have made the call to go beyond this dualistic model of examining transcultural media consumption. Among various attempts to reconcile the opposition, Wang (2009) suggests that we should avoid seeing the global and the local as two poles with one always threatening to take over the other. Instead, "as no one force necessarily processes a pre-determined advantage, the direction and nature of change is seldom totally dictated by a particular party" (Wang, 2009, p. 136). We are in favor of this new development to complicate the dynamics among the multiple layers and dimensions that are associated with the global and the local. We agree with Miller (2008) that our examination must integrate political-economic, cross-cultural, and aesthetic analyses of transcultural media. In the following part, we provide a description of the political economy of transnational cultural industries in China.

Popular Culture and the State

What is hidden in the global-local dualism is the intermediary role of the state. What makes the Chinese context especially interesting is also the dubious role of the state. Since its transformation into the postsocialist era, the Chinese state has relaxed its totalitarian reign over Chinese society (Yu, 2009). The most prominent new force is that of the market economy. However, the intertwining relationship between the state and market economy in China is exceptionally complicated: within the country, the state purposefully and carefully plans and implements marketization, whereas local capitalists consciously and willingly conform to state orders. Global capitalist forces eyeing the Chinese market are often faced with two challenges simultaneously: political control from the state and commercial competition from local corporations. The state, building its legitimacy upon nationalist morals and economic performance (Zheng, 2007), is caught up between the need to integrate with globalization trends and the desire to protect local industry from global competition.

Transcultural media conglomerates have to operate in this type of political economy, and the products they sell evoke mixed reactions from the state. Popular culture in the communist model was deemed to possess an ideological significance, and the Chinese state once had complete and intense control over the production of all kinds of cultural goods at various levels in the political hierarchy. Although commercialization of the mass media had been introduced a few decades ago (Zhao, 2008), the speed of opening up the cultural market is clearly slower than other kinds of markets. Policies and regulations are still very much effective in shaping the cultural market. A recent example of this sees that the Broadcasting Bureau banned the use of all forms of audience voting in television programs, which basically terminated the *American Idol*-type of reality shows that had been extremely popular around 2005 to 2007 (Wang, 2009). The close control of the cultural market by the state has resulted in a flow of information far from being fully free and purely market-driven.

Fung (2008, p. 61) finds that the localization of transnational media corporations in China has gone "from an exploratory stage of testing the governmental allowance of 'globalness,' through taking refuge from seeking joint projects with the local corporations, to the formation of the joint state-global-capital corporation." A mutually dependent relationship seems to take root when transcultural media conglomerates are co-opted to not challenge the state's ideological status, and the state collaborates with such conglomerates to produce cultural products that are politically correct and commercially attractive. This relationship helps to explain some of the self-contradictory state behaviors found in China. Transcultural media products that are considered to be inconsistent with the official ideology are made unavailable to the majority of Chinese by banning them from circulating through official channels (e.g., state-controlled theaters). Meanwhile, the state (intentionally or unintentionally) tolerates unofficial and illegal channels (e.g., pirated DVDs or free online downloads) to provide earnest and savvy consumers the access to such content. Commercial activities around the content (e.g., stars from popular American sitcoms featured in Chinese advertisements) are also allowed.

The influx of foreign information and entertainment via both official and illegal means, without doubt, has changed popular culture in China. From Hong Kongese/Taiwanese pop songs, to the Japanese and Korean waves, to British/American movies and TV shows, cultural products, produced outside mainland China, shown on official TV channels and sold by street vendors, have become an inherent part of the everyday lives of Chinese urbanites (W. Zhang, 2006). Tan (2011) observes that the cross-cultural consumption of *Friends*, an American sitcom that is mostly accessed through unauthorized ways in China, shows dissimilar readings that deploy both referential and critical frames. Although some local audiences yielded a dominant reading, cultural defense was also seen in their interpretation of the sitcom. When interviewing producers from a provincial TV station, a researcher (X. Zhang, 2006) finds that "local" is understood as a multidimensional concept that entails more than just the local versus the global divide (e.g., the local vs. the central refers to the political hierarchy that differentiates the state level from the province level). When terms such as *global* or *international* were used by these producers, the terms often signal quality and universality. Despite recognizing that young and enthusiastic fans of foreign content are immaterial labor for transcultural media conglomerates, Fung (2009) suggests that such collective consumptions have immense mobilizing potential, which can act as a conduit to challenging the state authority. Yang (2009) also sees such potential in the prosaic and playful style of online activism.

The Chinese context has rendered the scholarly inquiry of the implication of active consumption—or fandom—of transcultural media products more interesting by introducing the question of the omniscient presence of the state. How do we conduct our cross-cultural and aesthetic analyses when the political economy demonstrates the state as a powerful intermediary, which is by itself a complex actor (Zheng, 2007)? Our position is that we cannot bypass the state in our analyses, but we need not prioritize the state (Zhang & Wang, 2010). Both commercial exploitation and political mobilization can coexist in fans and their activities. With this balanced stance in mind, we ask the following questions: How do fans digitally access, consume, and reconstruct transcultural cultural products? What are the cultural and aesthetic values that have attracted these fans? How do fans perceive the impact of their active consumption of transcultural content on themselves?

Methods

We employed virtual ethnography—a combination of participant observations and in-depth interviews—as the key method in this research in order to gain insights into the lives and practices of Chinese fans in online fan communities. Virtual ethnography is the process of conducting and constructing an ethnography using an online environment as the site of the research (Evans, 2010). It enables the researchers to make observations of and participate in online communities through a number of computer-based methods. Described as an effective method to investigate the ways in which use of the Internet becomes socially meaningful, virtual ethnography can "be used to develop an enriched sense of the meanings of the technology and the cultures which enable it and are enabled by it" (Hine, 2000, p. 8).

The first step in conducting our virtual ethnography was to identify the most active online communities for Chinese fans of foreign reality TV shows, which served as our observation sites to find relevant textual materials and a sampling framework to locate interviewees. We decided to focus on foreign reality TV shows because of the high popularity of reality TV shows now in China as well as the relatively scarce academic examination of the topic. After careful scrutiny of various online fan communities such as BBSs (bulletin board systems), subtitle Web sites (i.e., yyets.com, 1000fr.net, ragbear.com, sfileydy.com, huahuakorean. Joinbbs.net, and hdbird.com), and Baidu post bars (i.e., forums), it was clear that post bars had become the primary arenas in which Chinese fans shared and expressed their enthusiasm for foreign reality TV shows.

The second step was to identify the most popular foreign reality TV shows among Chinese audiences. As previous research (Zhang & Mao, 2013) has shown, the majority of foreign entertainment content is not provided in official Chinese outlets and there are mainly two channels for Chinese audiences to access foreign reality TV shows: watching them on video-streaming Web sites and downloading free copies online. Therefore, our estimation of popularity relied on an overall consideration of numbers of downloads and views that can be obtained from video streaming and downloading Web sites. An initial list was compiled to include fifteen popular foreign reality TV shows.

The third step was to identify particular Baidu post bars based on both the popularity of shows and the activeness of user participation, since some of the highly ranked shows did not trigger heated discussions online, such as *Project Runway* and *The Voice UK*. We double-checked the initial list by examining the numbers of members, topics, and posts of each corresponding post bar. Two of the shows from the initial list were thus excluded. Our final list included thirteen Baidu post bars of foreign reality TV shows. Among them, eight were from the United States (*American Idol, America's Next Top Model, The Amazing Race, The X-Factor US, Survivor, So You Think You Can Dance, America's Got Talent, The Voice US*), four were from South Korea (*Kpop Star, We Got Married, The Romantic & Idol, Running Man*), and one was from to the United Kingdom (*Britain's Got Talent*).

After finalizing our target post bars, we conducted participant observation in these bars to discern how they operate in their day-to-day routines. One of the authors registered as a member of post bars in February 2013. The other author has been a passive observer since April 2012 and kept a close eye on the daily trends of these bars. The researchers took advantage of their experience to fully explore the activities provided by these post bars, such as checking in, reading and writing posts and comments, watching videos, browsing through images, in-site messaging, searching archives, and so on.

In-depth interviews through instant messaging tools (e.g., QQ and Baidu Message) were conducted with 23 members of these post bars during April and May of 2013. The interviewees included bar managers (moderators) both sitting and retired, as well as active and influential members (judging from the popularity of the posts they authored and recommendations from the managers). We started by contacting sitting managers who could be identified from the home page of each post bar. After that, we utilized the snowball sampling technique to recruit more interviewees. We intentionally sought a diverse sample in terms of personal background, community affiliations, and roles (see Table 10.1). Our interviewees are mostly young adults around their early twenties. Their geographic locations show that most of them are from economically affluent areas in China, with a few interviewees currently residing out of China. Their occupations ranged from college students to working professionals, coming from a variety of industries. Surprisingly, most of them (15 out of 23) are males. Considering that almost no refusals occurred when we invited interviewees, we tend

TABLE 10.1 Demographic Information of Interviewees

Username	Name of Post Bar	Role in Post Bar	Age	Gender	Location	Occupation
Satan Ujfalusi	American Idol, America's Got Talent	Active member	30	Male	Britain	Banking
Wow	American Idol, The Voice US	Active member	24	Male	Sichuan	Tourism
Sea-tangle of Caribbean	American Idol, So You Think You Can Dance	Active member	25	Male	Henan	Civil servant
Joemd	America's Next Top Model	Bar manager	23	Male	Macau	Student
Ginger Sauce Milk	America's Next Top Model	Active member	23	Female	Guangdong	Student
Cauchy	The Amazing Race	Bar manager	18	Male	Zhejiang	Student
Teddy KK	The Amazing Race	Bar manager	19	Male	Beijing	Student
Star Era	The Amazing Race	Bar manager	19	Male	Shanghai	Student
Fzkhello	The X-Factor US	Bar manager	20	Male	Guangdong	Student
Everyday Sunny	Survivor So You Think You Can Dance	Active member	31	Female	America	Student
Windy	So You Think You Can Dance	Bar manager	24	Female	Shanxi	Unemployed
Shi	So You Think You Can Dance	Ex-manager	25	Female	Singapore	IT product manager
1985tx4	America's Got Talent	Bar manager	27	Male	Beijing	Art designer
BiscuitHead	The Voice US	Active member	20	Male	America	Student
Marshburn	The Voice US	Active member	19	Male	Tianjin	Student
Angela_gao	Kpop Star	Bar manager	26	Female	Jiangsu	Finance
Jiexiao	We Got Married	Bar manager	21	Male	Jiangsu	Student
Jinshe	The Romantic & idol	Active member	23	Female	Shandong	Student
Han Zaixi	Running Man	Bar manager	20	Male	Unknown	Unknown
Spirit_han	Running Man	Bar manager	20	Female	Jilin	Student
A667809	Running Man	Active member	23	Male	Fujian	Management
Zhang Niannian	Britain's Got Talent	Bar manager	23	Male	Shandong	Student
Kikyo Kitty	Britain's Got Talent	Active member	24	Female	Beijing	Media

to think that the male dominance is a reflection of the gender composition of active members and managers of these fan communities.

We obtained written consent from the interviewees through Baidu Message when we first contacted them. Twenty-two of the interviews were conducted on QQ (a Chinese instant messaging tool) and one through Baidu Message, depending upon the interviewee's personal preference. Each interview took from 1 to 4 hours with an average of 2 hours. An interview guide with 50 questions divided into 4 sections was used as a rough guideline during the interviews. However, not all questions were asked of each of the interviewees, and new questions were added occasionally varying from interviewee to interviewee.

Textual materials were collected to serve as background information and examples. Throughout our observations of and participation in these post bars, we purposefully gathered heated discussion threads on a variety of topics, either recently posted or stored in historical archives. During the interviews, we also asked the interviewees to provide links of posts that they mentioned as examples. Finally, Baidu site documents (e.g., FAQs, announcement, help, and terms of use) and other relevant news reports were also studied.

Watching TV on the Internet

Most existing literature about online fandom treats fan activities on the Internet a continuation or extension of their offline experience of watching TV on televisions. The active participation of fans is often aimed at influencing the fan objects they have enjoyed through media channels other than the Internet. The online fan activities include the interpretation of the content (e.g., Costello & Morre, 2007), the reconstruction of the content (e.g., Helleskon, & Busse, 2006), and activism to reshape the production process and mechanisms (e.g., Rowe, Ruddock, & Hutchins, 2010), as well as to influence the artists or celebrities involved (e.g., Soukup, 2006; Theberge, 2005). As such, online fandom cannot be completely cut off from the production line assembled by corporate media.

The case of watching foreign reality shows in China is to a large extent an experience independent of the medium of television. Among the 23 interviewees, only a few of them mentioned that they first encountered the reality shows on TV. One interviewee said that he saw the reality show *Amazing Race* on a channel of Shanghai TV Station in 2002 but immediately told us that he is no longer watching this show on TV. The majority of our interviewees either serendipitously bumped into the reality shows when browsing the Web or were introduced to the shows by their friends and family members. Almost all of them watch the reality shows exclusively on the Internet now for the following reasons: first, some reality shows such as *American Idol* were banned in China due to its format being deemed inappropriate by the government; second, the import of foreign shows was often delayed for months or years due to the long process of getting official permissions; third, the import of foreign shows was also not continuous, with regular interruptions due to both economic and political reasons. In contrast, the Internet provides free, real time, and nondisrupted access to such foreign shows.

The online sources of these foreign reality shows contain official and unofficial, legal and illegal Internet services. Official sources include the Web sites of foreign TV networks that provide free live podcasting. Many Korean TV networks are pioneers in running this model. Other official sources are Chinese video Web sites such as Youku (similar to YouTube), which have agreements with foreign producers and streamline the official sources on their own Web pages. Some smaller video-streaming sites also do the same without having any agreements with the original producers. The last and most important source often falls into the grey area of being semi-legal or illegal. Zhang and Mao (2013) describe in detail how subtitle groups record, digitalize, translate, and disseminate foreign cultural products and provide them to Chinese audiences for free. Our interviewees indicated that they are used to consuming content from both types of sources because the official live podcasting is in its original language and the versions from the subtitles groups are in Chinese.

A typical online viewing process starts by searching for sources and schedules, important information found in fan communities such as Baidu post bars. After figuring out when and where they can watch the shows online, many fans watch the shows together with other fans. The way in which they watch together is through the so-called live-broadcasting posts. Since the live versions are still in their original language, most Chinese audiences who watch the shows in real time are not able to fully understand the content. Fans who have better language proficiency translate important content (e.g., rankings or elimination of contestants) in real time in the posts so that fans can discuss the content in real time. Watching the video streams online makes it easy to shift between discussion windows and video windows constantly. After the first round of viewing live broadcasts, almost all of the fans told us that they watch the video a second time using the subtitled version. An interviewee said that the discussions she had with fellow fans on the Internet sometimes reshaped her perceptions of contestants, and she watched the show with a new outlook the second time. The translated version is not entirely the same as the original version because the subtitle groups often creatively insert local jargon to make the foreign content more comprehensible and enjoyable to Chinese audiences. One interviewee, who is located in the United Kingdom right now, told us that although he is fully capable of watching the shows in their original form, he finds some of the localized translation amusing.

The remaining process of watching TV on the Internet is similar to previously documented fan activities. Fans cut the original episode into shorter sections in order to highlight the contestants or parts they enjoy the most. These so-called cuts are especially popular in post bars that are dedicated to particular stars or contestants. Fans express their fondness and loyalty to specific shows or their contestants by writing posts mixed with texts, images, and videos that attract fellow fans to reply. These support posts are called *Gailou* in Chinese, which literally means *building high-rises*, because the more replies, the longer the post, and the "higher" the "building." Fans of different shows and contestants often engage in highly emotional debates, as well. These posts are called *Qiajia* in Chinese, which literally means *fighting*. Although bar managers are concerned about the disturbing effect of debate posts, they admitted that these posts are regularly seen, and they themselves also engage in such fights under other user IDs.

Online fandom does not just stay online. Fans who met in the fan communities go offline and meet each other face-to-face. One interesting case is that of fans of *Amazing Race* and *Running Man* who organized their own online or offline competitions, borrowing the show structure. Fans also organize themselves to support their stars in real life by sending gifts to the stars, making trips to commercial events that feature their stars, and so on. One extreme case was mentioned by an interviewee who is a fan of Korean popular culture. She mentioned that her friend, also a passionate fan of the Korean wave, went to Korea to study for her college degree in order to be closer to her stars.

It is now evident that the process of watching TV on the Internet is distinct from watching TV on television sets. One interviewee felt that he has more power over his viewing experience when watching the shows online. He can fast forward the parts he does not like or go to post bars for discussions when commercial breaks appear in the live podcasting. The viewing experience, as pointed out by several interviewees, is also communal rather than individual. The discussions during and after the live podcasting not only bring pleasure to the viewers but also have significant influence on their interpretations of the content, especially when the foreign producers are not able to directly influence the fan communities yet.

Reading Reality Out of Reality Shows

This section provides cross-cultural and aesthetic analyses of the perceptions of Chinese audiences regarding the content of foreign reality TV shows and the impact of such content. Two questions are key to understanding fans' perceptions: First, how do foreign reality shows attract Chinese fans, and why do fans fail to find such attractions in local reality shows? Second, how do fans perceive the impact of such content on their understanding of both foreign and local cultures; their criteria for evaluating reality shows and cultural products in general; and their broader skills, knowledge, and values?

Many interviewees were attracted to the shows by either the format of the shows or the stars featured in the shows. A relatively clear difference was observed between British/American and Korean shows. Most Korean reality show fans were already fans of particular stars before they started watching the shows. Almost all of the Korean reality show fans were first drawn to the shows because they knew that their favorite stars would be featured in the shows. These Korean show fans kept watching the shows because they were able to see "the other sides" of their favorite stars. Watching such shows acts as an extension of their existing fandom of particular stars or Korean popular culture. A few Korean show fans mentioned that although some shows did not feature stars already known to them, they were still attracted because the unknown stars were "pretty," "entertaining," or "well-trained" by the Korean system. One interviewee referenced "the Big Three," the three biggest entertainment companies in South Korea, as guarantees for producing stars that cater to her taste.

In contrast, most of the British/American reality shows do not focus on celebrities but on ordinary contestants. Several interviewees answered that they particularly liked the component of featuring ordinary people who have talent. They also mentioned that they liked the component of competition, which is generally fair. When being probed about why they do not find such components in local reality shows, many of the answers included a key word, *Jia*. The Chinese word Jia is polysemous and can be used to refer to the opposite of being truthful, or sincere, or authentic, or original. The fans we interviewed have used the word in all four senses. They were often fast to point out that many local reality shows copied the format of successful foreign shows and, therefore, were rarely original. With regard to those local shows that had purchased franchise right from the foreign shows, the fans also found that the local versions were not consistent with the original versions. For instance, one of the managers of the post bar on the *Amazing Race* gave us a detailed summary on the differences between the original and local versions in choices of contestants, sites of shows, rules, and cutting and editing, as well as values conveyed. His conclusion was that the original version beat the local version hands down.

Fans generally thought that local reality shows tend to sell melodrama more than other components. They admitted that foreign reality shows also contain drama because the dramatic effect is one of the attractions that hooks-in audiences. However, they found the drama in foreign reality shows to be more authentic than those in local shows. To them, drama should not be scripted, rehearsed, and staged but should naturally emerge during the process of competition. An active member of the post bar on *America's Next Top Model* raised the example of one judge in the local version telling a contestant that if she could not lower her weight to a certain point within a few weeks, she would be eliminated immediately. The contestant turned out to pass the weight test with a marginal difference. This interviewee interpreted this drama as preplanned and overcooked. Even more intolerable for the fans, some drama in local shows is completely untruthful. They mentioned that some leaked news about contestants—such as their sexual orientation—is simply fake information released by the local producers in order to attract attention to the show. They also questioned the sincerity of both the producers and the contestants in playing out the drama. They interpreted that some contestants overemphasize their pitiful life in order to gain sympathy from audiences and linked that behavior to the producers' encouragement in promoting melodrama.

The critique of local reality shows based on the concept of Jia is further deepened when a minority of our interviewees reflected on the reasons of such lack of originality, authenticity, and sincerity. One of the reasons is the close control over the content from the government, which has put many constraints on local producers to work creatively. Another often-cited reason is the overcommercialization of local shows. Although foreign reality shows are also commercial, our interviewees argued that the foreign shows were not as "bloody" as the local shows. Quite a number of interviewees described how much the "in-your-face" kind of advertisements (e.g., TV hosts recite the advertisements verbally in the shows) disgusted them and thought that commercials in foreign shows were more "subtle" (e.g., commercial breaks can be skipped) and thus "appropriate." The fans cited local producers' motivation to "make fast money" as the reason why creativity, originality, and authenticity has been killed. Only a few interviewees addressed the level of cultural differences. One interviewee explained that Chinese culture stresses harmony, and the local shows tend to emphasize the image of one big family, which makes the show look pretentious. In contrast, foreign shows like to focus on the personality of individual contestants, and the individuals are encouraged to present their true selves, which makes the show look sincere. Another interviewee said that Chinese culture puts work in front of leisure, and entertainment is considered a meaningless activity. The foreign reality shows demonstrate that leisure activities have their purposes and should not be despised in a culture.

When asking about the perceived impact of these foreign shows, many interviewees mentioned that they became more knowledgeable about the subject, be it popular music or different varieties of dances. Some of them also became more knowledgeable about the culture/country of origin than before and believed that the reality shows were portraying the reality of the foreign culture. Most of our interviewees denied that the foreign reality shows have changed their worldviews and core values. However, they mostly agreed that their ability to judge the quality of reality shows was enhanced by being exposed to foreign shows. Believing that they have better taste than others, several interviewees referred to fans of local shows as "too young," "irrational," or "brain-dead." They occasionally got into fights with fans of local shows on the Internet, where they accused local fans of being ignorant and are, themselves, accused by local fans as being capitulated by foreign cultures. Interestingly, almost no one recognized that they were influenced by the global capital behind the transcultural media products. Even when we explicitly asked about their free labor invested in promoting the foreign content, they often responded with a simple answer such as "I don't care" or "I like the show so I want more people to like it."

Discussions and Conclusions

Our research found that Baidu post bars are currently the most prominent online arenas in which Chinese fans of foreign reality TV shows get together and share their fandom. Supported by other online tools such as Weibo and QQ, the post bar–based fan communities provide resources to access the content and facilitate a communal experience of watching TV on the Internet. The fans had to actively participate in production and circulation in order to locate the sources of content, translate the content into Chinese, and disseminate the subtitled versions to fellow fans. Their consumption, however, does not show a critical stance that resists the dominant reading of the global cultural products, partially due to the fans' perception that their consumption hardly makes any profits for the original producers. However, cultural defense (Tan, 2011) has been utilized to interpret foreign content and their compatibility with local values. Whereas the fans refused to admit that their worldviews and core values had been greatly changed by the shows, their evaluation of the quality of foreign versus local reality shows signaled the aesthetic transformation (i.e., changes in cultural and artistic standards) happening among these audiences.

We argue that this fandom of transcultural media products found in the Chinese cyber-sphere indicates the need to take a complex view on the process of globalization and its implications for the local. The nation-state plays an intermediary role that connects both global capital and local audiences. Proponents of cultural imperialism think that the only superpower now, the United States, reinforces its status by selling its cultural products to other parts of the world. Other nation-states are seen as either incapable of or unwilling to challenge the dominant status of the United States. Oftentimes, these less powerful states have to cooperate with global capital, through actions such as making policies that take away market barriers. We argue that the role of the state in globalization cannot simply be considered to be an agent of global capitalist forces because the state has its own need to survive as an entity. Our research shows that the Chinese state closely controls the official flow of information and entertainment in fear of losing ideological hegemony. Meanwhile, the state tolerates local capital (e.g., Baidu and various video Web sites) taking advantage of this shortage of foreign content by allowing a niche market to fulfill its needs. The local, in this case, is therefore comprised of multiple forces, including the nation-state, the local capitals, and the local audiences, with tensions existing among them.

If we understand globalization from the perspectives of the state, the market, and the society simultaneously, it becomes less confusing why active consumers of transcultural media products in China can be seen as both immaterial labor and fan activists. The fans' activism in obtaining foreign content and sharing their fandom can be viewed as a resistance to state control over the flow of information. New media such as the Internet provide users with an alternative channel to get access to such content. Meanwhile, their activism contains the value-adding potential to help multinational corporations to nurture the market, cultivate audience taste, and promote products, which enables profit-making via other means (e.g., sales of franchise rights) and prepares the readi-ness of consumers should the state decide to deregulate the cultural market. Due to the fact that the multinational corporations have yet to find ways to directly make profits from the fans, we argue that the immaterial labor is more exploited by local Web sites such as Baidu than by foreign cultural corporations. This exploitation is in line with the state's attempt to strengthen local capital, which can later export their products to other national markets. This complicated relationship between the state and capital helps us to understand why the state tolerates such fandom although it contains the possibility to mobilize ideologi-cal challenges.

Given the double potential of fandom regarding transcultural media prod-ucts, we are not going to make a holistic conclusion on the implications of such fandom. Instead, we propose that whether or not such fandom is able to lead to the building of a large active citizenry depends on how online activities influ-ence fans to behave in offline spheres. For example, how would the communal experience of watching TV on the Internet reshape the ways in which citizens organize themselves for offline collective action? Or, how do the changes in aesthetic standards (e.g., the emphasis on originality, authenticity, sincerity, and truthfulness) affect responses and reactions to all kinds of local cultural products, including the ones meant for promoting the official ideology? In addition to the nation-state, our analyses imply that both global and local economic capi-tals need to be examined carefully when we try to interpret the implications of online fandom of transcultural media products. We thus invite further research on the conditions that trigger the imbalance between the various forces that might lead to significant transformations in China.

References

Andrejevic, M. (2008). Watching television without pity: The productivity of online fans. *Television & New Media, 9*, 24–46.

Ang, I. (1985). *Watching Dallas.* London: Methuen.

Baym, N. (2007). The new shape of online community: The example of Swedish inde-pendent music fandom. *First Monday, 12*(8). Retrieved from http://firstmonday.org/ojs/index.php/fm/article/view/1978/1853

Costello, V., & Moore, B. (2007). Cultural outlaws: An examination of audience activity and online television fandom. *Television & New Media, 8*, 124–143.

Cote, M., & Pybus, J. (2007). Learning to immaterial labour 2.0: MySpace and social networks. *Ephemera: Theory and Politics in Organization, 7*(1), 88–106.

Curran, J., & Park, M. J. (2000). *De-Westernizing media studies.* New York: Routledge.

Evans, L. (2010). Authenticity online: Using webnography to address phenomenological concerns. Retrieved from http://www.inter-disciplinary.net/wp-content/uploads/2010/02/evanspaper.pdf

Fiske, J. (1989). *Understanding popular culture*. Boston: Unwin Hyman.

Fung, A. (2008). *Global capital, local culture: Transnational media corporations in China*. New York: Peter Lang.

Fung, A. (2009). Fandom, youth, and consumption in China. *European Journal of Cultural Studies, 12*, 285–303.

Hall, S. (1980). Encoding/decoding. In S. Hall, D. Hobson, A. Lowe, & P. Willis (Eds.), *Culture, media, language* (pp. 128–138). London: Hutchinson.

Hardt, M., & Negri, A. (2000). *Empire*. Cambridge, MA: Harvard University Press.

Helleskon, K., & Busse, K. (2006). *Fan fiction and fan communities in the age of the Internet*. Jefferson, NC: McFarland Press.

Hine, C. (2000). *Virtual ethnography*. London: Sage.

Hoskins, C., & Mirus, R. (1988). Reasons for the US dominance of the international trade in television programmes. *Media, Culture, & Society, 10*, 499–515.

Jameson, F. (1998). Notes on globalization as a philosophical issue. In F. Jameson & M. Miyoshi (Eds.), *The cultures of globalization* (pp. 54–80). Durham, NC: Duke University Press.

Jenkins, H. (2006). *Fans, bloggers, and gamers: Exploring participatory culture*. New York: New York University Press.

Miller, T. (2008). "Step away from the croissant": Media studies 3.0. In D. Hesmondhaigh & J. Toynbee (Eds.), *The media and social theory* (pp. 213–230). New York: Routledge.

Morley, D. (1993). Active audience theory: Pendulum and pitfalls. *Journal of Communication, 43*(4), 13–19.

Radway, J. (1984). *Reading the romance: Women, patriarchy and popular literature*. London: Verso.

Rowe, D., Ruddock, A., & Hutchins, B. (2010). Cultures of complaint: Online fan message boards and networked digital media sport. *Convergence: The International Journal of Research Into New Media Technologies, 16*(3), 298–315.

Soukup, C. (2006). Hitching a ride on a star: Celebrity, fandom, and identification on the World Wide Web. *Southern Communication Journal, 71*(4), 319–337.

Straubhaar, J. (1991). Beyond media imperialism: Asymmetrical interdependence and cultural proximity. *Critical Studies in Mass Communication, 8*, 39–59.

Tan, S. K. (2011). Global Hollywood, narrative transparency, and Chinese media poachers: Narrating cross-cultural negotiations of *Friends* in South China. *Television & New Media, 12*, 207–227.

Terranova, T. (2000). Free labor: Producing culture for the digital economy. *Social Text, 18*(2), 33–58.

Theberge, P. (2005). Everyday fandom: Fan clubs, blogging, and the quotidian rhythms of the Internet. *Canadian Journal of Communication, 30*, 485–502.

Van Zoonen, L. (2004). Imagining the fan democracy. *European Journal of Communication, 19*(1), 39–52.

Wang, G. (2009). Going beyond the dualistic view of culture and market economy: Learning from the localization of reality television in Greater China. *Chinese Journal of Communication, 2*(2), 127–139.

Yang, G. (2009). *The power of the Internet in China: Citizen activism online*. New York: Columbia University Press.

Yu, H. (2009). *Media and cultural transformation in China*. New York: Routledge.

Zhang, W. (2006). Constructing and disseminating subaltern public discourses in China. *Javnost—The Public, 13*(2), 41–64.

Zhang, W., & Mao, C. (2013). Fan activism sustained and challenged: Participatory culture in Chinese online translation communities. *Chinese Journal of Communication, 6*(1), 45–61.

Zhang, W., & Wang, R. (2010). Interest-oriented versus relationship-oriented social network sites in China. *First Monday, 15*(8). Retrieved from http://firstmonday.org/htbin/cgiwrap/bin/ojs/index.php/fm/article/view/2836/2582

Zhang, X. (2006). The concept of "local" in local Chinese television: A case study of Southwest China's Chongqing Television. *Westminster Paper in Communication and Culture, 3*(1), 28–41.

Zhao, Y. (2008). *Communication in China: Political economy, power, and conflict.* Lanham, MD: Rowman & Littlefield.

Zheng, Y. (2007). *Technological empowerment: The Internet, state, and society in China.* Stanford, CA: Stanford University Press.

11

THE NEW POLITICAL OF MEDIATED ACTIVISM IN CHINA

A Critical Review

Elaine J. Yuan

Amid enthusiastic scholarly discourses about the waves of technological developments in recent years has been a growing interest in the political effects of the Internet and mobile communication in Chinese communication studies. Researchers from media studies, political communication, and various other social disciplines have focused their attention on new forms of popular and grassroots political activities enabled by digital media.

Despite the long tradition of centralized control over the media system, various forms of mediated activism have been crucial components in struggles for political change in China. The Democracy Wall movement in the 1970s, featuring wall posters advocating for broad social changes, and the "Culture Fever," endorsed by the influential TV documentary *River Elegy* in the 1980s, are only two prominent examples of such struggles for Enlightenment ideals of freedom and democracy in an earlier age of contemporary Chinese social movements (Yang, 2009c).

The new epoch of mediated activism in contemporary China, however, is delineated by profound social and economic reforms and their subsequent consequences. These include the establishment of a market economy, rapid urbanization, and growing social inequality. Significant developments in the country's media landscape, such as media marketization and the speedy diffusion of information and communication technologies (ICTs) are not only one of the propelling forces behind these changes but also one of the main avenues where the dynamics of change play out (e.g., Lee, 2000; Zhao, 1998, 2008). Consequently, mediated activism in China is defined by the emerging "middle classes" and their claims for citizenship and rights, the articulation of new political demands by marginalized social strata, and the changing forms of political struggle enabled by new media. Indeed, as Chu and Cheng (2011) keenly point out, the modern

Chinese experience is defined by the simultaneous rise of modern capitalism and rapid cyberization, while also quickly moving toward a more open society in an increasingly globalized world (p. 26).

New forms of networked communication enabled by digital ICTs have augmented the mode of nonreciprocal "quasi-interaction" in the era of mass media with mediated interactive communication (Thompson, 1995). Social media may serve to mediate social processes by which sociopolitical power dynamics struggle over "truth regimes" (Zhao, 2012, p. 146). At the same time, increasingly personalized modes of political association (Bakardjieva, 2009; Rosen, 2010) has spawned new issues with collective identification in social activism. In light of these new developments, research into mediated activism is pressed to provide a contextualized understanding of important aspects of the modern political process in contemporary China.

A notable feature of a rapidly growing body of literature on mediated activism in China is the case study approach. Existing studies have documented and analyzed numerous episodes of "new media events (*xinmeiti shijian*, 新媒体事件)," "online events (*wangluo shijian*, 网络事件)" (Qiu & Chan, 2011), online "mass incidents" (Jiang, 2012), "collective actions," "cyberprotests," and "social movements" (e.g., Tai, 2006; Yang, 2009c; Zheng & Wu, 2005). These often-isolated cases are noted for their mass scales, dynamic processes, political and cultural consequences, and, more importantly, spontaneous and contentious nature. Scholars have also made considerable efforts to apply relevant theoretical frameworks in relating patterns of communication in these cases to broader social factors and concerns.

This chapter intends to survey existing literature, identify its main trends, critique its theoretical approaches, and relate it to the urgent call for a new agenda for Chinese communication research in general. In the remainder of this chapter, I make my comments along three distinct yet interrelated lines of inquiry: (1) structuralist assumptions underlying the understanding of the state-society relation in (mediated) activism scholarship; (2) mediated cultural practices and processes of civic agency; and (3) understanding of *the political* as situated in new dynamics of social structures, cultural agency, and the mediated interaction among them. In the conclusion, I briefly reiterate the agenda for future research in this area.

Civil Society and Its Discontents

A prevalent framework common in the majority of studies focused on mediated activism and online events is civil society (Yang, 2003a, 2003b). The application of such a framework often indicates that (1) various forms of online activism are evidence demonstrating the role of the Internet as an exuberant space for information dissemination, opinion formation, and civic association, and (2) the often contentious nature of these activities only reflects the struggle of a fledgling civil society against a monolithic, oppressive authoritarian party-state in China (e.g., Tai, 2006; Zhang & Zheng, 2009). The liberal-normative expectations explicit in these frames have been embodied in the popular "liberation discourse" (e.g., Xiao, 2004; Zittrain & Edelman, 2003) and "control discourse" (e.g., Damm & Thomas, 2006; MacKinnon, 2008; Marolt, 2011; Qiu, 1999; Taubman, 1998), which have been present to varying degrees in virtually every study of the Chinese Internet (Chu & Cheng, 2011; Damm, 2007). While the former started with the initial enthusiasm about the liberating power of "open network" technology, the latter shifted the focus to explaining how "closed regimes" employed the Internet for policing and censoring purposes (Kalathil & Boas, 2003).

With a primary focus on examining *how* contentious struggles and activities are enabled by new media networks, this approach tends to take for granted *why* these activities happen. It often assumes that the causes are inherent to the antagonism of control and resistance between the authoritarian state and liberal society. Implicit in this model of understanding are structuralist assumptions about the nature of society and power. Such assumptions prioritize and privilege the primacy of institutionalized power, typically embodied in the state and dominant political and economic structures, while overlooking or discounting other sources of power and forms of oppression in explaining the causes and effects of (mediated) activism (Armstrong & Bernstein, 2008).

Arguments along these lines are premised on the rapid and uneven growth of urbanization, privatization, and marketization, insensitive to the subsequent structural polarization and fracturing in contemporary China. With the authoritarian state as the single-most pervasive source of dominance, the struggles of social actors are organized around and against this source of power (Armstrong & Bernstein, 2008). It is only natural that the media has become one of the many sites of a great amount of literal and metaphorical resistance by economically and politically dispossessed people (Yang, 2009c).

This state-centric perspective fails to pay adequate attention to the multiplicity of interests and goals of various social groups in the increasingly fragmented contemporary Chinese society, imbued with a variety of conflicts and resistance (Hsing & Lee, 2010; O'Brien, 2008; Perry, 1994; Perry & Selden, 2003; Wasserstrom & Perry, 1992). Increasingly divided by class/social strata, gender, regional, ethnic, and other divisions, Chinese society is susceptible to profound crises in meaning, identity, and ethics (Damm, 2007; Yang, 2009c; Zhao, 2008). Consequently, this structuralist framework does not fare well with the rising level of contentious activities challenging nonstate institutions or hegemonic cultural meanings. Episodes of the popular *Human Search Engine* (Herold, 2011) and online *egao*, a parody of remixed cultural imageries or playful satire in multimedia forms (Li, 2011; Meng, 2011; Tang & Yang, 2011), for instance, often target economic and cultural elites and contest sociocultural institutions such as marriage and privacy. These online activities are often presented as "carnivals," "fun, freak-shows, masquerade" (Herold & Marolt, 2011) that characterize an online universe outside the sphere of political activism.

A most helpful approach, I would like to suggest, is to adopt a multi-institutional model to reflect both the structures and substances of social relation in flux (Armstrong & Bernstein, 2008). This model defines all collective and public challenges to all forms of constituted authority, by all peoples of the periphery, as the realm of the political.[1] This realm takes its shape and preserves its character in constant contestations between the central and the peripheral on various socioeconomic and cultural fronts. Such an approach affords us opportunities to examine domination exerted by multiple sources of material and symbolic power. The sociocultural heterogeneity and diversity embodied in various collective actions is celebrated as integral to a progressive civic culture (Meng, 2011).

All this, however, is not to deny the central role of the state in sociopolitical life in China. Yet the role of the Chinese state is complex. Scholars have noted the engagement of the state by activists in such fields as the environmental movement, the consumer-rights movement, and popular crusades against corruption of officials (Yang, 2009c). There has also been a growing degree of flexibility and versatility on the part of the state in its responses to social activism (Perry, 2009). What we need is a more sophisticated approach that recognizes the complex role of state power and the ambivalent nature of civil society in relation to it (Hsing & Lee, 2010; Zhao, 2008).

Zhao (2008), for instance, argues that the government constructs its rules for control in the communication and ideological arena through the selective implication of neoliberal policies. From this perspective, it's more important to understand how the power of the party-state has been reconfigured than how much power it has been able to retain. Along similar lines, Wang and Wu (2013) point out that what defines the Internet as a shared discursive space is not so much the direct opposition between the dominant political power and the Internet as the public sphere but the effects of political practices performed by various intermediary agents within the mediated public sphere.

While the Chinese state and its censorship regime are an important context in which we understand the parameters of online activism, this should not overshadow our efforts to arrive at a historical understanding of the complicated role of the state in the Chinese media system. The state has played a transformative role as the designer and manager of Chinese modernity in general (Zhao, 2012). Such an understanding may free us from the limits of the liberal media model and open up new ground for understanding mediated activism beyond simplistic dichotomies. Instead of seeing social contention as a sign of "social unrest" weakening a stable social order, perhaps we should seriously consider the proposition made by Hsing and Lee (2010) that we understand social activism as constitutive of an evolving social order of a Chinese society in a state of "dynamic stability" (p. 12).

Cultural Forms and Agents

Parallel to the overwhelming interest in collective contention aimed at the state and institutionalized politics, there has been greater attention to the symbolic practices, agency, and discourse of mediated activism playing out in social arenas (Li, 2011; Meng, 2011; Tang & Yang, 2011, Yang, 2009a, 2009b; Yang & Zheng, 2012; Yu, 2009). Attesting to the porous boundaries of the political, expressive and creative symbolic practices are often discussed as alternative political acts. Though often without explicit political goals, scholars argue, meaningful cultural practices effectively challenge or deconstruct traditional and often oppressive cultural hierarchies and social classifications. In her study of some popular cases of *egao*, for instance, Meng (2011) contends that although these episodes are neither qualified as consensus-oriented rational debates nor capable of producing visible consequences for policies, the encoding and decoding of these spoofs involve a wide array of critiques of sociopolitical issues and offer emotional bonding for participants. In this sense, they "set up inside and outside positions, which renders it politically potent" (p. 47).

Such creative activities are also analyzed with an emphasis on their use of new cultural forms, characterized by plastic formats of presentation and a remix culture (Lessig, 2008) enabled by the digital media (Yang, 2009b). But the notion of cultural form, as Yang (2009b) points out, is not defined simply by technological capability. He reminds us that new cultural forms, emerging out of the interactions between the Internet and society, are the products of both cultural tradition and innovation—creative forms of response to new social conditions.

Moreover, researchers have noted, "many shapes of and possibilities for grassroots agency . . . visible in myriad narratives of creative power that have become ubiquitous on the Chinese internet" (Marolt, 2011, p. 53). Marolt (2011) maintains that "the Chinese internet is a diverse and ever-changing civil sphere that, rooted in subjectivity, fosters people's awareness and agency" (p. 63).

There has been insufficient scholarship, however, that goes beyond the residual and reflective role of the cultural in order to probe cultural contexts, mechanisms, and processes of such agency in the social context of Chinese communication. One notable line of inquiry subsumes issues of civic agency and competence under the liberal notion of civic culture. The concept of civic culture has obvious roots in a long tradition of historical and sociological research on civic engagement and democracy in Western sociology (e.g., de Tocqueville, 1835; Putnam, 1995; Putnam, Leonardi, & Nanetti, 1994). Advocates maintain that cultures of citizenship, growing out of meaningful civic practices, promote, sustain, or diminish democratic participation. Dahlgren (2005), for instance, argues that civic culture is "anchored in the mind-sets and symbolic milieu of everyday life" and concerns with "the processes of becoming—how people develop into citizens, how they come to see themselves as members of and potential participants in societal development" (p. 158). Applying cultural theory to issues of political communication, scholars of civic culture consider dimensions such as "meaning, identity, and subjectivity" to be crucial elements of political communication (p. 158).

Issues of agency and subjectivity remind us of two important questions for understanding mediated activism in any context: First, what sort of social identity qualifies one to participate in public discourses that influence policy and power? The dominant models of liberal democracy, for instance, assume as their subjects individual actors making rational decisions in relation to self-regulating market system. Second, what is the role of communication in the formation of subjectivity? Habermas, for instance, emphasized an intersubjective model of rationality that is constituted through communication (Habermas, 1989).

A. X. Wu (2012) notes that the existing research on the Chinese Internet has tended to take for granted this consistent, self-motivated liberal subject as one capable of being transposed directly into a citizen of formal liberal democracies. The few studies that address such issues in the cultural and historical contexts of China, however, report the general online population to be conservative or apathetic (Dahlgren, 2006; Damm, 2007; Farrer, 2007; Giese, 2004; Wallis, 2011). Nevertheless, the discourse of civic culture serves to shift our attention fixated on elite- and dissident-led activities to the social processes of communication in which the broader population for democratic cultural purposes participates (Wu, 2012).

Moreover, political participation is often conceptualized as the enactment of citizenship as a form of social agency (Dahlgren, 2000). Yu (2009), for instance, believes that "citizenship can no longer be thought of as a formal and institutional given, but as a concept of fluidity and flexibility that rests on the spatial and subjective positions of the socio-cultural agents in question" (p. 107). She further argues that media users are transformed into media citizens by "exercising citizenship, not through overt resistance, but through a process of re-subjectification via mediated expression, social interaction, and circulation their own media stories" (p. 110).

However, Dahlgren (2005) reminds us that the progressive and subversive role of the Internet should not be overestimated. Coming from a liberal pluralist perspective, he maintains that while different social and cultural groups can express civic culture in different ways, a functioning civic culture "suggests minimal shared commitments to the vision and procedures of democracy" and that this "entails a capacity to express civic commonality beyond the immediate interests of one's own group" (p. 158). In light of this cautious note, it is imperative to interrogate the often taken-for-granted concept of the public. Rather than a fixed category, the public, as Calhoun (1998) suggests, is a self-producing and self-aware body that develops from the project of public good through discursive interactional processes. It is such deliberative processes that safeguard the collective from degenerating into chaotic populism (Dahlgren, 2005).

Equally important is the question of the political nature of the subject that a public media space is supposed to nurture and sustain in the social historical context of China. Scholars have long noted a unique repertoire of traditional (and modern) beliefs, values, and symbols that has been passed down through socialization in Chinese political communication (Wasserstrom & Perry, 1992). Chinese political culture is heavily influenced by the cultural tradition of Confucianism and the historical experience with the communist revolutions (Perry, 2007). In contemporary China, these relatively stable meaning systems are brought into contact with other ideological complexes and mechanisms such as neoliberalism, consumerism, and populism. Much work is needed to examine how these cultural currents influence activist subjectivity and collective identity formation through mediation processes.

Disputing the liberal notion of civil society, China's leftist intellectuals and their allied social forces—including the State, to a certain extent—hold onto Chinese revolutionary legacies and socialist discourse in developing their view of the political subject and political agency for building a just society. They claim to speak for "the masses"; that is, China's vast working classes in whose name the revolution was fought (Zhao, 2011). They embrace the Marxist idea that the nature of the human being is the sum of all of his or her social economic relations embedded in concrete sociohistorical contexts. No individuals exist outside such social relations. Treating society as an integrated whole consisting of abstract individuals with equal rights, the concept of civil society ignores class disparities in concrete social relations. For this reason, they believe the so-called civil society is more of a neoliberal fabrication than a historical reality (Wang, 2013).

Mediated communication has long played a significant role in creating and performing political subjectivities in contemporary China. Zhang (2000), for instance, examines the historical trajectory and significance of conceptual change from "masses" to "audience" in Chinese political communication. He points out that this change eroded Mao's "Party–masses model" of propaganda, prescribed a new political and ideological relationship between the press and readers in both the discursive and practical domains of Chinese journalism, and opened up an institutional space for further reform activities. More recently, in his critique of the state-corporatist logic in recent media developments, Pan (2010) noted that the media have served to activate the subjectivity of consumers rather than that of citizens.

Along these lines, China's growing urban "middle-class" and its potential political agency has attracted much attention in recent years. Empirical analyses of the media's role in the making of the "middle class," however, are quite limited, as are those of the political consciousness and communicative practices of identifiable segments of this class (Wu, 2012). The remainder of this section is a crude account of the "middle stratum" on the Chinese Internet. It aims to provide an alternative way to think about the relationship between the socially constructed process of collective identity—as dialectically interrelated combinations of structural positions and consciousness (Buechler, 1995)—and social activism.

It has long been noted that Chinese Internet users are demographically distinct. Typical Chinese users are urban, young (between 15 and 30 years old), and relatively better educated (with some high school or college education). With an average monthly salary under 5,000 RMB Yuan, the majority of online users are students (28.8%), middle- or lower-ranking company employees (15%), small-business owners and the self-employed (13%), and professionals and skilled vocational workers (10.4%) (CNNIC, 2010).

Although large in size (564 million), this online population represents less than 30% of the country's total population, leaving out a vast number of rural villagers and workers. Chinese Internet users occupy different and fluid socio-economic positions. Since education is a major means of social mobility in Chinese society (Bian, 2002; Huang, 2008), the student group is especially mobile. Middle-ranking managers and white-collar workers, though small in proportion, make up the more affluent layer of the online population (Huang, 2008). In addition, liberal humanistic intellectuals and social critics, the group with traditional cultural power, are also active online and often serve as advocates and opinion leaders on contentious social issues (Zhao, 2008).

Despite its internal socioeconomic differentiation, this online population is defined by a common political position, what Huang (2008) calls a "middle social stratum"[2] in the rapidly stratifying Chinese society. This middle stratum mediates between the ruling classes and their social-elite allies, on the one hand, and the underclasses of rural peasants and the urban poor, on the other (Huang, 2008; Zhao, 2008). Subject to the volatility brought about by the country's ongoing market reforms in employment, housing, and health care, members of this particular social stratum face a precarious socioeconomic future of their own. They are vulnerable to the drawbacks of the party-state's authoritarian regime, such as corruption, ineffective public services, and arbitrary governmental administrative power. Most of them, therefore, are sensitive to social justice and motivated to speak on behalf of unprivileged social groups (Zhao, 2008).

Moreover, this particularly mobile social stratum is at the forefront of the ongoing "individualization" process of Chinese society (Yan, 2010). Increasingly "disembedded" from traditional social categories (e.g., family, community, etc.) and collective institutions (e.g., Danwei), members of the middle stratum have led the trend toward self-reliant individualism in a society experiencing rapid modernization. The emergence of the new consumption-based sociality has further rendered the individuals "liberated" consumers, who have to struggle for social status on the diverse markets of the quickly marketized Chinese society (Liu, 2011; Yan, 2010). The logic of its social-structural situation sets the middle stratum apart from the underclasses, who are subject to the relatively stable needs of daily life.

Affected by its objective position, the middle stratum develops its own subjective class consciousness. The norms and values of this stratum are neither propelled merely by the constraints of daily life, nor can they be justified by universalistic reasoning. Consequently, the middle stratum often drifts away from—and sometimes even operates in opposition to—the instrumental interests of the lower classes and demands to establish its own needs as the true social needs (Buechler, 1995; Eder, 1985). With both the objective structure of their social position and the subjective consciousness of their social position, the actors of the middle stratum together constitute a collective disposition, what Bourdieu calls a "habitus." Eder (1985) argues that the central explanatory variable in the analysis of contentious collective action is the collective acquisition of such a habitus in interaction with other individuals in a life world that is simultaneously objectively structured and the prerequisite for the construction of a collective consciousness.

The precarious middle stratum reflects the fluidity and fragility of contemporary social structures in Chinese society (Huang, 2008). The making of a new middle-class as a group with a distinct identity and consciousness is dialectically intertwined with the rise of collective sociopolitical actions on the Chinese Internet. The various expressive and contentious collective actions are manifestations of "a class-specific response to the middle-class realities of upward mobility, cultural capital, and the lack of a clear group identity" in the ongoing social construction project in China (Buechler, 1995, p. 455).

Perhaps the notion of a middle stratum is still too totalizing as an analytic concept for understanding the workings of a cultural agency both enabled and bound by the structural positions of the various social groups active online. Recent data have documented changing demographics of Internet users. The Internet has penetrated users further down the ladder of social and economic status. The percentages of less-educated users have been steadily increasing. So have those of seniors and users from rural areas. These trends suggest that there will soon be palpable changes in political perspectives voiced online. We expect to see more nuanced and in-depth analyses of subjectivity and civic cultures anchored at the level of lived experiences, personal resources, and subjective dispositions of these groups. These elements of agency both embody and manifest collective and social relations, which in turn provide resources and constraints for meaningful cultural life. The dynamics of the new political, consequently, play out in this structuration process.

The New Political

The new political takes place in the dynamics between the changing social structures and cultural agency discussed above. While socioeconomic and cultural structures both enable and limit the possibilities of the formation and expression of culture agency, the latter embodies, reinforces, and, in the long run, reconfigures changing structures. Yet, there are a couple of additional elements to the structuration process of the new political—networked communication and new forms of political association.

Chinese online activism has unique characteristics. Unlike its counterparts in democratic societies, online activism in China is more likely to be episodic and spontaneous, often without formal organization (Yang, 2006). While in Western societies the Internet is mainly a mobilizing device for preexisting movements that have recently adopted online tactics, in China, the Internet provides both the form and substance for online activism. For this reason, the classical social movement models of political opportunity, organizational resources, and cultural framing are not fully applicable to Internet activism in the Chinese context (Armstrong & Bernstein, 2008; O'Brien, 2008; Tarrow, 1996).

The informal, episodic, and emergent character of online activism in China (Yang, 2006) is attributable in part to the technological network as the de facto organizational structure. The decentralized, distributed, networked, organizational forms that the Internet affords are robust, adaptable, and highly maneuverable in the face of conflicts (Garrett, 2006). Bimber, Flanagin, and Stohl (2005) argue that transient, fragmented, and pluralistic structures have elevated the importance of short-term issue groups. As a result, cycles of mobilization and response are more rapid, causing issue support to wax and wane more quickly.

Moreover, the Internet has proven to be a versatile vehicle for navigating the structures of the social world. Collective action, in essence, is the process of transforming private interests or actions into public expressions for the creation of collective identities and demands in conjunction with a public good (Cohen, 1985). In the same vein, the "problem articulation" function of the Habermasian public sphere refers to the notion that private-life spheres at the civil-social periphery have greater sensitivity than the political center in detecting and identifying new problem situations (Yang, 2009c). While personal problems of social importance may not be brought to public attention because of the lack of institutionalized channels, they are likely to attract more attention when articulated on the Internet (Yang, 2009c). In this sense, the boundaries between private and public domains that have traditionally shaped modern societies and identity have become porous and easily crossed with the help of the Internet (Bimmer, Flanagin, & Stohl, 2005).

Accompanying the technological network is a new form of political association: personalized engagement in event-centered contention facilitated by individualized personal connective networks (Bennett & Segerberg, 2012). Rosen (2010) maintains that Chinese society has experienced the "secularization" of youth, whose "participation" in politics has primarily been a private participation, through friends and family, and in anonymous Internet activities (p. 512). Damm (2007) also observed the rise of urban and consumerist lifestyles and a stronger focus on identity politics in an increasingly fragmented Chinese society.

Both new technological developments and emerging political practices bear complex implications for political communication. Hallin (2008) concludes that contemporary media culture is a contradictory joint product of two opposing currents. On the one hand, the blurring of conventional boundaries between the public and the private, as well as between the cultural and the political, "represents an opening to actors previously excluded from the institutionalized public sphere and a politicization of areas of social life not previously subject to political contestation." On the other hand, there has been "the increased personalization of public communication, the focus of media on 'private' life and on individual experience. This can be seen in some ways as a de-politicization of public communication, and hence a shrinking away of the public sphere, which increases the power of elites by leaving important areas of social life outside the arena of public debate" (p. 55).

Perhaps these broad observations could serve as a point of departure for hypotheses formulation and empirical observation in the Chinese context. The role of the Internet for social activism needs be studied within frameworks that connect us to the central concerns of the political process: the restructuring of center-periphery relations, politicizing the demands of various sectors of society, and the struggle over the definition of the realm of the political (Eisenstadt, 2000, p. 6).

For these purposes, the media have been conceived in three distinct ways: (1) as technological networks and infrastructures for distributed and flexible communication and mobilization; (2) as symbolic spaces for struggles to influence and direct the public's perceptions of sociopolitical issues (Blumler & Gurevitch, 2005); and (3) as social institutions of varied political economic configuration that shape the flow of political communication in society (Blumler & Gurevitch, 2005).

Heavily focusing on the Internet and related online social networks as technological structures and instrumental platforms, research on mediated activism has yet to pay more attention to new forms of mediated communications as a discursive field or space in which competing discourses struggle for visibility and legitimacy. Moreover, the increasingly important role of social media attests to the importance of people's overall social connections, which substantiates the view that social structures such as class are dynamic social formations, renewed by social action and practice (Murdock & Golding, 2005). Such a perspective unites the traditional research focuses of both political economy—seeking to explain cultural consequences with structural and material determinants; that is, people's overall location in the economic system—and critical cultural studies, which asserts the sovereignty of social agents to impose their own meanings and interpretations.

Still the questions remain: How are dominant political and media institutions adapting to these new developments? Does the Internet supplement or supplant institutionalized political communication? Working in the framework of representative democracy, Blumler and Gurevitch (2005) are keen to acknowledge the challenge of social activism and movements that are participatory, plebiscitary, and populist in character. They argue against uncritical faith in implicitly anarchic notions of civic communication and believe that democratic deliberation and participation can be augmented "only through institutions and procedures that are specifically designed to realize such goals" (p. 1).

Similarly, Beck (1992), contemplating the divergence between political institutions and civil society, is critical of the increasing trend of "subpolitics"—the politicizing activities of social movements and advocacy and single-issue pressure groups. He argues that subpolitical social actors exercise political power by mobilizing communication pressures through media events. Subpolitical practices are potentially divisive because they promote group-specific values, interests, and demands with little concern for other values and claims or for the availability of public resources. Consequently, it has become progressively more challenging to operate effectively in the public space of communication. All potential political actors must resort to professional media public relations personnel skilled in the business of planning publicity campaigns and monitoring and managing public opinions (Beck, 1992).

The above criticisms have demonstrated the predicament the Habermasian public sphere faces in representative democracy. As a mechanism to put issues at the center, the notion of the public sphere was created to work against "the system." But when the system itself undergoes fundamental transformations, the public sphere loses its theoretical foothold in a process of refeudalization. For advocates of liberal democracy following the Habermasian tradition in China, these issues are worth pondering in debates about the directions of political reform in light of the rapid development of social stratification and fragmentation in Chinese society.

Within China's media ecology, however, the Internet has also been the unofficial forum for leftist intellectuals and social forces to express socialist ideas and defend the country's revolutionary legacies. This leftist social coalition upholds a reinvigorated concept of "people's democracy" as a way to realize "the subordination of market and state to the self-regulating society" (Zhao, 2011, p. 229). This ideology has been the foundational framework for China's lower social classes to engage in various (mediated) social struggles against the negative consequences of economic reforms (Zhao, 2011).

Conclusion: A Renewed Agenda for the New Political?

This review chapter took the effort to identify the major issues and theoretical frameworks in research focused on mediated activism against the backdrop of unprecedented social transformations in contemporary Chinese society. It started with a critique of the simplistic characterization of social power structures and argued for a more nuanced understanding of the relationship between state and society. The chapter suggested a multi-institutional framework to define the new political as a structuration process between changing structures and cultural agency. The chapter also surveyed the important topics of cultural form, agency, and subjectivity situated in both the liberal tradition of civil society and civic culture, as well as leftist tendencies that uphold the country's communist legacies. Finally, the chapter noted the changing patterns of political association enabled by new forms of networked communication.

On a final note, it is timely to share what Zhao (2010) proposed for a new agenda for researchers of Chinese communication—reroot the area in history, reembed the area in the social terrain, redefine the agency of social change, reengage with meaning and community, and, finally, recover utopian imaginations. These five "Rs" may work to integrate meaning-making processes into structures of political economy and instill cultural sensibility in scholarship on communication and social change (Zhao, 2010, p. 175). As a conclusion, the problematics of the new political concern the understanding of the new dynamics of social structures and cultural agency, and the way they interact. These developments, as Zhao eloquently put, not only defy any linear logic and dichotomous characterization but also are fraught with complication, contingency, and compromise. It would take much reflexivity on our part as scholars to grasp changes amid continuities, patterns within chaos, and, ultimately, fluid processes with indeterminate outcomes in this great historical moment of change (Zhao, 2008).

Notes

1. What is also applicable here is the distinction between politics and "the political" by Mouffe (1999, p. 754). Also see Dahlgren (2002).
2. This "middle social stratum" in the Chinese context differs from the conventional concept of "middle-class" majority groups mediating between the traditional poles of capital and labor in a developed capitalist society (Huang, 2008).

References

Armstrong, E. A., & Bernstein, M. (2008). Culture, power, and institutions: A multi institutional politics approach to social movements. *Sociological Theory, 26*(1), 74–99.

Bakardjieva, M. (2009). Subactivism: Lifeworld and politics in the age of the Internet. *Information Society, 25*(2), 91–104.

Beck, U. (1992). *Risk society: Towards a new modernity.* London: Sage.

Bennett, W. L., & Segerberg, A. (2012). The logic of connective action: Digital media and the personalization of contentious politics. *Information, Communication & Society, 15*(5), 739–768.

Bian, Y. (2002). Chinese social stratification and social mobility. *Annual Review of Sociology, 28*, 91–116.

Bimber, B., Flanagin, A. J., & Stohl, C. (2005). Reconceptualizing collective action in the contemporary media environment. *Communication Theory, 15*(4), 365–388.

Blumler, J. G., & Gurevitch, M. (2005). Rethinking the study of political communication. In J. Curran & M. Gurevitch (Eds.), *Mass media and society* (pp. 155–172). London: Hodder Arnold.

Buechler, S. M. (1995). New social movement theories. *Sociological Quarterly, 36*(3), 441–464.

Calhoun, C. (1998). The public good as a social and cultural project. In W. W. Powell & E. S. Clemens (Eds.), *Private action and the public good* (pp. 20–35). New Haven, CT: Yale University Press.

China Internet Network Information Center (CNNIC). (2010). *Statistical survey report on the Internet development in China.* Beijing: Author.

Chu, R. W., & Cheng, C. (2011). Cultural convulsions: Examining the Chineseness of cyber China. In D. K. Herold & P. Marolt (Eds.), *Online society in China: Creating, celebrating and instrumentalising the online carnival* (pp. 23–39). Oxford: Taylor & Francis.

Cohen, J. L. (1985). Strategy or identity: New theoretical paradigms and contemporary social movements. *Social Research, 52*(4), 663–716.

Dahlgren, P. (2000). The Internet and the democratization of civic culture. *Political Communication, 17*(4), 335–340.

Dahlgren, P. (2002). In search of the talkative public: Media, deliberative democracy and civic culture. *Public, 9*(3), 5–26.

Dahlgren, P. (2005). The Internet, public spheres, and political communication: Dispersion and deliberation. *Political Communication, 22*(2), 147–162.

Dahlgren, P. (2006). Doing citizenship: The cultural origins of civic agency in the public sphere. *European Journal of Cultural Studies, 9*(3), 267–286.

Damm, J. (2007). The Internet and the fragmentation of Chinese society. *Critical Asian Studies, 39*(2), 273–294.

Damm, J., & Thomas, S. (Eds.). (2006). *Chinese cyberspace: Technological changes and political effects.* New York: Routledge.

de Tocqueville, A. (1835). *Democracy in America.* New York: Vintage.

Eder, K. (1985). The "new social movements": Moral crusades, political pressure groups, or social movements? *Social Research, 52*(4), 869–890.

Eisenstadt, S. N. (2000). Multiple modernities. *Daedalus, 129*(1), 1–29.

Farrer, J. (2007). China's women sex bloggers and dialogic sexual politics on the Chinese Internet. *China Aktuell, 36*(4), 10–44.

Garrett, R. K. (2006). Protest in an information society: A review of literature on social movements and new ICTs. *Information, Communication & Society, 9*(2), 202–224.

Giese, K. (2004). Speaker's corner or virtual panopticon: Discursive construction of Chinese identities online. In F. Mengin (Ed.), *Cyber China* (pp. 19–36). New York: Palgrave.

Habermas, J. (1989). *The theory of communicative action: Lifeworld and system: A critique of functionalist reason* (Vol. 2). Boston, MA: Beacon Press.

Hallin, D. C. (2008). Neoliberalism, social movements and change in media systems in the late twentieth century. In D. Hesmondhalgh & J. Toynbee (Eds.), *The media of social theory* (pp. 43–59). New York: Routledge.

Herold, D. K. (2011). Human flesh search engines: Carnivalesque riots as components of a "Chinese democracy." In D. K. Herold & P. Marolt (Eds.), *Online society in China: Creating, celebrating and instrumentalising the online carnival* (pp. 127–145). New York: Routledge.

Herold, D. K., & Marolt, P. (2011). *Online society in China: Creating, celebrating and instrumentalising the online carnival.* New York: Routledge.

Hsing, Y., & Lee, C. K. (2010). *Reclaiming Chinese society: The new social activism.* New York: Routledge.

Huang, P.C.C. (2008). Zhongguo de xiaozichanjieji he zhongjian jieceng: beilun de shehui xingtai [Petty-bourgeoisie and middle social stratum in China: The paradox of social formation]. *Leaders, 22.* Retrieved from http://www.21ccom.net/articles/rwcq/article_20100120381.html

Jiang, M. (2012). Chinese Internet events. In A. Esarey & R. Kluver (Eds.), *The Internet in China: Online business, information, distribution and social connectivity*. New York: Berkshire.

Kalathil, S., & Boas, T. (2003). *Open networks, closed regimes*. Washington, DC: Carnegie Endowment for International Peace.

Lee, C. C. (2000). *Power, money, and media: Communication patterns and bureaucratic control in cultural China*. Evanston, IL: Northwestern University Press.

Lessig, L. (2008). *Remix: Making art and commerce thrive in the hybrid economy*. New York: Penguin.

Li, H. (2011). Parody and resistance on the Chinese Internet. In D. K. Herold & P. Marolt (Eds.), *Online society in China: Creating, celebrating and instrumentalising the online carnival* (pp. 71–88). Oxford: Taylor & Francis.

Liu, F. (2011). *Urban youth in China: Modernity, the Internet and the self*. London: Routledge.

MacKinnon, R. (2008). Flatter world and thicker walls? Blogs, censorship and civic discourse in China. *Public Choice, 134*, 31–46.

Marolt, P. (2011). Grassroots agency in a civil sphere? Rethinking Internet control in China. In D. K. Herold & P. Marolt (Eds.), *Online society in China: Creating, celebrating and instrumentalising the online carnival* (pp. 53–67). Oxford: Taylor & Francis.

Meng, B. (2011). From steamed bun to grass mud horse: E Gao as alternative political discourse on the Chinese internet. *Global Media and Communication, 7*(1), 33–51.

Mouffe, C. (1999). Deliberative democracy or agonistic pluralism. *Social Research, 66*(3), 745–758.

Murdock, G., & Golding, P. (2005). Culture, communications and political economy. In J. Curran & M. Gurevitch (Eds.), *Mass media and society* (pp. 70–92). London: Hodder Arnold.

O'Brien, K. J. (2008). *Popular protest in China*. Cambridge, MA: Harvard University Press.

Pan, Z. (2010). Articulation and re-articulation: Agendas for understanding media and communication in China. *International Journal of Communication, 4*, 517–530.

Perry, E. J. (1994). Trends in the study of Chinese politics: State-society relations. *China Quarterly, 139*, 704–713.

Perry, E. J. (2007). Studying Chinese politics: Farewell to revolution? *China Journal, 57*, 1–22.

Perry, E. J. (2009). A new rights consciousness? *Journal of Democracy, 20*(3), 17–20.

Perry, E. J., & Selden, M. (2003). *Chinese society: Change, conflict and resistance*. New York: Routledge.

Putnam, R. D. (1995). Bowling alone: America's declining social capital. *Journal of Democracy, 6*(1), 65–78.

Putnam, R. D., Leonardi, R., & Nanetti, R. Y. (1994). *Making democracy work: Civic traditions in modern Italy*. Princeton, NJ: Princeton University Press.

Qiu, J. L. (1999). Virtual censorship in China: Keeping the gate between the cyberspaces. *International Journal of Communications Law and Policy, 4*(Winter), 1–25.

Qiu, L., & Chan, T. (2011). Studies of new media events. Beijing: People's University Press. 新媒体事件研究. 中国人民大学出版社.

Rosen, S. (2010). Is the Internet a positive force in the development of civil society, a public sphere, and democratization in China? *International Journal of Communication, 4*, 509–516.

Tai, Z. (2006). *The Internet in China: Cyberspace and civil society*. New York: Routledge.

Tang, L., & Yang, P. (2011). Symbolic power and the Internet: The power of a "horse." *Media, Culture & Society, 33*(5), 675–691.

Tarrow, S. (1996). Social movements in contentious politics: A review article. *American Political Science Review, 90*(4), 874–883.

Taubman, G. (1998). A not-so World Wide Web: The Internet, China, and the challenges to nondemocratic rule. *Political Communication, 15*(2), 255–272.

Thompson, J. (1995). *The media & modernity*. Cambridge: Polity Press.

Wallis, C. (2011). New media practices in China: Youth patterns, process, and politics. *International Journal of Communication, 5*, 406–426.

Wang, H., & Wu, J. (2013). The story of "In the Spring" – from a grass-roots cry to a carnival in the media. *Xinwen ChunQiu, 3*, 33–41. "春天里"的故事——从草根呐喊到媒体 狂欢,《新闻春秋》, 2013年第三期。

Wang, S. (2013). Civil society is a myth of Neoliberalism. The Observer. 王绍光: "公民社会"是新自由主义需要的神话。观察者网. Retrieved from http://www.cul-studies.com/index.php?m=special&c=index&a=show&id=115&catids=26

Wasserstrom, J. N., & Perry, E. J. (Eds.). (1992). *Popular protest and political culture in modern China: Learning from 1989*. Boulder, CO: Westview Press.

Wu, A. X. (2012). Hail the independent thinker: The emergence of public debate culture on the Chinese Internet. *International Journal of Communication, 6*, 25.

Xiao, Q. (2004, November). The "blog" revolution sweeps across China. *New Scientist, 24*.

Yan, Y. (2010). The Chinese path to individualization. *British Journal of Sociology, 61*(3), 489–512.

Yang, G. (2003a). The co-evolution of the internet and civil society in China. *Asian Survey, 43*(3), 405–422.

Yang, G. (2003b). The Internet and civil society in China: A preliminary assessment. *Journal of Contemporary China, 12*(36), 453–475.

Yang, G. (2006). Activists beyond virtual borders: Internet-mediated networks and informational politics in china. *First Monday*. Available at http://pear.accc.uic.edu/ojs/index.php/fm/article/view/1609/1524

Yang, G. (2009a). The Internet as cultural form: Technology and the human condition in China. *Knowledge, Technology & Policy, 22*(2), 109–115.

Yang, G. (2009b). Online activism. *Journal of Democracy, 20*(3), 33–36.

Yang, G. (2009c). *The power of the Internet in China: Citizen activism online*. New York: Columbia University Press.

Yang, L., & Zheng, Y. (2012). Fen qings (angry youth) in contemporary China. *Journal of Contemporary China, 21*(76), 637–653.

Yu, H. (2009). *Media and cultural transformation in China*. New York: Routledge.

Zhang, X., & Zheng, Y. (Eds.). (2009). *China's information and communications technology revolution: Social changes and state responses*. Oxford: Taylor & Francis.

Zhang, Y. (2000). From masses to audience: Changing media ideologies and practices in reform china. *Journalism Studies, 1*(4), 617–635.

Zhao, Y. (1998). *Media, market, and democracy in china: Between the party line and the bottom line*. Urbana: University of Illinois Press.

Zhao, Y. (2008). *Communication in China: Political economy, power, and conflict*. Lanham, MD: Rowman & Littlefield.

Zhao, Y. (2010). Directions for research on communication and China: An introductory and overview essay. *International Journal of Communication, 4*, 573–583.

Zhao, Y. (2011). Sustaining and contesting revolutionary legacies in media and ideology. In S. Heilmann & E. J. Perry (Eds.), *Mao's invisible hand: The political foundations of adaptive governance in China* (pp. 201–236). Cambridge, MA: Harvard University.

Zhao, Y. (2012). Understanding China's media system in a world historical context. In D. C. Hallin & P. Mancini (Eds.), *Comparing media systems beyond the Western world* (pp. 143–173). Cambridge: Cambridge University Press.

Zheng, Y., & Wu, G. (2005). Information technology, public space, and collective action in China. *Comparative Political Studies, 38*(5), 507–536.

Zittrain, J., & Edelman, B. (2003). Internet filtering in China. *Internet Computing, IEEE, 7*(2), 70–77.

INDEX

Note: Page numbers with *f* indicate figures; those with *t* indicate tables.

For Product Safety Concerns and Information please contact our EU
representative GPSR@taylorandfrancis.com
Taylor & Francis Verlag GmbH, Kaufingerstraße 24, 80331 München, Germany